COMPLETE GUIDE TO
MODERN REAL ESTATE TRANSACTIONS

Don Owens

Prentice-Hall, Inc.

Englewood Cliffs, N.J.

Prentice-Hall International, Inc., *London*
Prentice-Hall of Australia, Pty. Ltd., *Sydney*
Prentice-Hall of Canada, Ltd., *Toronto*
Prentice-Hall of India Private Ltd., *New Delhi*
Prentice-Hall of Japan, Inc., *Tokyo*

Library of Congress Cataloging in Publication Data

Owens, Don
    Complete guide to modern real estate transactions.

    1. Real estate business--United States--Handbooks,
manuals, etc. I. Title.
HD255.O86   643   74-17364
ISBN 0-13-160218-7

*This publication is designed to provide accurate and authoritative information in regard
to the subject matter covered. It is sold with the understanding that the publisher is not
engaged in rendering legal, accounting, or other professional service. If legal advice or
other expert assistance is required, the services of a competent professional person
should be sought.*

> *—From a Declaration of Principles jointly adopted by
> a Committee of the American Bar Association and a
> Committee of Publishers and Associations.*

Printed in the United States of America

About the Author

Don Owens is a Realtor who has been actively engaged in the general brokerage of real estate listings, sales, exchanging, and leasing since 1954. He was one of the early pioneers of the Sacramento Multiple Listing Bureau and served as Chairman, Director, and Vice President of that organization for a number of years.

In addition to operating the Don Owens Realty Company from 1956 until his recent retirement, Mr. Owens was a lifetime state accredited College Instructor of Real Estate. For many years he taught Real Estate Practice and Real Estate Financing in the American River College at Sacramento, California.

Mr. Owens is author–publisher of the book, *Real Estate Financing and Closing Costs,* directed primarily to California laws and customs and extensively used by real estate brokers, salespeople, attorneys, mortgage lenders, and numerous California colleges in real estate courses.

What This Book Will Do for You

The technical aspects of most real estate transactions require varied degrees of experience and knowledge in our modern times. In some instances the transfer of real property from one owner to another may be fairly simple. Other transactions may become more complex and should be processed only by experts who have received special training in the real estate profession. Such practice would assure the client that all factors have been considered.

The language of the real estate profession as applied to terms, closing costs, financing, legal documents, listing and sales agreements, settlement procedures, and so on, is often confusing even to the more experienced real estate agent. The purpose of this book is to reduce the complexities of normal real estate transactions and procedures to simplified terms providing a comprehensive guide for clearer general understanding.

In the sale of property a concise property description along with the terms and conditions under which the property is to be sold are of extreme importance. Equally important is the phrasing of terms and conditions under which the property is being purchased in order to avoid future misunderstandings as to the purchaser's intent. Listings, deposit receipts, the phrasing of financial arrangements, and other essential factors of this type of transaction are fully explained in this book.

Closing costs in real estate transactions are the inevitable charges that are involved in finalizing the sale. Buyers and sellers may consider these costs to be mysterious extractions of funds that appear on the settlement papers. To aid the real estate agent in explaining the subject to his clients, this book discusses each item of buyer's and seller's costs in connection with transactions involving new loans and loan assumptions.

There are many methods of financing the purchase of a home or other properties, such as through government-sponsored and conventional type loan programs. These methods and procedures are discussed in detail.

The differences between security instruments, such as mortgages, trust deeds, and contracts of sale, are also dealt with, along with other legal documents used in various sections of the country.

The numerous forms provided throughout the book serve as examples of agreements commonly used in the real estate profession nationwide. Interest charts and amortization schedules also contained herein are invaluable reference tools of the trade.

The laws and customs concerning real estate transactions as they are practiced in various states and localities are individualized to some extent to conform with local conditions and circumstances. However, the primary objectives and purposes of state and national legislation to protect the general public and to establish certain guidelines and procedures under which to perform are the same regardless of the locality in which a property may lie. The professional real estate practitioner must be as well informed as possible of the practices and laws pertaining to the purchase, sale, lease, and exchange of real estate in the area in which he practices. The information in this book may be applied to any particular locality providing it conforms with prevailing local real estate laws and customs.

Don Owens

Contents

13

17

List of Forms

1

Appraisal Methods

The market value of property has been defined as, "Price in terms of money for which a property would sell in the open market, seller not obligated to sell, the buyer not obligated to buy, with a reasonable length of time to effect the sale."

Since the sale of real estate begins with the establishment of a realistic market value on which to base the listing price, it is essential that real estate brokers and salesmen practice, to some degree, the procedures involved in three basic methods of appraisal approach normally utilized by professional appraisers. These methods are: Comparison, Replacement Cost, and Capitalization. The factors and considerations employed within these methods will depend largely on conditions and facts concerning past, present and future contingencies found to exist in connection with individual properties.

Most professional appraisers will correlate the results of their findings, through employment of each of the basic methods, to arrive at an analytical and conclusive value of subject properties. In the last analysis, an appraisal is an expression of expert opinion based on available pertinent facts and figures. Frequently, an appraiser's personal opinion as to how the property appeals to him will create an involuntary influence in his final report concerning market value.

Personal preference is often an influential factor in instances whereby a real estate agent is called upon for an opinion of value and sales price when listing an owner's property for sale. For example, an agent may not care for the distinctive style or construction of certain homes and will subconsciously reflect his opinion of value accordingly. Not everyone is prone to be of the same opinion from the standpoint of buyer's appeal. Therefore, the establishment of value should be based on that potentiality, since real estate agents are seldom prospective buyers regardless of their preferences. In the event of an over-estimate in value, where little or no interest is shown in a listed property, a price adjustment may be necessary in order to remedy the situation within the first month of the listing term. There is seldom anything wrong with a parcel of real estate that cannot be cured through a material price adjustment.

The utility value of a property is an important factor in considering market value. Utility value consists of the value in use of the property to an owner, value in warranted use to an owner and the amenities that may attach to the property.

Owners are motivated to place their properties for sale on the market for various reasons. In some instances, an owner may desire to sell his property only at an abundant personal gain or he will not sell at all because otherwise he can retain a beneficial use and need for the property. Another owner may be motivated to dispose of his property because of an employment transfer to a distant city whereby his use potential is vastly decreased.

When a property is capable of fulfilling the exact needs and requirements of a prospective purchaser, the utility value may be increased from the standpoint of warranted use.

The amenities of a property such as location, improvements and other enhancements may have a more effective utility value to one prospective purchaser than it would to another. For example, a large home with a swimming pool and located near a high school, may have more utilization appeal to a family with children of high school age than it would have to an older couple with no children or a family consisting of very small children. Older people are usually more interested in a smaller home near shopping and public transportation and have little or no interest in a swimming pool. Families with small children frequently fear the hazard of a child falling into the pool when no one else is around.

COMPARISON METHOD

This approach is normally applied more than other methods in arriving at a realistic market value for the sale of residential property. A considerable amount of research and knowledge is required as to the sales of comparable properties sold under approximately the same terms and to the conditions that may apply to the property being evaluated for a listing price.

A market data analysis of comparable properties is of an immense value when compiled to indicate properties for sale on the current market, properties sold within the past twelve months and properties listed for sale on the market within the past year, but which were never sold. This type of analysis reveals information concerning listing prices, sales prices, terms and conditions of individual property sales, appraisals and the length of time each property was on the market prior to being sold.

Listing prices of properties normally indicate the probable top market value, while actual sales prices are more reflective of a true market value. Where a listing has expired, the chances are that the listed price was too high and was not adjusted from the beginning of the listing term.

In the interest of more accurate research, a physical inspection of comparable properties noted on the analysis should be accomplished whenever possible, as the conditions of general repair are often reflected in price. The factor of physical deterioration is a consideration when a property is in poor condition. When the design of a structure and the amenities attached to it are of an age or condition not acceptable to most prospective purchasers, it is referred to as functional obsolescence. The location of a property in an undesirable neighborhood may suffer economic obsolescence.

Amenities of a property such as built in appliances, patios, landscaping, air conditioning, etc., are to be considered in comparing properties being used on a market data analysis sheet.

When an agent prepares information, as outlined above, and presents it in the proper manner to a prospective seller, the chances of obtaining a good saleable listing are excellent.

REPLACEMENT COST METHOD

This approach to establishing the market value of a property is frequently applied along with the Comparison Method. Residential salespeople employ this method in a rule of thumb estimate of construction costs of similar homes and attached amenities. For example, a similar home consisting of three bedrooms, a family room, two baths, built in appliances and carpeted hardwood flooring may cost approximately fifteen dollars per square foot of living area in the finished state of construction. That figure may then be used as the replacement cost of a similarly constructed home with the same features and approximate size. If the living area of the home should happen to be two thousand square feet, the cost would be $30,000.00 ($15 X 2,000 square feet). Nonliving areas such as the garage, patio, landscaping and other amenities would be added to that figure from the standpoint of known replacement costs.

The lot on which the home is constructed is researched regarding costs of similar lots in comparable neighborhoods and added to the other figures. Depreciation and obsolescence are then deducted from the total amount. The remaining balance will normally reflect a close estimate of market value.

Professional appraisers ordinarily employ the Comparison and Replacement Cost methods of approach on a more detailed and technical basis in property appraisals, but to do so generally requires a considerable amount of training and experience, which is not usually accorded to the average real estate salesperson.

It is almost essential for professional appraisers to use the Replacement Cost Method of approach when establishing values on public properties and buildings where there is no comparative sales information of similar properties and no monetary income on which to base the Capitalization Method.

CAPITALIZATION METHOD

In formulating an appraisal report on income producing property, the Capitalization Method of approach is ordinarily employed along with the Comparison and Replacement Cost methods by professional appraisers, as a check and balance of value. Investors often rely solely on Capitalization results as a guideline to market value.

The first step in Capitalizing is to establish the Adjusted Gross Income by deducting the vacancy and collection loss allowances from the Gross Annual Income. Annual property expenses are then deducted from the Adjusted Gross Income to find the Net Annual Income.

Annual property expenses may include:

1. Management
2. Property Taxes
3. Services (janitorial, gardening, etc.)
4. Utilities (lights, fuel, water, refuse removal, etc.)
5. Insurance
6. Maintenance and Repairs
7. Replacement Reserve (furniture, appliances)
8. Other Fixed Expenses

After determining the Net Annual Income, consideration is given to the projected Future Income. In this connection, the past and present income may be used as a guide, but past figures are not necessarily the basis for a true estimate of income for the remaining productive life of the property. Neighborhood trends and other factors are also to be taken into account.

The next step is to establish a reasonable Capitalization Rate of return, or yield, normally demanded by the average prospective investor-purchaser, according to the current money market, interest rates and individual income tax potentials. Some investors may require a high percentage of yield for their purposes while others may feel it more beneficial to accept a lower percentage of yield basis from the standpoint of an income tax shelter.

In any case, the Capitalization Rate is important since only a fraction of a percent may make a material difference in determining the market value of income properties by Capitalizing the income. To Capitalize the income is to divide the projected Future Income by the established Capitalization Rate. The quotient (results) will indicate a market value of the property, as a whole, commensurate with the selected rate.

EXAMPLE OF CAPITALIZATION APPROACH

A ten unit apartment house. Age—4 years. Projected monthly rental per unit—$150.00 (10 X $150 = $1,500 per month or $18,000 per year). Indicated vacancy and collection loss factor—10%. (10% X $18,000 = $1,800 per year).

Gross Annual Income Projected	$18,000	
Less Vacancy and Coll. loss	1,800	
Adjusted Gross Annual Income Projected		$16,200

Annual Property Expenses:

1. Management	$1,200	
2. Property Taxes	960	
3. Services	360	
4. Utilities	240	
5. Insurance	250	
6. Maintenance & Repairs	240	
7. Replacement Reserve	500	
8. Other Fixed Expenses	100	
		3,850
Net Annual Income		$12,350

Capitalization Rate—10% $\dfrac{\$12,350}{.10}$ = $123,500 Approximate Value

Capitalization Rate — 9% $\dfrac{\$12,350}{.09}$ = $137,222 Approximate Value

APPRAISER'S REPORTS

Ordinarily, the appraiser's report is submitted in a form that is commensurate with the purpose of the appraisal, the intended use of the derived information and the type of property being appraised.

A descriptive "letter form" report may be sufficient in instances where the client is already familiar with the property. It could be the case of a tenant who plans to purchase or improve the premises, or it could be the property owner who plans to sell or lease the premises. This type of report is often a verification of what the client already knows plus pertinent data and

25

information concerning comparable properties and the surrounding area of the subject property.

A "short form" type of report consisting of an outlined drawing and measurements of the land and improvements is often required of some clients such as lending institutions for mortgage loan purposes or insurance companies for insuring purposes. The form contains checklists and spaces to be filled in for pertinent data by the appraiser. In most instances, a photograph of the subject property and adjoining properties is required to be submitted along with the report.

The more complex "narrative report" form is normally required in the event of court action cases, taxation, large income producing properties involved in a sale or lease and condemnation procedures. This type of report is usually substantiated by maps, photographs, charts and plot plans. It is complete with all pertinent information concerning the subject property and the area surrounding it. The report is explanatory as to the line of reasoning and various computations of the value conclusions.

Professional appraisers normally arrive at the reported value conclusions through the correlation of the results determined in each of the three methods of appraisal.

It is recognized that it would be impractical to engage the services of a professional appraiser each time it is necessary for the real estate agent to reach a conclusion of value as to a client's property. However, it would be practical to assimilate all the pertinent facts possible and test those facts through application of the three methods of approach that are professionally utilized.

Property values continually fluctuate due to the factors of labor and material costs, neighborhood changes and local economic trends. Therefore, it is extremely important for the real estate agent to keep abreast with current events in addition to the many other factors to be considered in arriving at a conclusive value of property for listing and sale purposes.

2

Listing Contracts

Due to the complexities of an average real estate transaction and the influences of state and national associations of real estate boards, most states' laws require anyone who is engaged in the normal activities of the real estate profession to be a licensed real estate agent.

Some states impose severe penalties against unlicensed persons who for compensation, solicit listings, sales, purchases, exchanges, leases, loan funds or in any way perform as agents for others in real estate transactions. The penalty in other states may be limited to the denial of a commission or fee for services performed, if collection should become a matter of litigation in a court of law.

The laws of some states require an attorney-at-law to be a licensed real estate broker when performing certain services for the purpose of collecting a commission. The exception may be when it is evident that he is acting in the capacity of an attorney and not as a real estate broker.

Most states' laws provide that the contract of employment, as it pertains to real estate, must be contained in a written agreement if the agent is to be entitled to collect a commission. Therefore listing contracts are essential from the standpoint of the agent's protection for services performed.

OPTIONS

An option, as applied to real estate, is a written agreement between two principals, whereby one principal is given the right to purchase, lease or exchange property, as the case may be, within a certain time and at a fixed price.

A cash consideration paid to the owner is to represent compensation for the holding of property until the buyer either exercises his option or allows it to expire and become void. Since an option normally runs from seller to buyer, the seller is the optionor and the buyer is the optionee.

27

Terms of the purchase should be set forth in the option agreement as to price, financing, expenses, prorations and any other factors pertinent to the ultimate transaction. If the buyer exercises his option within the prescribed time, the terms and conditions outlined in the agreement will apply.

Prior to expiration of the specified time or date for the option to be exercised, the seller is deprived of his right to revocation of the agreement. However, under normal circumstances, by forfeiture of any consideration paid to the seller, the buyer may revoke the agreement at any time prior to exercising the option. The option agreement does not usually bind the optionee to any performance, although he is given the right to demand performance.

In negotiating an option type of transaction, a real estate agent is not generally entitled to a commission unless and until the option is exercised by the purchaser.

LISTINGS

A listing agreement, in real estate, is a contract of employment for an agent to perform certain services. The services are normally connected with the sale, leasing or exchanging of real estate in behalf of the principal and the listing forms are generally captioned according to the primary intended purpose of the authorization, for example, "Authorization to Sell," "Authorization to Lease," and so on.

Since a listing is an agency contract between principal and agent, the agent is bound under the laws of the agency to perform as agreed and has certain obligations to his principal that do not exist between two principals. The principal also has certain obligations to the listing broker and agent that do not apply to anyone else.

In some instances, listing forms are extremely simplified and provide only the essential information as to names of principal and agent, address and description of the property, sales price and terms, effective date and expiration date, amount of commission to be paid and agreement as to the type of listing. Other listing forms contain more elaborate and detailed information on properties with improvements such as residences, apartment buildings and commercial structures.

An exchange of listing information may be accomplished through organized groups of real estate brokerage offices providing copies of their listings to a central administrative office for distribution to the other members. Such organizations are usually known as Multiple Listing Service groups.

Multiple listing services are often organized by members of local real estate boards which are now known as "Board of Realtors." However, in many localities, organized groups of real estate brokers exchange copies of their listings for cooperative sales and have no connection in any manner with the Board of Realtors from the standpoint of organization of members.

The basic concept of a multiple listing service is to provide a broader scope of exposure of properties for sale to clients. It is thus possible for one agent to lead his client to another agent's listing and provide all the available facts regarding the property from a copy of the listing agreement.

A division of the commission between the "listing" member and the "selling" member is varied according to organizational policy. Of course, when the listing and the sale is accomplished by the same member, there is no division of the commission. Administrative expenses of the organization are provided through membership fees and dues in various forms such as a small percentage of the commission upon sale of the property or an advance fee at the time a listing is published for distribution.

A supply of good saleable listings is essential to the successful operation of a brokerage office as well as to the professional salesperson's career. To survive in the real estate business without good listings is indeed a rare circumstance. Therefore, it is not only necessary to maintain a supply of listings, it is also essential to create saleable listings that are properly written to include accurate information to be passed on to a prospective purchaser.

Whenever possible, it is advisable to verify some of the information, provided by the seller, to be written into the information portion of the listing contract. Generally this includes loan balances, interest rates, monthly payments, bond balances, property taxes, lot size and sewer connections.

Those items concerning existing loans may usually be verified and/or computed from the lender's most recent year-end loan statement mailed to the owner for general accounting and tax deduction purposes. In the event such a loan statement is not available, the lender should be contacted for the information. Exhibit 2-1 is an example of a form letter used for this purpose.

Property taxes may be verified by a phone call to the local assessor's office or to the tax collector's office. Bond balances can normally be verified by the county treasurer or the local agency in charge of assessment bond collections. Sewer connections may be verified through the city or county agency that issues permits for work of this nature.

These verifications should be made, because owners are not always sure of the division of payments to principal and interest on liens and in some cases may have been misinformed as to existing conditions when purchasing the property. Under certain circumstances, the listing agent may be held responsible for erroneous information passed on to a new purchaser.

29

Listing Form

ADDRESS 2115 Agency St., Your City SIDE OF STREET South NR. CORNER Mission Way

NO. BDRMS. 3	NO. ROOMS 6 BATHS 2	GARAGE 2-car attach	PRICE $ $23,950
BDRM. SIZE (1) 11' X 14'	LOT 69' X 144' TILE yes	WATER SOURCE Arcade Dist.	DN. PAY. $ 6,950
(2) 11' X 12'	AGE 16 yrs. SHWR. stall	PRESENT ZONING residential	1ST T.D. $ 17,000
(3) 11' X 11'	APPROX SQ. FT. not measured CONST. frame	SEPTIC IN CONN yes SEWER PAID yes	MO. $ 149.30 5¼ % INT. + ½%
(4) ———	STYLE cottage ROOF wood shingle	ASS'MT. BAL. none	LENDER XYZ Mortgage Co.
FAM. RM. no	HEAT central F/A FLRS. hardwood	CURBS yes WALKS no	LN. NO. 551-55835 TYPE F.H.A.
LV. RM. 16' X 26'	FIRPL. yes FENCES completely	ALLEY no	2ND. T.D. $1,000 % INT.
DN. RM. 10' X 12'	T.V. ANT. color TRADE no	OCC. MO. RENT owner	MO. $ (not assumable)
BKFST. RM. in kitchen LNDRY. yes 220 yes	LAWNS yes	POSS. plus 15 days Recording date	LENDER (private party)
SHEET ROCK PLASTER yes no	EX. BLDGS. no TREES large shade	HI. SCH. Tech	DUE DATE (to be paid on sale)
BASMT. no	BAR BQ yes INSUL. ceiling	GR. SCH. English	TAXES $400 VET. EX.? yes
ENT. HALL yes	PATIO yes SPKLR. complete	MKTS. 4 blocks	OWNER'S FINANCING Possible - Submit
KIT. 10' X 16' 220 yes	KEY In lock box - porch railing	TRANS. 4 blocks	WATER. GAS or HEATER ELECT. 40 GALS.

HOW SHOWN Any time- Please call first - 989-7080 - if no answer - use key in lock box.

REMARKS: W/W carpeting less than 2 yrs. old. 4 ton central air conditioning. Large flagstone barbecue pit. Water softener not included in listed price, but can be purchased separately for $500. Immaculate home near schools, shopping, transportation and recreational park. FHA appraisal applied for. Seller will pay necessary discount points for new financing. Excellent loan assumption provided owner is relieved of loan responsibility through FHA 2210 procedures.

DIRECTIONS: East on Post Ave. to Mission Way - North on Mission Way to Agency St. - turn West to prop.

The above information is not a part of this listing agreement. It has been furnished by the owner and/or other sources, and is not guaranteed by the agent.

For and in consideration of services to be performed by Your Realty Company hereinafter called agent, I hereby employ said agent as my sole agent and grant him the exclusive right to sell and accept a deposit thereon, that said real property, situated in the City of Your City County of Your County Legally described as: Lot 115 - Glen Subdivision # 2. Known as: 2115 Agency St., Your City and State.

I hereby grant said agent the right to sell same for the price of $ 23,950 on the following terms $ 6,950 in cash; balance payable Assume present loan through 2210 - FHA procedures or refinance. Seller will pay necessary discount points for new financing.

This employment and sole right to sell shall continue irrevocably from the date hereof until the expiration date below and I agree to pay agent 6 per cent of the selling price or any other price acceptable to me as and for the compensation of said agent hereunder in the event of a sale or exchange of said real property by said agent or any other, including myself, while this contract is in force or if sold within ninety (90) days after such termination to anyone whose name has, during the life hereof or within ten days after its termination, been submitted to me in writing personally or by mail to me at my address given below. I agree to pay Broker said per cent of the listing price if I withdraw said property from sale or exchange, or otherwise prevent performance hereunder by Broker.

Evidence of good merchantable title to be in the form of Policy of Title Insurance herein issued by a responsible title company, to be furnished and paid for by the seller. Interest, insurance, taxes and rent to be prorated from close of escrow unless otherwise designated.

If a purchaser shall forfeit his deposit, agent in consideration of the work performed, shall retain out of said deposit an amount equal to the commission above named, or without notice to seller may return deposit to purchaser.

Seller, if occupying property, may retain possession not exceeding fifteen days after date of recording at rent of $ 6.00 per day.

Dated at Your City & State this 17th day of January, 19____ We have read and received a copy of this exclusive listing.

Expiration date: 17th day of May, 19____

x James A. Howe (signature) Owner 1-17-7_ DATE SIGNED 2115 Agency St., Your City & State

x Marie A. Howe (signature) Owner 1-17-7_ 989-7080 ADDRESS

Print Owner's Name (Howe) DATE SIGNED PHONE

In consideration of the above employment, the undersigned agent agrees to use diligence in procuring a purchaser.

Joseph Martin , Salesman Tel. 798-8080

Your Realty Company , Broker Tel. 897-1423 Address Your Company Address

EXHIBIT 2-1 LISTING FORM

NET LISTINGS

This type of listing is not ordinarily acceptable to Multiple Listing Service organizations because the compensation for services is not specific. Net listings are used when the occasional seller establishes a set amount of money, net to himself, after expenses. The agent's compensation is to be in the form of any monies or other assets in excess of that amount set forth in the listing by the seller.

Net listings are perfectly legitimate contracts, although often an unsatisfactory arrangement from the standpoint of "goodwill" in the event the agent realizes an amount materially in excess of a normal commission. In such cases, the principals have been known to claim fraud. The laws of some states are stringent as to the procedures in the handling of net listings. Other states' laws, in this connection, may be more relaxed. It would be advisable to become familiar with these laws pertaining to the locality in which the property lies.

OPEN LISTINGS

Prior to the establishment and operations of multiple listing services, it was common practice for an owner to engage several real estate brokerage offices to expose property for sale to prospective purchasers. The owner would provide an open listing to any interested broker and at the same time reserve the right to sell the property himself without obligation to pay a commission.

With the advent of multiple listing services, it is no longer necessary to employ open listing practices for the purpose of creating a greater number of prospective buyers. To list the property with one member of a multiple listing group may provide for all other members and their salespeople copies of the listing and the authority to show the property to their clients on a cooperative basis.

Open listings are not usually acceptable to multiple listing organizations for distribution among the members, since there is always the possibility of clients later dealing directly with the owner after being exposed to the property. There is no absolute protection for the agent in this type of listing unless a relationship of complete loyalty exists between agents and principals.

Where several open listings are given, the sale of the property is considered to cancel all outstanding listings. Therefore, no time limit is usually specified in the employment agreement. The commission is considered to be earned by the broker who is first to find a buyer, who meets the terms of the listing, or whose offer is accepted by the seller. When the owner himself sells the property, he is not obligated to pay a commission to anyone holding an open listing.

EXCLUSIVE AGENCY LISTINGS

An exclusive agency listing is an employment agreement that must contain the words "exclusive agency." This type of listing provides for the payment of a commission to the listing agent regardless of the property being sold by another agent. However, the owner retains the right to sell the property himself without obligation to pay a commission to anyone.

Where one agent holds an exclusive agency listing and another agent sells the property, the owner may be in a position of being obligated to pay a full commission to both agents. An exclusive agency listing is not normally acceptable for distribution in multiple listing service organizations, since an owner's position may be placed inadvertently in jeopardy.

The term of the listing must be set forth in the agreement, with a specified expiration date, in order to be effective and lawful in most states.

EXCLUSIVE RIGHT TO SELL LISTINGS

The exclusive right to sell listing is a contract of employment that provides for payment of a commission to the listing broker regardless of who, including the owner, may actually find a buyer and consummate a sale during the term of the contract. An effective date and expiration date of the listing is mandatory by law in order to be considered a valid contract. Failure to do so may bring severe disciplinary action against the agent licensed under the jurisdiction of the laws of some states.

Ordinarily, the forms for this type of listing contain a provision for the payment of a commission for a period after the expiration date, where the purchaser was exposed to the property during the effective period of the contract by the listing broker or subagent. This may be accomplished by the listing agent submitting a list of the names of the persons with whom he or his subagents negotiated a transaction to purchase the subject property during the listing period. The provision has an effect of discouraging a prospective client from attempting to wait until after the listing has expired in order to deal directly with the owner.

The exclusive right to sell contract is normally the only type of listing acceptable to multiple listing service organizations. The contract forms are usually formulated, printed and used exclusively by members of the group, with no other forms acceptable, for the sake of uniformity in information and agreement.

As a matter of full disclosure to prospective purchasers, it would be advisable to reveal complete information and facts concerning each listed property. Unexpected complications frequently arise prior to the completion of a transaction when the information portion of a cooperative listing is either incomplete or inaccurate.

Listing forms vary from the standpoint of content and format in every state and locality from coast to coast. For example, the listing form for residential property in one locality may simply state the price, terms, conditions, address, dates of effectiveness and contain the signatures of seller and agent. Anything more than that may be unnecessary and considered superfluous. In other localities, it may be important, from the matter of merchandising the property, to supplement the listing contract with a complete description and resume of the property. It is customary in some areas to combine the information portion of the listing with the contract portion, while in other districts it is customary to separate the two forms.

As it is with residential listings, the same will apply to listings on other types of property such as residential income, commercial, industrial, farms, and so on. It is strictly a matter of local laws and customs as to the necessity of legal phrasing, content and the format used in merchandising the listed property for prospective purchasers and cooperative real estate offices.

Exhibit 2-2 is a representative example of a combined listing contract and information sheet form, with an "exclusive right to sell" provision used by a great many brokerage offices throughout the country. The form structure and substance of the information and contract may vary substantially with individual brokerage firms, multiple listing services and local laws and customs. In any case, the basic fundamentals are all to the same purpose, which is to list, merchandise, and sell real property.

The format of this letter may be used to verify information for listing purposes or for notification to the lender in the event of sale.

Letter Of Inquiry To Lender

X-Y-Z Mortgage Company
2468 Control St.   Re: Loan #2-6734928
Certain City, State

Gentlemen:

You hold a mortgage on the property located at (address) under the above loan
number. We have (listed this property for sale) or (sold this property and recording
date is anticipated to be on or about (date)). In order to verify certain conditions
of the existing loan, will you please provide us with the following information:

Original Loan Amount	Monthly Payment	Principal & Int.	Interest Rate
$	$	$	$

Present Loan Balance	Impound Balance	Type of Loan	Date Interest Paid To
$	$	$	$

Conditions Affecting Prepayment Of The Loan_____ .

Conditions Pertaining To Assumption Of The Loan_____ .

Hazard Insurance Information_____ .

Very truly yours,

(Owner's Names)

(Address)

(Date)

EXHIBIT 2-2 LETTER OF INQUIRY TO LENDER

Sales Contracts

STEPS TO TAKE

It is the law throughout the nation for some type of a "binder" to be written and signed by buyer and seller in connection with a buyer's offer to purchase real property, if the agreement is to be considered enforceable. The binder, in some localities, may be merely a form of memorandum drawn up by a real estate agent. It may contain the buyer's name, address, the property address, the purchase price offered and the agent's name and address. An enforceable contract of sale or sales agreement would be drawn up by the buyer's attorney who would then submit the document to the seller's attorney for negotiation and/or acceptance.

The binder, in many instances, also serves as a receipt to the purchaser for any earnest money deposits received. Laws and customs may differ to a considerable degree concerning the buyer's signed offer to purchase. In a few localities, real estate agents are encouraged, but not required to allow the sales agreement to be drawn by an attorney for the purchaser.

Some states permit the real estate broker or his agent to draw up the combined "deposit receipt" and "binder" whereby certain terms and conditions are specified. However, the details are to be polished and processed by an attorney and the entire transaction is subsequently completed under the supervision of legal counsel.

The laws and customs of other states do not require the involvement of attorneys into real estate transactions under normal and ordinary circumstances, although attorneys are often employed in the event of complex negotiations and details. In such states where attorneys are not normally involved in real estate transactions, it is a legal custom for real estate brokers, or their agents, to use a deposit receipt form combined with the sales agreement when accepting an "earnest money deposit" to bind an offer received from a prospective buyer, at which point it is merely an "offer to purchase."

Details of the agreement, including all the terms and conditions pertaining to the transaction, are either written in or are already contained in the printed form. The "offer to purchase" is then submitted to the seller, by his real estate agent, for acceptance or negotiation in connection with some of the terms or conditions. When there is a complete meeting of the minds between buyer and seller and when the seller signs the buyer's offer to purchase, an enforceable contract is created.

Regardless of whether a sales agreement, or contract of sale, is drawn by an attorney or a real estate agent, in accordance with local laws and customs, it is a legal and valid contract when properly executed. Therefore, all eventualities such as price, terms and conditions, financial arrangements, personal property to be included in the sale, possession date, buyer's assurance of receiving marketable title, agent's commission and other pertinent details should be set forth in the contract. Provision should also be made for a complete understanding as to the return of deposits in the event an offer is not accepted and for disposition of deposit monies if the buyer fails to perform as agreed.

Although local laws and customs may provide adequately for some eventualities and performances, even though not written into the contract, it is often more prudent and expedient to include them in the contract of sale.

Under normal circumstances, real estate brokers, or agents working under their supervision, are not technically obligated to perform other than to bring a ready, willing and able buyer to a ready, willing and able seller who has authorized such performance. It is not required of him to draw up any type of sales or purchase agreement in order to have earned a commission, provided he has authorization from the seller to bring him a buyer and can prove that he did so act.

However, some form of "binder," "sales agreement" or "contract of sale" is normally prepared by the agent in order to verify that he is the procuring cause of the sale. Where the seller has authorized the broker to accept an earnest money deposit from the buyer, it would also be necessary to hand the buyer a receipt for such deposit. Listing agreements most usually provide for the agent to accept deposit monies in behalf of the seller, but if there is no such provision, the agent may accept deposit monies in the buyer's behalf until the offer to purchase or contract of sale has been accepted and signed by the seller. In such case a receipt for the deposit would also be handed to the purchaser, with the funds retained in the broker's "escrow" or "trust account."

In the localities where the drawing of the formal contract of sale is customarily performed by attorneys, the agent may take the buyer to an attorney who will draw up a preliminary offer to purchase and receive any deposits in connection with the purchase, to be held in the attorney's "escrow" or "trust account."

Attorneys in localities where the formal contract of sale is drawn by them, are often apprehensive about "binders" and "deposit receipts" being written by real estate agents, as there may be some limitations as to the details of the formal contract of sale, due to defective phrasing, which may provide loopholes for the offeror, or otherwise not be legally binding.

However, in most states, the accepted practice is for the broker, or his salespeople, to write up some form of an originating agreement for the buyer and seller to sign and have a detailed form of sales contract drawn by an attorney. In such localities, real estate agents are aware of local laws and customs to the extent of creating valid and binding contracts without later repercussions.

As mentioned previously, there are some states in which the real estate agent draws up the contract of sale or sales agreement himself without benefit of legal counsel, except in difficult or complex transactions. In such states, the agent is required to possess a practical working knowledge of local real estate law in order to be licensed. Brokers are required to have even a higher level in knowledge of local real estate laws in order to assume the responsibility for the acts of salespeople working under them.

The public is well-protected through most established laws and it is considered to be the fault of the broker if and when defective contracts are prepared by him or someone under his supervision. His real estate license could be revoked or suspended for the violation of certain laws and acts of his agents working under him. The seriousness of defective sales agreements and consequences suffered by clients are included in those violations. The above is generally true in practically all states. However, without legal counsel to guide him and his clients it is necessary for the broker and agent to exercise a little more care and caution than may be necessary to exercise in other states, where attorneys are always employed to handle the details.

As a general rule, the prudent real estate broker will at least employ the services of an attorney to edit and help formulate a sales agreement form whereby as many contingencies as possible are provided for in print. Thus, it is a matter of filling in the blank spaces correctly.

It would be impossible to set forth every detail concerning a transaction in the printed form of contract. However, it is possible to provide for the normal requisites and usual occurrences.

Exhibit 3-1 is a representative example of a printed form of an "agreement for sale of real estate" including purchaser's deposit receipt and

Sales Contracts

(1) Date ___March 1, 197—___

AGREEMENT FOR THE SALE OF REAL ESTATE
Including purchasers deposit receipt and sellers authorization for sale

☐ Cash   ☒ Check   ☐ Note

(2) This will acknowledge receipt from ___John J. Jones and Mary F. Jones___

(3) hereinafter called "buyer" whose address is ___115 Park Street, Your City and State___

(4) ___the sum of $ __500__ (Five Hundred)__ dollars as a deposit on account of the

purchase price of the following described property which buyer hereby offers to purchase, situated in the City of ___Your City___

(5) County of ___Your County and State___

___2115 Agency Street, Your City and State. Lot 115 Glen Subdivision # 2.___

This offer to purchase shall constitute an agreement to sell and purchase the above described real property upon the terms herein set forth upon
seller accepting this offer by signing below

(6) Said deposit shall be increased to ___Twelve Hundred – no – 00___ dollars ($ __1,200__) within ___three___
days after execution of this agreement by the seller.

(7) The total purchase price is ___Twenty Three Thousand Nine Hundred Fifty___ dollars ($ __23,950__) on
which said deposit shall apply, the balance to be paid as follows

(8) This agreement is conditioned on buyer's immediate application and subsequent approval, within
30 days, for a new conventional loan in the amount of $20,000 for 30 years, payable at approx.
$146.80 per month, including principal and interest of 8% per annum, plus taxes and insurance
payments. Loan fees of approximately $600 to be paid by seller. Buyer to pay a cash down
payment of $3,950 plus normal Non-Recurring and Recurring closing costs, except loan fees, for
said new loan when escrow is in position to close. Above earnest money deposits to apply towards
said purchase price and closing costs. Seller to pay seller's normal closing costs and expenses
plus the new loan fees from proceeds of sale. Buyer to pay additional $500 to seller for water
softener upon final settlement of this transaction.

AND IT IS HEREBY AGREED

(9) 1 Possession and Occupancy Agreement Seller shall give buyer possession of premises ___May 15, 197—___
If buyer is given possession before legal title passes, buyer shall be a tenant at will and shall pay rent in advance of $ __6.00__ per day
If seller retains possession after legal title passes, seller shall be a tenant at will and shall pay rent in advance of $ __6.00__ per day
In any litigation involving occupancy under this paragraph, prevailing party shall be entitled to reasonable attorney's fees

(10) 2 Termite Clearance. If, within 7 days from date, seller has not submitted a termite clearance report into escrow which is dated less than six months
before the date escrow will close, then buyer hereby instructs _____ Realty to order a structural pest control and dry rot inspection by a
licensed operator ___Buyer___ shall pay cost of any inspection report ordered after date of this agreement and seller shall pay for any
recommended corrective work ___or conventional___

(11) 3 That in the event a new loan is to be obtained through the F.H.A. or V.A in conjunction with the purchase of the herein described property, the
seller shall deliver to the buyer, upon receipt of same by seller, the official form as issued by the F.H.A. or the V.A. showing their valuation to be in
the amount of at least ($ __23,950__) and if this is not done the buyer shall have the option of demanding and receiving back all
monies paid hereon excepting occupancy charge if any, and rescinding or enforcing this agreement. Both buyer and seller further agree that they
will abide by all rules and regulations as set forth by the governmental agency processing the loan and the loaning agent. In the event a current
F.H.A. or V.A. appraisal does not exist the cost to secure one will be paid by ___seller has already paid for FHA app. fee.___

(12) 4 That existing insurance policies are to be ___cancelled___ as of ___recording date___ 19___
If possession is prior to recording of the deed, the buyer agrees to provide insurance with loss payable to the seller in an amount satisfactory to
the seller

(13) 5 Taxes are to be pro-rated as of ___recording date___ 19___

(14) 6 That any existing street, sewer or special assessment bonds shall be paid by the ___seller if any balance exists.___

(15) 7 That this writing including the terms and conditions on the reverse side hereof expresses the entire contract of the parties and there are no other
understandings or representations, oral or written, which in any manner alter its terms

(16) REALTY by ___Gertrude Smith (sig)___ (Broker's Initials) D.O.

I (or We) agree to purchase the above described property on the terms and conditions herein stated

(17) MAKE DEED TO ___John J. Jones and Mary F. Jones – his wife – as joint tenants___

(18) ___John J. Jones (sig)___ Phone ___231-9160___ ___Mary J. Jones (sig)___
BUYER   BUYER

(19) I (or We) agree to sell and convey the above described property on the terms and conditions as herein stated and the undersigned seller hereby agrees
to pay an amount equal to (__6__%) of sales price to _____ Realty, as commission for effecting said sale Said commission to be paid by escrow
agent handling the transaction or any part thereof may be retained by the said agent from the first money received on account of said purchase price
The undersigned acknowledges receipt of a copy hereof

(20) ___James A. Howe (sig)___ ___Marie A. Howe (sig)___
SELLER   SELLER

EXHIBIT 3-1 AGREEMENT FOR SALE (FRONT SIDE)

The contract on the reverse side is subject to the following terms and conditions

1. That title to said property shall be subject only to any existing restrictions, conditions, reservations, easements of record, and other zoning ordinances and governmental regulations. If any other encumbrances or defect of title be found to exist, the seller shall remove same within a reasonable length of time, and if he does not do so the purchaser shall have the option of rescinding this agreement and demanding and receiving back said deposit, or of paying and retiring said defect or encumbrance and deducting said sum from the purchase price.

2. That evidence of title is to be a policy of title insurance, issued by a responsible title company, furnished and paid for by the seller. Escrow handling charges are also to be paid by seller.

3. That in the event a new G.I. loan is to be placed on the herein described property and a termite or pest inspection is required for the completion of said loan, the seller shall cause the premises to be inspected by a licensed termite inspector and comply with all recommendations as set forth in the inspection report. Fees and cost of repairs, if any, shall be at the expense of the seller. In the event the report is required by the buyer, F.H.A. or lender, the buyer agrees to pay the cost of such inspection. Repairs, if any, to be paid for by the seller. The buyer expressly agrees that in the event such repairs are necessary to comply with said licensed inspectors report, that such repairs shall be made to inspectors satisfaction and any dispute concerning said repairs shall not be deemed material in an avoidance of this agreement.

4. That the buyer shall reimburse the seller for any Impound Account deposits held by the mortgagee.

5. That if, before delivery of deed or the taking of possession, (whichever is first), any of the improvements on said property are destroyed or materially damaged by fire or other cause, the buyer shall have the option of enforcing this agreement or cancelling by written notice within ten (10) days thereafter. If cancelled, all monies paid hereon shall be returned to the buyer.

6. That in the event new financing should fail (due to restrictions as set forth by the F.H.A. or the V.A. or the loaning agency) and the purchaser is in possession of the premises under the occupancy agreement herein contained, the purchaser specifically agrees that he will waive all rights that may be acquired by virtue of this agreement, and will quit and leave the premises (in as good a condition as of date of possession) within 30 days after receiving notice of failure of such financing. The purchaser further agrees that monies pro-rated as of date of possession on the basis of the occupancy clause may be retained and passed to the seller as agreed compensation for the use and occupancy of the premises.

7. That the act of taking possession of the premises by the buyer under the terms of the occupancy agreement contained on the reverse side hereof shall be deemed conclusive evidence of his prior inspection and satisfaction as to the condition of the property and improvements thereon and that there are no warranties or representations express or implied by the owner or the agent not herein contained. The buyer further agrees that the said taking of possession shall constitute his acceptance of liability as to the maintenance and upkeep of the premises and any improvements thereon including lawns, shrubs and trees, and that he shall be fully responsible for any damage to the premises caused by his acts or omissions or from any cause whatsoever, excepting overt acts of the seller subsequent to the date of possession.

8. That if the seller has kept his part of the contract and the buyer fails to comply with the contract on his part as herein provided (unless such failure shall be caused by restrictions as set forth by the F.H.A. or the V.A. or the loaning agency), then the monies deposited by the buyer shall be retained by the seller, and this contract may or may not be operative thereafter at the option of the seller. Agent may retain one-half of any deposit monies forfeited by buyer, provided such shall not exceed the full amount of the commission.

9. That if either the buyer or seller, after execution of this agreement, causes this agreement to fail (excepting as provided in Clause 8), the offending party promises to pay all attorney fees that may be incurred in the enforcement of this agreement.

10. That said property is sold subject to the approval of the owner, and in consideration of the execution of this agreement, the agent is granted the right for a period of fifteen (15) days to obtain such approval.

11. That the agent agrees to use due diligence in the completion of the sale as herein provided, and in consideration thereof, both buyer and seller promise and agree that if either party should cause this agreement to fail (excepting as provided in Clause 8), the offending party shall pay the agent a commission in an amount as set forth by the local Real Estate Board in transactions of this type, and all attorney fees that may be incurred in the enforcement of the payment of said commission, such fees being due and payable at the time of failure.

12. That the agent shall not be held responsible for the failure to comply with the terms of this agreement by either the buyer or the seller.

13. That time is the essence of this agreement.

Additional terms and conditions:
_____
_____
_____
_____
_____
_____
_____

EXHIBIT 3-1 REVERSE SIDE

seller's authorization for sale. The format, terms, conditions and provisions may differ in some instances, in accordance with local laws and customs in the various states, but in general, all the necessary stipulations required are contained in this form. Standard terms and conditions printed in the form will apply according to the type of transaction and financial arrangements to which agreement is made.

Each step to take in filling in the spaces is in numerical order below and corresponds with those numbers indicated on the form.

1. Date of agreement.
2. Full names of purchasers.
3. Complete address of the purchasers.
4. Amount of "earnest money" deposited.
5. Complete address and legal description of property.
6. Amount of increase in "earnest money" deposit and when to be, if at all.
7. Total purchase price of the property.
8. Financial arrangement for payment to the seller. Other conditions.
9. Possession date. Rental amount for prior possession by buyer or future retention of the property by the seller.
10. Termite and dry rot agreement. Which party to pay inspection and repair fees and charges.
11. New loan appraisal agreement. Appraisal amount should at least equal purchase price on FHA and VA transactions. Who pays appraisal fees.
12. Date hazard insurance is to be "cancelled" or "prorated."
13. Date taxes to be prorated.
14. Assessment bonds to be paid by seller or assumed by buyer.
15. Refers to terms and conditions on reverse side of agreement.
16. Name of real estate firm and salesman's signature.
17. How title of ownership is to be indicated on deed when it is drawn.
18. Purchaser's signatures.
19. Amount of commission (agent's fee). Use percentage of sales price rather than dollar amounts in the event of change of price on a counter-offer. Dollar amounts of commissions may have to be changed, but percentages of sales price remain constant.
20. Sellers' signatures.

Additional space is provided on the reverse side of the form, which is shown as Exhibit 3-1, in the event more space is needed for other terms and conditions, financial arrangements or counter-offers.

Reference to the reverse side of the form should be made on the front when the additional space is used, for example, "See reverse side of this agreement for additional terms and conditions, etc."

Buyer and seller should both be made aware of the printed conditions on the reverse side of the form in any case.

COUNTER-OFFERS

When an agent is employed by a seller, through a listing contract, to sell the property at a certain price and under certain terms and conditions and the purchaser submits his offer to purchase on the exact same price, terms and conditions, the property is normally considered sold upon communication of such fact to the seller. However, local laws may differ or be more specific under certain circumstances.

On the other hand, it is not uncommon for a buyer to offer a lower price or condition his offer under different terms and conditions than those specified in the listing contract. In such cases, the seller may accept the offer as it is submitted by the buyer or he may either insist on the listed price, terms and conditions or offer to compromise with the buyer on certain aspects.

If the seller changes the offer submitted, in any manner or form, it is considered a counter-offer and the contract is not complete until the buyer accepts the change.

PHRASING FINANCIAL ARRANGEMENTS

It is extremely important in a real estate transaction for a complete understanding and agreement between buyer and seller. This, of course, includes terms, conditions and the manner in which the purchaser intends to pay for the property being purchased. Unless the phrasing of financial arrangements is clear, an offer to purchase may be intended one way by the purchaser and his agent, but interpreted in another way by the seller, his agent, or the lender in the event the transaction is dependent on the obtaining of new loan funds.

When the terms for payment involve a new loan, which is to be secured by the property being purchased, it is essential that the lender and/or government sponsoring agency know exactly what the loan applicant is requesting in the way of new financing. Since real estate loans are normally granted according to terms and conditions outlined in the sale and purchase agreement, accurate phrasing of the financial arrangements is mandatory. Otherwise, the buyer may not receive the expected or required loan amount.

Although it is common practice by a great number of real estate agents

41

to specify the exact amount of loan, the exact interest rate, the exact amount of payments, etc., these terms often constitute "built-in" loopholes for a buyer. If there should happen to be some differential between the amounts written into a sales agreement and the figures that may later develop, there could be a problem in closing escrow.

For example, an error of $50 in an F.H.A. loan computation written into a sales agreement could be fatal to the transaction ever closing in escrow. Whereas, if it had been written that the buyer was to receive the maximum loan available, under the conditions of that particular F.H.A. program, and received the maximum loan, there would be no problem. The lender and F.H.A. will compute the maximum loan and will allow it when the buyer, the property and other factors involved justify it.

In our present economic trend of fluctuating interest rates, when a specific interest rate is written into the agreement, it may be equally as bad for the buyer as it may be good.

For example, when interest rates reduce, the lender will normally increase discount points to be paid by the seller, if the buyer takes advantage of the reduced rate. If a higher rate is specified in the sale and purchase agreement, the seller would be justified in holding the buyer to the higher rate in order that he may receive advantage of lower discount points. This could be a problem in closing escrow.

However, if both buyer and seller agree to accept prevailing interest rates and to pay necessary discount points, respectively, at the close of escrow, the matter is resolved for both parties regardless of what would happen to interest rates or the money market.

Naturally, a change in interest rates will have an effect on monthly payments. When monthly payments are specified in the sale and purchase agreement and if interest rates increase, the buyer may want to renegotiate the entire transaction or withdraw completely from the purchase. Such a situation places the seller at a distinct disadvantage and possible financial loss.

While it is necessary for the real estate agent to protect his buyer, it is also necessary to protect the seller. Therefore, loopholes should never be provided whereby either party may place the other in a position of disadvantage.

The phrasing of financial arrangements, outlined herein, are provided for the purpose of saving time in the composition of financial terms and conditions in a clearly stated form. Variations and modifications may be utilized in some localities in order to conform with local laws, customs and individual company policies in writing offers to purchase and sales agreements pertaining to real estate transactions. In any case, it is a good business practice to provide real estate salespeople with an outline of phrasing financial arrangements for the types of transactions most commonly developed in their working area.

ALL CASH TO SELLER—SUBJECT TO NEW LOAN FUNDS

When the buyer's purchase depends on his ability to obtain new loan funds to be secured by the property being purchased, the seller will receive all cash from the sale, after expenses, provided the funds are granted to the buyer and escrow closes.

Under those circumstances, it is necessary to inform the seller of all known facts as to the buyer's requirements in securing such loan funds. It is also necessary to inform the seller as to the type of loan to be obtained, when application for the loan is to be instigated and an approximate period of time required to finalize the entire transaction if the loan is approved. Such information is important to the seller in order that he may plan accordingly prior to his acceptance of an offer to purchase.

On the other hand, the buyer's deposit monies and other interests must be protected in the event he is unable to secure the anticipated loan funds. If and when there is to be some delay in making loan application, loan approval and finalization, the details should be written into the sales agreement and approved by the seller prior to acceptance of the proposal in order to avoid later complications.

F.H.A. LOAN PROGRAMS

The phrasing shown below will apply to all F.H.A. programs by specifying the applicable program in the space provided. The financial arrangement should be written as follows:

This agreement is conditioned on buyer's immediate application and approval for the maximum new F.H.A. (specify FHA program) loan based on total F.H.A. value. Said loan to be secured by a note and (trust deed) or (mortgage) on the subject property for a term of _____ years at the lowest interest rate prevailing at close of escrow. Balance of purchase price to be paid in cash (or other described liquid assets owned by buyer.) Buyer to pay buyer's normal non-recurring and recurring closing costs and expenses to obtain said new loan when escrow is in position to close. Above earnest money deposits to apply towards said purchase price, closing costs and expenses.

Seller is to pay seller's normal closing costs, expenses and required discount points to obtain said new loan, from proceeds of sale. (Or in advance for appraisal fee if seller is to pay it.)

Pest control inspection fee is to be paid by _____. Pest control repairs

43

and expenses to be paid by _____. Appraisal fee, If no commitment exists, to be paid by _____. Appraised value to be in an amount of at least $ _____.

VARIED CONDITIONS—ON F.H.A. LOANS

Sweat Equity

When an F.H.A. Loan Commitment specifies certain conditions to be met such as painting and repairs to the improvements, prior to insuring the loan, the seller is permitted to credit the buyer for labor and materials supplied by the buyer, towards the required amount of buyer's down payment and closing costs. Such a credit allowance is called a "sweat equity."

The allowable credit cannot exceed a reasonable amount the seller would have to pay a contractor, carpenter or painter to do the required work. However, it may exceed the total amount of cash normally required of a buyer under ordinary circumstances. The buyer must be in a financial position to pay cash for any labor and materials involved in the necessary painting or repairs.

It is advisable for a buyer to prolong doing the "sweat equity" work until after his loan has been approved by F.H.A. and he sees that no problems exist which may prevent escrow from closing. Although escrow cannot close until the work is completed, it is better to wait, as the buyer may lose his time and materials if he does not otherwise qualify for the loan.

In the event a "sweat equity" is possible and is one of the conditions to the purchase, it should be written into the financial arrangements of the offer to purchase as follows:

Buyer to receive credit in the amount of $_____, from seller in escrow, for the following "sweat equity"—Panel D work as required by the F.H.A. loan commitment issued on the subject property. (Describe work to be done by buyer.)

SECONDARY FINANCING—OTHER THAN SUBJECT PROPERTY

At the time of originating a new F.H.A. loan there can be no secondary mortgages or trust deeds secured by the subject property in lieu of the buyer's down payment and closing cost requirements. However, it is allowable, by F.H.A., for the buyer to give a willing seller a trust deed or mortgage on another property, owned by the buyer, in lieu of cash for the down payment and closing costs or as a portion of the purchase price. If it is necessary, or desired, for the buyer to purchase under these terms and conditions, it should be written additionally into the financial arrangements as follows:

> Buyer will give Seller a (1st or 2nd, etc.) note and (trust deed) (mortgage) in the amount of $_____ in lieu of cash for the required down payment and closing costs. Said (trust deed)–(mortgage) to be secured by property located at (address of property). Buyer's equity is approximately $ _____ in said securing property. Note and (trust deed)–(mortgage) is to bear an interest rate of ____% per annum with monthly principal and interest payments of $_____, or more, and to be paid in full within _____ years or upon sale of the property whichever occurs first.

When payments of a certain amount are stated and followed by the words, "or more," the entire balance could be paid off anytime the mortgagor wants prior to maturity.

An existing note and trust deed or mortgage held by the buyer may also be used in the same manner when purchasing property. In such case, it should be described in the financial arrangements in order that the seller may understand what he would be accepting in lieu of cash.

F.H.A. will allow a purchaser to trade in any of his assets the seller may be willing to accept, as long as it has a value equal to, or exceeding, the amount required under ordinary circumstances, provided it is properly described.

SELLER TO PAY BUYER'S NONRECURRING CLOSING COSTS

In instances where a property is being purchased at total F.H.A. value, which is value plus nonrecurring closing costs, the seller should pay the buyer's nonrecurring closing costs. Otherwise, the buyer would be paying them twice, once by financing them and again in cash. However, when the purchase is at value, excluding closing costs, the buyer must pay his own nonrecurring closing costs in order to obtain the maximum loan. (See F.H.A. Programs in Financing chapters.)

The seller is permitted to pay buyer's nonrecurring costs, but is not allowed to pay any of the buyer's recurring costs which are used for the purpose of establishing the buyer's impound account. These items are normally referred to as "Prepaids." (See Closing Costs for Buyer's in New Loan chapters.)

When the seller is to pay buyer's nonrecurring costs, it should be specified in the financial arrangements as follows:

This agreement is conditioned on buyer's immediate application and approval for the maximum new F.H.A. (specify FHA program) loan based on total F.H.A. value. Said loan to be secured by a note and (trust deed) or (mortgage) on the subject property for a term of _____ years at the lowest interest rate prevailing at close of escrow. Balance of purchase price to be paid in cash (or other described liquid assets owned by buyer). Buyer to pay only normal recurring closing costs and expenses to obtain said new loan when escrow is in position to close. Above earnest money deposits to apply towards said purchase price, closing costs and expenses. Seller is to pay buyer's nonrecurring closing costs plus seller's normal closing costs, expenses and required discount points to obtain said new loan, from proceeds of sale. (Appraisal fee in advance if seller is to pay it.) Pest control inspection fee, repairs and expenses to be paid by seller. Appraisal fee, if no commitment exists, to be paid by seller. Appraised value to be in an amount of at least $_____ .

VETERANS ADMINISTRATION—G.I. LOANS

The Veterans Administration will allow a 100% loan based on their appraisal (Certificate of Reasonable Value). The buyer is not required to make a down payment when purchasing the property at a price equal to, or lower than, the appraisal amount indicated on the C.R.V. However, he may pay any amount of down payment he chooses unless he is paying more than the C.R.V. appraisal for the property. In that case he must pay the excess amount in cash from his own assets and sign a statement to that effect when applying for his loan or when offering to purchase.

A veteran is not required to pay any of his closing costs in establishing a new G.I. loan if the seller is willing to pay them for him. Thus, the veteran could purchase a single family residence, or a two, three or four-unit residence without any cash invested, if he otherwise qualifies, and if the seller is willing to sell on the basis of paying all the buyer's closing costs. (See *New G.I. Loans* in financing chapters.)

CASH DOWN PAYMENT—G.I. LOAN

When a qualified veteran purchases property under his G.I. loan entitlement and the transaction involves the necessity of his paying a down payment or in the event he desires to do so, the financial arrangements should be written as follows:

This agreement is conditioned on buyer's immediate application and approval for a new G.I. loan in the amount of $(loan amount desired). Said loan to be secured by a note and (trust deed) or (mortgage) on the subject property for a term of _____ years at the lowest interest rate prevailing for G.I. loans at close of escrow. Balance of purchase price to be paid in cash by buyer. Buyer to pay all of buyer's normal closing costs and expenses to obtain said new loan when escrow is in position to close. Above earnest money deposits to apply towards purchase price, closing costs and expenses.

Seller to pay seller's normal closing costs, expenses and required discount points, involved with this transaction, from proceeds of sale. Pest control inspection fee to be paid by seller (buyer not allowed to pay). Pest control repairs and expenses to be paid by seller.

Appraisal fee, if no current C.R.V. exists, to be paid in advance by _____ .

Appraised value to be in an amount of at least $_____ .

100% G.I. LOANS

Most G.I. loans are granted on a 100% of the purchase price basis, where there is no down payment required and should be written as follows:

This agreement is conditioned on buyer's immediate application and approval for a new G.I. loan in the amount of $(purchase price). Said loan to be secured by a note and (trust deed) or (mortgage) on the subject property for a term of _____ years at the lowest interest rate prevailing for G.I. loans at close of escrow. Buyer to pay all of buyer's normal closing costs and expenses to obtain said new loan when escrow is in position to close. Above earnest money deposits to apply towards closing costs and expenses.

Seller to pay seller's normal closing costs, expenses and required discount points, involved with this transaction, from proceeds of sale. Pest control inspection fee to be paid by seller (buyer not allowed to pay). Pest control repairs and expenses to be paid by seller.

Appraisal fee, if no current C.R.V. exists, to be paid in advance by _____ .

Appraised Value to be in an amount of at least $_____ .

100% G.I. LOAN—BUYER'S CLOSING COSTS PAID BY SELLER

In some instances, a qualified veteran has no cash on hand with which to pay a down payment or his closing costs, but is financially capable of making payments on the home being purchased. Sellers are often under some sort of circumstances whereby they are willing to do almost anything within reason in order to sell their property, including paying the buyer's closing costs. When such conditions are prevalent, the financial arrangements are specified as follows:

This agreement is conditioned on buyer's immediate application and approval for a new G.I. loan in the amount of $(purchase price). Said loan to be secured by a note and (trust deed) or (mortgage) on the subject property for a term of _____ years at the lowest interest rate prevailing for G.I. loans at close of escrow.

Seller to pay all of buyer's normal closing costs and expenses to obtain said new

47

loan plus all seller's normal closing costs, expenses and required discount points involved with this transaction, from proceeds of sale.

All pest control inspection fees and repairs to be paid by <u>seller</u>. Appraisal fee, if no current C.R.V. exists, to be paid in advance by _____ .

Above earnest money deposits to be returned to buyer upon close of escrow.

Appraised value to be in an amount of at least $_____ .

CALIFORNIA VETERANS LOANS

In the state of California, a special loan is offered to veterans who are native born in California or were inducted into military service from there. It is covered here in order to illustrate the writing of financial arrangements for similiar types of veterans assistance programs existing in other states.

Loan funds are usually available only on a priority basis; therefore, the California Department of Veterans Affairs would be contacted by the veteran and agent prior to submitting an offer to purchase on the basis of a new Cal-Vet loan.

The financial arrangements for this type of purchase should be written as follows:

This agreement is conditioned on buyer's immediate application and subsequent approval for a new Cal-Vet loan, on the subject property, in the amount of $ _____ . Balance of purchase price to be paid in cash (or other assets). Buyer to pay buyer's normal closing costs and expenses to obtain said new loan when escrow is in position to close.

Seller to pay seller's normal closing costs and expenses, involved with this transaction, from proceeds of sale.

Pest control inspection fee to be paid by _____ .

Pest control repairs and expenses to be paid by _____ .

CONVENTIONAL LOANS

Conventional loans are those granted by lending institutions without government agency sponsorship or backing. Therefore, the conventional type loan normally requires a larger cash investment and higher interest rates.

Since conventional loan terms, conditions and interest rates are not regulated by F.H.A. or the Veterans Administration, they become a matter of the lender's policies in connection with the purchaser's capabilities and property location and condition.

Conventional lenders are usually local institutions or are represented by local correspondents who are in a position to issue quotations and verbal commitments on an almost daily basis. The effect is an established rate of interest, maximum loan and definite loan fees at the time an offer to purchase is written. Under those circumstances these details may be specified in the financial arrangements without the possibility of having to renegotiate at the close of escrow because of a change in the money market or government regulated interest rates.

The financial arrangements for conventional loans could be stated as follows:

> This agreement is conditioned on buyer's immediate application and subsequent approval, within _____ days, for a new conventional loan in the amount of $(loan desired) for _____ years, payable at approximately $ _____ per month, including principal and interest of _____% per annum plus taxes and insurance payments. Loan fees of approximately $_____ to be paid by_____ .
>
> Buyer to pay cash down payment of $_____plus normal nonrecurring and recurring closing costs for said new loan when escrow is in position to close. Above earnest money deposits to apply towards said purchase price and closing costs.
>
> Seller to pay seller's normal closing costs and expenses from proceeds of sale.
>
> Pest control inspection fee to be paid by _____ .
>
> Pest control repairs and expenses to be paid by _____ .

CONVENTIONAL LOAN—SELLER TO CARRY

In instances where the purchaser does not have sufficient cash funds to pay the entire amount to the available maximum conventional loan, it may be possible that the lender will permit the buyer to pay half of the down payment in cash and allow the seller to carry the balance of the down payment in secondary financing. Such arrangements should be verified prior to writing the offer to purchase and if the lender is willing, the financial arrangements could be written as follows:

> This agreement is conditioned on buyer's immediate application and subsequent approval, within _____ days, for a new conventional loan in the amount of $ _____ for _____years, payable at approximately $ _____per month, including principal and interest of _____% per annum plus taxes and insurance. Loan fees of approximately $_____to be paid by _____ .
>
> Buyer to pay a cash down payment of $_____ plus buyer's normal nonrecurring and recurring closing costs for said new loan when escrow is in position to close. Above earnest money deposits to apply towards said purchase price and closing costs.
>
> Seller to carry a second note and (trust deed) or (mortgage) in the amount of $_____ for balance of purchase price. Said note and (trust deed) or

(mortgage) to be payable at $_____ or more, per month, including principal and interest of _____% per annum (until paid) or (to be paid in full) within _____ years.

Said security instrument to contain the following special clauses—(acceleration) (alienation) (escalation) (prepayment) (others).

Pest control inspection fee to be paid by _____ .

Pest control repairs and expenses to be paid by _____ .

Note: When monthly payments are stated at "$ _____ or more," it provides the mortgagor with the option of paying off the entire principal balance at any time prior to maturity. This should be eliminated if the seller insists on having some sort of prepayment penalty clause contained in the mortgage security instrument.

All special clauses must be mutually agreed on offer and acceptance and cannot be inserted or deleted later.

LOAN ASSUMPTION—STRAIGHT

When the buyer intends to pay cash for the difference between purchase price and existing loan or loans, the agreement should indicate whether the buyer is to pay cash down to the loan "subject to the loan" or "assuming the existing loan." If the purchase is "subject to the loan," the buyer is not taking any responsibility for the loan obligation other than to make payments. In the event of foreclosure, only the seller is to be held responsible for any deficiencies resulting from foreclosure action.

To "assume the loan" means the buyer is taking responsibility of the loan obligation and may be held liable to the lender for any deficiencies resulting from foreclosure action. (See *Loan Assumption* in financing chapters.)

Loan assumption financial arrangements should be written as follows:

Buyer to pay a cash down payment in the approximate amount of $_____and (assume the existing (describe) loan) or (purchase subject to the existing (describe) loan) in the approximate amount of $_____. Buyer to replace seller's impound account and pay buyer's normal closing costs and expenses when escrow is in position to close. Above earnest money deposits to apply towards down payment and closing costs.

Pest control inspection fee to be paid by _____ .

Pest control repairs and expenses to be paid by _____ .

LOAN ASSUMPTION—SELLER TO CARRY

In a loan assumption transaction where the purchaser does not have sufficient cash to pay the entire amount of the seller's equity between sales price and existing loan balance, the seller may be willing to carry a portion of his equity in secondary financing.

There are times when a seller may not want all his equity in cash in one year for tax reasons. In that case the words, "or more," should be eliminated and not indicated after the amount of monthly payment as shown in the phrasing below, as these two words give the mortgagor (buyer) the option of paying the full principal balance at any time prior to maturity, or any portion thereof.

The financial arrangements for this type of transaction should be written as follows:

Buyer to pay a cash down payment in the amount of $_____ and (assume the existing (type) loan) or (purchase subject to the existing (type) loan) in the approximate amount of $_____.

Seller to carry balance of his equity on a note and (trust deed) or (mortgage) in the approximate amount of $_____ payable at $_____, or more, per month, including principal and interest of _____% per annum (for _____ years) or (to be paid in full within _____ years.) Said mortgage security instrument to contain the following special clauses—(acceleration) (alienation) (escalation) (prepayment) (others).

Buyer to replace seller's impound account in cash or (to be added to note) plus balance of down payment and buyer's normal closing costs and expenses when escrow is in position to close. Above earnest money deposits to apply towards down payment and closing costs.

Pest control inspection fee to be paid by _____.

Pest control repairs and expenses to be paid by _____.

LOAN ASSUMPTION—NO PRORATIONS

There are times when a buyer has only a specific amount of available cash to invest in a purchase and not a dollar more. If the existing loan balance should be lower than estimated or the seller's impound account higher than anticipated or if the buyer had to pay the seller some tax and insurance prorations, the buyer would be short of funds.

In order that the buyer may know exactly where he stands in cash outlay, and the seller may know exactly what he will receive, the transaction could be written as follows:

Buyer to pay a total of $_____ cash for seller's equity and (assume the existing (type) loan) or (purchase subject to the existing (type) loan) in the approximate amount of $_____, but not to exceed $_____.*

---

*Prevents buyer from having to assume an excessive existing loan balance.

Seller's impound account to be transferred free to buyer with no prorations of taxes or insurance. Existing monthly loan payments are to be currently paid. Current earned interest to be charged to the seller and credited to the buyer in escrow.

Pest control inspection fee to be paid by _____ .

Pest control repairs and expenses to be paid by _____ .

LOAN ASSUMPTION—INSTALLMENT CONTRACTS

Installment Contract of Sale

When the buyer has limited funds to invest in a purchase of real estate, from the standpoint of down payment, the seller may be willing to sell provided he may have control of the property and existing loan obligations until such time the buyer has paid in sufficient monies to accumulate a substantial equity or until some other condition has been modified. In some instances, it may involve full payment of the purchase price before the seller conveys title to the property to the buyer.

In such transactions, where the seller retains title to the property, the written agreement is called an Installment Contract of Sale or an Installment Sales Contract. The purchaser normally pays the seller in monthly payments on the remaining balance, after the down payment, plus interest, taxes and insurance. Interest is based on the balance due to the seller and the rate of interest is usually considerably higher than the interest the seller pays on any loans which may exist against the property. (See the financing chapter on *Installment Contract of Sale* for more details.)

This instrument is widely used in some sections of the country, but has limited usage in other states and localities.

It is normally impossible to insert all the details of such transactions into the original sales agreement or offer to purchase agreement. In any case, the details of this form of sale should be worked out and drawn by legal counsel.

However, since all agreements must have a starting point, the following phrasing will show intent as to how the buyer proposes to pay for his purchase:

Buyer to pay a total cash down payment in the amount of $_____ .

Seller to carry balance of purchase price on an Installment Contract of Sale payable at $_____ or more per month, including principal and interest of _____% per annum plus impound account payments for taxes, insurance and assessments.

When $ _____ has been applied to the principal balance, seller is to transfer title of property ownership to buyer and impound account is to be transferred free to

52

buyer, with the remaining principal balance to be converted and secured by a note and (trust deed) or (mortgage). Buyer then to (assume existing loan balance) or (to take property subject to the loan).

All-inclusive Mortgage or Trust Deed

This type of sales contract is similiar to the Installment Contract of Sale described in previous paragraphs. The primary difference is in the fact that the seller conveys ownership title to the property to the buyer upon close of escrow and carries junior mortgage or trust deed for the balance of purchase price less the down payment.

The buyer pays interest on the full amount of principal balance to the seller, plus amortization payments on the principal and taxes, insurance and assessment balance payments due on the property. These payments are usually made on a monthly basis.

This contract is sometimes called a "Wrap Around Mortgage or Trust Deed," since it includes any other previously existing mortgage loans against the property.

As it is with the Installment Contract of Sale, the buyer pays the seller a specified amount each month and the seller in turn pays any existing mortgage payments, taxes, insurance, etc., which become due, out of such payment received from the buyer. Usually, when the seller has received all his equity, which is the difference between sales price and existing loan balances at the time of sale, the buyer is released from the "All-Inclusive" security instrument and assumes obligation of any remaining mortgage loan balances. (See the financing chapter on *All-inclusive mortgages.)*

The phrasing of financial arrangements for this type of contract should be written as follows:

Buyer to pay a total cash down payment of $_____ and replace seller's impound account on existing loan.

Seller to carry balance of purchase price in the amount of $_____ on an all inclusive mortgage or (trust deed) payable at $_____ or more per month including principal, interest, taxes, assessments and insurance.

Interest to be at the rate of _____% per annum.

Seller to transfer title (customary with locality) and buyer to assume existing loan balance as of recording date, with all payments currently paid.

Any existing loan payments are to be paid first from buyer's payments to seller and the balance applied to the principal balance remaining on this contract.

All payments to be collected and disbursed by a third party financial institution.

When a total of $_____ has been applied to principal balance due seller, buyer is to be released from this obligation of mortgage debt.

Buyer and seller to pay their respective normal closing costs and equally divide

53

any attorney fees charged for drawing the details of a subsequent agreement and examination of any documents pertinent to this transaction.

Pest control inspection fee to be paid by _____ .

Pest control repairs and recommendations to be paid by _____ .

Any existing assessment and/or improvement bonds shall be (paid) or (assumed) by (buyer)—(seller).

In the Installment Contract of Sale and the all-inclusive mortgage or trust deed type of transactions, it is often advisable for the buyer to pay his monthly payments to a reliable, mutually agreed, third party who in turn is to pay current payments on existing loans, taxes, insurance, etc., with funds received from the buyer, and forward the balance to the seller.

Mutually agreed details, involving the transaction, should be drawn by a competent attorney at law and his fees equally divided between buyer and seller. In the event the security instruments on existing loans contain special clauses, which would prevent the loans from being assumed, do not use these contracts as written above as the seller must be in position to deliver good and marketable title at a certain point in time.

4

Promissory Notes

Laws and customs pertaining to valid negotiable promissory notes and other security instruments in real property may vary from state to state, but the basic concepts of their utilization are similar throughout the nation.

Promissory notes play an important role in normal usage in connection with mortgages and trust deeds as security devices in granting real estate loans. The note is evidence of the debt while terms, conditions and obligations of the debt are recited in the mortgage instruments to which the evidence is attached.

Negotiable notes are two party instruments. The person who signs the note is the "maker" and the person to whom it is made is the "payee." There are three kinds of notes generally employed in real estate loan transactions. The differences lie in the manner of payment to principal and interest in retirement of the obligation.

STRAIGHT NOTE

This type of note provides for payment of interest only during the term of the note. When the note is due, the full amount of principal is paid at that time. Straight notes are often used when the maker anticipates the availability of sufficient future funds with which to clear up the obligation, but is limited in ability to pay large monthly payments until such future time. Exhibit 4-1 is an example of the form of this type note used in connection with a trust deed.

INSTALLMENT NOTE—PLUS INTEREST

Periodic payments are applied to the principal balance at a fixed amount. Interest payments are computed on the remaining balances and are considered as separate payments, although normally included as additional to the principal payment. Interest payments are reduced each time paid, due to amortization of the principal balance.

Promissory Note

(STRAIGHT)

$ ....

.... 19 ....

For value received ....

.... promise .... to pay to

....

or order, at ....

the sum of ....

.... DOLLARS,

with interest from .... until paid at the rate of

.... per cent per annum; interest payable ....

principal payable .... ;

....

....

....

Should interest not be so paid it shall thereafter bear like interest as the principal. Should default be made in payment of interest when due the whole sum of principal and interest shall become immediately due, at the option of the holder of this note. Principal and interest payable in lawful money of the United States. If action be instituted on this note, I promise to pay such sum as the Court may fix as attorney's fees. This note is secured by a DEED OF TRUST.

....

....

EXHIBIT 4-1 PROMISSORY NOTE (STRAIGHT)

Promissory Note

(INTEREST INCLUDED — DUE DATE)

$... ...., 19.....

For value received,... promise...... to pay to

.... ,

or order, at...

the sum of... DOLLARS,

with interest from...on unpaid principal at the

rate of..................................per cent per annum; principal and interest payable in installments of

.... Dollars

or more on the..day of each...............................

on the......................................day of.............................month, beginning

...., 19.....

....

and continuing until the..............................day of.........................., 19.....,

on which day the unpaid balance of principal with unpaid interest due thereon shall be due and payable.

Each payment shall be credited first on interest then due and the remainder on principal; and interest shall thereupon cease upon the principal so credited. Should default be made in payment of any installment when due the whole sum of principal and interest shall become immediately due at the option of the holder of this note. Principal and interest payable in lawful money of the United States. If action be instituted on this note, I promise to pay such sum as the Court may fix as attorney's fees. This note is secured by a DEED OF TRUST.

....

....

EXHIBIT 4-2 PROMISSORY NOTE (INTEREST INCLUDED–DUE DATE)

INSTALLMENT NOTE—INCLUDING PRINCIPAL AND INTEREST

This type of installment note is more often used than the other. Fixed periodic payments are first applied to interest and the remaining amount is applied to the principal balance. With each successive payment, the amount applied to interest is decreased and the amount applied to principal is increased.

Most institutional lenders use this type of note in amortizing real estate mortgage loans. It is required in the event of F.H.A. insured and Veterans Administration guaranteed mortgage loans, on their specified forms. Exhibit 4-2 is an example of this form of note.

Notes of all kinds are normally negotiable instruments when properly prepared. They may be declared invalid when drawn with an intent of fraud or forgery and when a material alteration is made on the face of it. The maker must be legally competent and the note cannot be signed under duress if it is to be a valid instrument.

By conforming to the terms and conditions of the security instruments to which the note is attached such as a mortgage or trust deed, it may be transferred from one holder to another, along with the security instrument, by endorsement or assignment.

Trust deeds and mortgages are always under the control of the provisions contained in the note as to maturity, interest rate, manner of payment, and so on.

On the other hand, certain provisions contained in the security instruments may control the note. For example, an alienation or acceleration clause in a trust deed or mortgage may cause the note to mature prior to the specified maturity date on the note in the event of a violation of a provisional clause. The entire amount of the obligation could be "called" even though the clause is not specified in the note.

Since the note and mortgage are to be construed together, the assignment of a mortgage transfers nothing to the assignee unless the note is also assigned. However, to transfer the note without the mortgage may provide the assignee a right to the mortgage instrument.

REQUIREMENTS—NEGOTIABLE NOTES

In order for a promissory note to be regarded as a negotiable instrument, it must contain certain elements of statement of fact in conformity with a strict definition according to the statutes. The requirements are:

1. The note must be an unconditional promise to pay.

2. It must be in writing.
3. It must be made by one person and payable to another.
4. It must be signed by the maker.
5. The promise to pay must be on demand or at a fixed or determinable time in the future.
6. It must be for a certain sum of money.
7. It must be payable to order or to bearer.

Should one of the elements not be contained, the document may still be transferable the same as an ordinary contract. In the event of a missing element and the note is transferred or assigned from one payee to another, the assignee receives no more than the assignor had and defenses that were good against the assignor are good against the assignee.

HOLDER IN DUE COURSE

When the note qualifies as a valid negotiable instrument containing the essential elements and it is transferred or assigned to a third party, that third party may enjoy a more favorable position by taking the note as "a holder in due course." Under those circumstances, it is not necessary to make a full and careful investigation of the maker's reliability or situation at the time of signing the note and creating the instrument.

A holder in due course is one who has taken a negotiable instrument under the following conditions:

1. That the instrument is complete and regular on its face.
2. That he became the holder before it was overdue and without notice of its previous dishonor, if such was the fact.
3. That he took the instrument in good faith and for a valuable consideration.
4. That at the time the instrument was negotiated to him he had no knowledge of any infirmity in the instrument, or any defect in title of the negotiator.

If it should become necessary for anyone, who qualifies as a holder in due course to bring an action to collect on the instrument, the maker of the note cannot refuse to make payment on the basis of the following defenses:

1. Fraud in the inducement to sign the note. (False statements of payee.)
2. Lack or failure of consideration. (Payee failed to deliver as promised.)
3. Prior payment or cancellation. (Maker failed to receive note and

payee negotiated instrument to a third party "holder in due course.")

4. A set-off. (Cancellation of a debt payee owes to maker.)

The above defenses would normally be good as against the original payee, but not against a subsequent holder in due course.

The defenses listed below are good against the world, including any holder in due course.

1. Incapacity. (If the maker was an infant or mentally incompetent at the time of signing the note.)
2. Illegality of the instrument. (If the instrument was executed in some connection with illegal conduct such as gambling, or carries a usurious interest rate.)
3. Forgery. (When the maker himself never signed the instrument.)
4. Material alteration. (If the holder makes an important change in the instrument such as the amount, date or rate of interest without the maker's consent.)

ENDORSEMENTS

The greatest attribute to a valid negotiable instrument lies in its transferability from one party to another. Therefore, when notes are secured by a mortgage or trust deed, they are normally more highly acceptable to subsequent holders in due course. Transfer by delivery can be made if the note is made payable "to bearer." When the note is made payable to the order of a named person, that person must "order" the maker to pay the transferee by endorsement.

The various types of endorsement of negotiable instruments such as notes, checks, drafts, etc., include the following:

1. Endorsement in Blank. (Holder signs name on back of the instrument.)
2. Special endorsement. (Holder writes "Pay to the order of name of transferee" on back of instrument and signs name below.)
3. Restrictive endorsement. (Holder writes "Pay to order of _____ Bank, for deposit only" on back of instrument and signs below.)
4. Qualified endorsement. (Holder writes "Without Recourse" on back of the instrument and signs his name below.)

A qualified endorsement is to provide notice to the transferee that the transferor will not be liable for payment in the event the maker refuses to pay. However, a qualified endorsement does not eliminate the transferor's contingent liability on certain warranties implied by law. By negotiating a note by simple delivery, or by endorsing the instrument, he still warrants the following:

1. That the instrument is genuine and what it purports to be.
2. Good title to the instrument is held by the transferor.
3. All prior parties had capacity to contract.
4. Transferor does not know any fact that would impair the validity of the instrument or render it valueless.

When negotiation is by delivery only, the above warranties extend only in favor of the immediate transferee. If there is a conventional endorsement without qualification with the exception of the fourth warranty, the above warranties are implied by law to protect subsequent holders in due course. The fourth warranty, also implied by law, by modification would read that "the instrument *is,* at the time of the transferor's endorsement, valid and subsisting." In order to eliminate or avoid the above warranties, the transferor would have to write in the words "without recourse or warranties" to his endorsement.

Without a qualified endorsement, the endorser is liable to subsequent holders, who are unable to collect from the maker, through proper presentation and notice. If that situation should exist with an instrument containing a qualified endorsement, the transferee cannot look to the endorser for payment. On the other hand, a qualified endorsement may render the instrument as being less desirable in acceptance by a third party under some circumstances.

The negotiability of a note, written in the proper form for validity of being a negotiable instrument, is not affected by the statement that it is secured by a mortgage or trust deed, nor by any conditions contained in the security instrument. If anything, it normally becomes more desirable and marketable with such security.

Most notes secured by a mortgage or trust deed include a clause which adds attorney's fees and court costs in the event collection of the note becomes a matter of litigation. Other clauses such as acceleration, alienation, etc., may be included in the note in detail or it may be merely noted on the face of the note that such clauses exist in the mortgage or trust deed. When these clauses run with the note, and/or security instrument, they are more acceptable to holders and subsequent holders because of the added protection. Therefore, their value is enhanced as negotiable instruments.

5

Mortgages and Trust Deeds

A majority of the states adhere to the operational laws and customs of regular mortgages as security instruments in real estate loans. Other states favor the operational legal procedures of trust deeds.

Some of the states, where mortgages normally prevail, also provide legislation for the use of trust deeds although the latter may seldom be utilized as a security instrument. Other states have enacted laws which restrain the use of trust deeds in any form.

A few states have combined conveyancing of title to the property and the mortgage into one instrument. For example, a "Deed of Mortgage" is used in Alabama, the state of Georgia uses a "Deed To Secure A Debt" form of mortgage, while the state of Maine uses a "Mortgage Deed" form in real estate transactions.

In the states where trust deeds are primarily used, mortgages are sometimes also utilized, although such usage may vary and in most instances, such mortgages contain a power of sale provision, which is discussed later in this chapter.

The states in which trust deeds are most often used are: Arkansas, California, Colorado, Maryland, Mississippi, Missouri, North Carolina, Tennessee, Texas, Virginia, West Virginia and Washington, D.C. All the other states use mortgages in form according to the individual state's laws and customs.

Although trust deeds are, in effect, mortgages and are often referred to as such, there are many material differences between the two security instruments. There are also some degrees of variance in the operational methods and laws pertaining to both forms of mortgage from state to state. For example, the foreclosure and redemption laws as to regular mortgages may be entirely different from one state to another. The same may also be true in connection with trust deeds.

Therefore, verification of procedures and points of law should be examined carefully or obtained from a competent attorney who practices in the general locality of a property or issue in question.

The primary distinctions between mortgages and trust deeds prevail in application to:

1. Parties
2. Title
3. Statute of Limitations
4. Remedy
5. Redemption
6. Satisfaction
7. Deficiencies and personal liability

It is advisable to become familiar with the legal aspects of the above as they apply in the real estate agent's locality of listings and sales. However, legal advice to the agent's client should come only from an attorney at law.

PARTIES

Mortgages: There are two parties to a mortgage. The mortgagor is the borrower and the mortgagee is the lender. The giving of a mortgage, by a mortgagor to a mortgagee, creates a lien against the mortgagor's property as security for a loan, or some other consideration, advanced by the mortgagor.

Trust Deeds: There are three parties to a trust deed. They consist of the trustor (borrower—mortgagor), trustee (third party—holder of legal title) and the beneficiary (lender). A certain degree of title to the property is conveyed to the trustee as security for an obligation owed to the beneficiary.

When the trustor has performed the obligation, as provided in the terms and conditions of the note and trust deed, title is reconveyed, by the trustee, to the trustor. If the trustor should fail to perform, the trustee is empowered to sell the secured property at public sale and satisfy the debt in behalf of the beneficiary.

TITLE

Mortgages: A mortgage does not convey title. It merely creates a lien against the property. The mortgagor enjoys legal title and possession while satisfying the obligation. Some degree of title may be accorded to the mortgagee, depending on local laws, concerning the mortgagee's rights to rents and possession.

Trust Deeds: In a trust deed, the trustor remains owner of record and retains equitable title and possession, but conveys legal title of his property to the trustee as security for an obligation owed to the beneficiary. Although legal title is transferred, from trustor to trustee, the trust deed is, in effect, a lien against the property and is treated as such.

STATUTE OF LIMITATIONS

Mortgages: With a mortgage, an action of foreclosure is barred when the statute of limitations has run on the principal obligation such as a mortgage note. The length of time varies, from state to state, as to when this may occur. In some states the mortgage is barred along with the note. However, in most states, the effect is only the prevention of obtaining a deficiency judgment when the nonpayment of a debt exceeds the statute of limitations, but may not prevent foreclosure of the mortgage.

Trust Deeds: In a trust deed, foreclosure rights of the creditor are never ended. Even though the statute of limitations may run on the note, the trustee, as holder of legal title and under power of sale provided in the trust deed, may sell the secured property to satisfy the debt.

REMEDY

Mortgages: In a mortgage, the only remedy of the mortgagee is by a foreclosure suit through a court of law. However, in the event "power of sale" is contained in the mortgage, it may not be necessary to foreclose through court action.

Trust Deeds: With a trust deed, when a trustor defaults in payment, or violates other terms contained in the security instrument, there are alternative methods of remedy. The trustee may exercise his power of sale or a judicial foreclosure may be accomplished through court action similar to a mortgage foreclosure.

REDEMPTION

Mortgages: When a mortgage is foreclosed through court action, the mortgagor may have certain rights to redeem the property after the foreclosure sale as well as prior to the sale. Redemption periods may vary from none at all, to two months or up to two years according to the laws of various states. A mortgage foreclosed under the "power of sale" contained in the instrument does not provide a redemption period and the sale is final.

Trust Deeds: Under a trust deed, the trustor has a limited right of reinstatement of the loan after default, but will lose all rights of redemption after the trustee's sale is completed. A trustee's sale is final and absolute and the purchaser of the foreclosed property will receive a trustee's deed vesting title in the new owner's name. Entitlement to immediate possession is also given to the new owner of record.

SATISFACTION

Mortgages: In the case of a mortgage, when the mortgagor performs as to satisfaction of the debt, the mortgagee will execute and deliver a certificate that the mortgage has been satisfied or discharged. In form, the certificate is often captioned "Satisfaction of Mortgage" and when the document is recorded, the lien is removed from against the mortgagor's property. The laws in some states impose certain penalties against the mortgagee for failure to deliver a certificate of satisfaction within a specified period of time.

Trust Deeds: When performance is completed or final payment is made on a note and trust deed, the trustor should request full reconveyance from the beneficiary. The beneficiary will, in turn, forward the original note and trust deed instruments to the trustee along with an authorization for the trustee to issue a "Deed of Reconveyance" to the trustor. The trustee will in turn provide the mortgage instruments and the Deed of Reconveyance to the trustor and collect a trustee's fee for the services.

The trustor is responsible to have the "Deed of Reconveyance" recorded, which will remove the lien from against his property in the public records.

DEFICIENCIES AND PERSONAL LIABILITY

Mortgages: In a foreclosure sale, initiated through court action, it is possible the sale price may be less than the debt, in which case the mortgagee will suffer a deficiency in receiving all the money due him. The laws of most states provide for the recovery of such deficiencies by holding the mortgagor personally liable for payment thereof. Thus, the mortgagee may file for a deficiency judgment against the mortgagor. The laws may vary from state to state with respect to time and circumstances involved with the mortgage note.

For example, in some states, the decree or judgment of foreclosure is in itself a personal judgment for the amount of the mortgage debt, against the mortgagor and proceeds from the sale merely apply to the personal judgment debt.

The laws of other states may provide for the personal judgment to be entered by the court after the foreclosure sale, thereby creating a deficiency judgment. In some instances, the amount of judgment is limited to the difference between the mortgage debt and an opinion of the court as to fair market value of the property. However, the amount of the deficiency judgment is more often determined in the difference between the mortgage debt, plus necessary expenditures and interest and the amount of monies received by the mortgagee from the foreclosure sale.

In a few states such as California, Montana and North Carolina, a deficiency judgment cannot be obtained on "purchase money mortgages." That is when money has been loaned or credit extended to purchase the subject property.

Some states have abolished deficiency judgments altogether, while others have enacted restrictive and limiting legislation in connection with such court actions.

Trust Deeds: When foreclosure is accomplished through a trustee's power of sale, there can be no deficiency judgment in most states. This is particularly true in the case of a purchase money trust deed. The exception may be in foreclosure through the trustee's power of sale on a nonpurchase money trust deed in some states under certain circumstances. A few states have abolished deficiency judgments altogether, regardless of the circumstances surrounding foreclosure on the mortgage debt.

ASSIGNMENT OF MORTGAGES AND TRUST DEEDS

Investors often sell, trade or assign mortgages and trust deeds when it may be to some advantage. Consequently, these debt security instruments may be assigned several times before being fully paid and retired as liens.

Mortgages: When the assignment of a mortgage occurs, it is necessary to provide an "assignment of mortgage" instrument to be recorded in the public records, as a general rule, because such recording gives constructive notice to all persons. It may also provide additional protection to the assignee.

The note must be properly endorsed and delivered and should be accompanied by the original mortgage instrument. The assignment of a debt, secured by a mortgage, carries with it the security. An attempted assignment of the mortgage without the note transfers nothing to the assignee and a

67

transfer of the note without the mortgage gives the assignee the right to the security.

Trust Deeds: In the case of a trust deed and note, the trust deed is given as security of the note. If it is a negotiable note made out merely to "bearer," endorsement is acceptable, but not necessary. However, when the note is made out to a specific party, or order, endorsement of it is necessary upon transfer and delivery.

The transfer of a trust deed from one party to another normally is accomplished on a transfer instrument captioned, "Assignment of Trust Deed," for later recording in the public records. It contains a description of the trust deed, the date of the instrument, names of the trustor and trustee and necessary information for identification in the public records. Upon recording, the assignment is a matter of constructive notice.

SALE OR TRANSFER OF SECURED PROPERTY

Mortgages: Property secured by a mortgage remains *subject to* the mortgage debt in the event of a sale or transfer of ownership. The grantee cannot be held personally liable for a deficiency judgment unless he has *assumed* the mortgage debt. The laws of most states provide that when the grantee is to be held responsible for payment of the debt, it must be in writing that he "assumes the mortgage" or that he "assumes and agrees to pay the mortgage."

In assuming the debt the grantee becomes the principal debtor, but the grantor remains liable to the mortgagee as surety for any deficiency resulting in a foreclosure sale of the mortgaged property, unless there has been a complete novation. It is possible the mortgagee may agree to new conditions in this respect, but it is not probable.

In the event the mortgage debt is guaranteed by the Veterans Administration on a G.I. loan, the original mortgagor remains liable for any deficiencies arising from a foreclosure sale unless the V.A. releases him from liability and accepts the new owner as being personally liable. This may be accomplished through request of application forms from the nearest Veterans Administration area office. Even though some states have abolished deficiency judgments either partially or altogether, the Veterans Administration may collect deficiencies on any loan guaranteed by the agency.

In the transfer of ownership of secured mortgaged property, the grantee may refuse to take personal liability of the debt. He will agree to pay the obligation, but may prefer to confine any foreclosure losses on his part to his cash investment and subsequent payments. In that case, the sales contract, agreement of sale or deed should stipulate that the purchaser is taking the property "subject to the loan." Personal liability for the debt would remain with the grantor or those before him. The laws of some states provide for liability against the owner of record, regardless of stipulations or waivers to the contrary.

Trust Deeds: The same general conditions prevail in the transfer of property on which a debt is secured by a trust deed as they do with a mortgage. However, in some states where a purchase money trust deed is involved, in the event of default, the remedy of the mortgagee would be against the property only and no deficiency judgment can be obtained.

Loan Statements

Loan statements pertaining to the condition of loans are often referred to as "off-set" statements. In a real estate transaction, where the purchaser intends to assume an existing loan, an off-set statement may be supplied by the seller at the time of listing the property for sale, or soon thereafter, through contact with the lender. The statement will contain information regarding the loan balance, interest rate, monthly payments to principal and interest, payments to the impound account, the impound account balance, insurance coverage and other vital information concerning assumption of the loan.

As a general rule, escrow agents and title companies do not rely on information, as outlined above, furnished by the seller. They will require a statement, concerning this type of information, direct from the mortgagee or the loan servicing agency for the mortgagee.

The lender, or servicing agency, may demand a nominal "statement fee" for providing the information on a current basis and will also instruct the escrow agent to collect an assumption fee from the buyer. If the security instrument should contain special conditions such as an alienation and/or acceleration clause, that information is disclosed in the statement.

Although there may be some expense involved with a lender's statement, the purchaser will have a clear understanding as to the obligations of the mortgagor to the mortgagee prior to actual transfer of ownership; therefore, it is well worth the cost.

Alienation—Acceleration Clause

When a trust deed or a mortgage exists as security of a debt against a property, the owner may transfer his interests in title to another party, along

69

with the debt, provided the security instrument in use does not contain conditions that prohibit such action. These conditions are normally contained in the security instruments such as an alienation clause. In effect, the conditions are that the mortgagor, or trustor, may not transfer title or any interest in the property to another party without written permission from the mortgagee or beneficiary. Violation of the conditions would give the holder of the security instrument the right to "call the note" and demand full payment of the debt or place the property in position of foreclosure.

It is common practice for lenders to insert this clause into their security instruments when granting conventional loans. It adds strength to their investment in that it may provide an opportunity to revise the terms and interest rates commensurate with the current money market, if and when a new purchaser desires to assume the loan.

Real estate loans insured by the Federal Housing Administration or guaranteed by the Veterans Administration are not permitted to be granted under such conditions of an alienation clause. Therefore, ownership title may be transferred at any time without the lender's approval.

Default—Acceleration Clause

The holder of a trust deed or mortgage may instigate foreclosure proceedings against the trustor or mortgagor when the debtor defaults in the principal and interest payments, the payment of taxes, assessments, insurance premiums or advancements made by the lender in payment of necessary expenses.

The debtor may cure the default by payment of the amount of default and costs, including attorney fees and/or other foreclosure proceedings costs. In order to reinstate the loan and cause proceedings to be dismissed, payment in full of the default amount must be made within a specified period which may vary with the laws of different states. The full amount of loan balance may be demanded in some instances if the default is to be cured, depending upon terms and conditions contained in the security instrument and the state in which the property is located.

Redemption laws differ in practically all states. However, in most areas, payment of default on a regular mortgage may be made any time prior to entry of foreclosure decree in order to obtain dismissal of foreclosure proceedings. This fact would normally apply in the case of trust deeds also.

Lien Priorities

The priority of a lien over another depends mainly upon the time of

70

recordation in which constructive notice is given. A mortgage lien has precedence over any subsequently recorded liens, which may include second, third or more mortgage liens or judgment liens. However, in the case of tax liens by the federal, state, county or city governments, a priority is given over the mortgage lien even though the tax lien was recorded behind the others.

In the event of successive tax liens on the same property, priority is given on an inverse order of their creation and those attaching later are superior over earlier tax liens recorded.

In transferring ownership and title, the seller should be prepared to remove any liens that may have attached to the property or there should be a definite meeting of the minds and agreement set forth from the first sales agreement as to the purchaser taking responsibility for payment of recorded liens.

FORECLOSURE

When a borrower is in default on a mortgage instrument, the mortgagee may remedy by foreclosure action or, in the event the mortgage contains a provision for "power of sale," the mortgagee may exercise his rights in a more expedient manner. If the mortgage instrument is a trust deed, remedy may be accomplished through a trustee's sale.

The laws of many states differ as to remedy in default of security instruments and the operational procedures in remedy, but in all cases, the objectives are similar.

Mortgages: The primary objective in remedy through foreclosure is to obtain the right, title and interest in the property that the mortgagor had at the time of the execution of the mortgage. Adverse or superior claims to that of the mortgagee are not affected by the decree of foreclosure.

In several states, a foreclosure suit is the only method of remedy to default in a mortgage instrument. The suit is usually instigated by the mortgagee by the filing of a petition to foreclose in the office of a court clerk. The petition may name, in addition to the mortgagor of record, all persons who may have an equitable right to the property. The persons so named may be tenants, holders of junior lines and judgment creditors in order that they may defend their positions in some manner or means.

When the court finds in favor of the mortgagee, a decree, or judgment of foreclosure is entered. The decree recites the finding of the amount due the mortgagee, a description of the property to be sold, the designated official who is to administer the sale, and, in some instances, the decree may specify the notice of sale to be published.

The notice must be written to describe the property and the time and place of the foreclosure sale plus all terms of the sale. As a general rule, the terms are specified as cash for payment by the highest bidder. The mortgagee may bid up to the amount of money due him and apply the debt against the bid price. The notice of sale is intended for the primary purpose of securing additional bids in excess of the amount due the mortgagee if possible. Excessive amounts may then be turned over to the mortgagor.

The notice is posted in a public place of the city or county in which the property is located for a number of days as specified by local laws. It must also be published at least once a week, ordinarily in a newspaper of general circulation in the township in which the property, or some portion of it, is situated. If no such paper is published in the township, publication of the notice may be in the county where the foreclosure proceedings are to be held.

Ownership title of the successful bidder is deemed to relate back to the title of the mortgagor as of the date of execution of the mortgage and intervening liens, except for some tax liens, are eliminated by the foreclosure sale and purchase.

In states where no statutory redemption period exists, the successful bidder will receive a deed giving him title to the property free and clear of the mortgagor's rights. In states where the mortgagor has a statutory right of redemption, the purchaser will receive only a Certificate of Sale from the appointed official who controlled the foreclosure sale. Upon expiration of the period of statutory right of redemption, if the mortgagor has not redeemed the property, the purchaser is given a deed of title to the property.

Power of Sale Mortgage

Under the laws of several states, mortgages may contain a power of sale condition. This allows the mortgagee to sell the property in the event of default without resorting to court proceedings for a decree of foreclosure.

With the exception of the necessity of obtaining a court decree of foreclosure, all other factors, including the posting and advertising of foreclosure notices and bidding at the sale, remain the same as in the procedures of regular mortgage foreclosures. In any case, there must be a strict adherence to the state laws of the localities in which the property lies.

Some states, in which the power of sale mortgage is permitted, may have laws prohibiting the mortgagee from bidding on the property in his own foreclosure sale. This may be to some disadvantage to the mortgagee, as the property may not sell for the amount due him. A public official may be required to conduct a foreclosure sale under a power of sale mortgage in some states. The mortgagor may not have any rights of redemption, under certain circumstances involving third party purchasers, according to the laws of certain states.

Redemption—Mortgages

The primary purpose of a foreclosure suit is to remove and discharge the mortgagor's equitable rights of redemption. However, most states reserve a statutory right of redemption for the mortgagor to redeem the foreclosed property within a certain period of time.

Redemption laws differ from state to state and the allotted period of time may vary from two months to two years. Some states do not have a statutory right of redemption law and merely defer final foreclosure for a period of time to allow the mortgagor to redeem which, in effect, serves the same purpose.

There may be no provision for redemption rights in some states and upon the foreclosure sale, the purchaser is given a deed of title to complete ownership whereby the mortgagor has no further rights to the property.

Equitable redemption is made prior to the mortgagee's obtaining a decree or judgment of foreclosure. In order to detain such judgment or decree from being processed, the mortgagor or anyone who may have a direct or indirect interest in the property, must pay the defaulted debt in full plus involved expenses in instigating foreclosure proceedings, advanced taxes, interest, maintenance, etc., to redeem their equity.

In states where the statutory right of redemption is provided, the law becomes effective after the judgment or decree of foreclosure has been entered.

Generally, the laws of most states provide for redemption upon the payment of the full price plus expenses and interest that the purchaser paid at the foreclosure sale, which may be more or less than the original debt balance. The laws of other states may require the mortgagor to pay at least the full amount of the debt, regardless of the sale price in foreclosure being lower.

Since there is such a vast difference in the manner, methods and redemption periods applied according to the various states' laws, it is always advisable to seek the advice and interpretations of local legal counsel.

Strict Foreclosure—Mortgages

This type of mortgage foreclosure involves a foreclosure suit and the processes of it up to the point of receiving the decree or judgment of foreclosure. It does not provide for immediate sale of the property, but will allow the mortgagor a specified time to make redemption. If redemption is not accomplished within the specified period of time, the mortgagor's rights of redemption are terminated.

Trustee's Sale

The laws and statutes pertaining to trust deeds are varied in the states where this type of mortgage security instrument is utilized. This is particularly true in the redemption of equitable interests and statutory redemption periods. For example, the trustor may have only fifteen days in which to reinstate a loan in one state, but may redeem by paying the entire debt within ninety days. In another state the trustor may reinstate the loan within ninety days and may redeem by paying the entire debt plus expenses within twenty-one days after the ninety-day period. The circumstances surrounding the creation of the trust deed may also be considered in applicable laws.

In some states, where trust deeds are generally preferred over mortgages and other security instruments, it is sometimes optional as to whether foreclosure is to be by court action or through the trustee's third party power of sale. In the latter case, the redemption period is greatly reduced and the trustee's sale is final and absolute.

When a trustor (borrower) defaults on a note secured by a trust deed, the beneficiary (lender) will demand the default be rectified. Usually, it involves failure to make specified payments of principal and interest or other obligations due against the property. Partial payment on the default is not ordinarily acceptable. If the situation is not cleared up within a specified period of time, the beneficiary will mail or deliver a "Notice of Intent to Foreclose" to the trustor.

If the trustor fails to perform within the specified time, the beneficiary may instruct the trustee to commence foreclosure proceedings against the property by virtue of the trustee holding legal title and power of sale. Upon being so instructed, the trustee will deliver a copy of a recorded Notice of Default to the trustor. Thus begins a legalized period of equitable redemption by the trustor or anyone who may have an interest in the property such as a junior mortgage or another type of lien that may be eliminated by the trustee's sale. A copy of the Notice of Default is also mailed to any party who has recorded a Request for a Notice of Default against the property.

At the end of the period provided by law in which the trustor may cure the default and reinstate the loan, the trustee must post a notice of the sale in a public place; usually the courthouse of the county in which the property is located. In addition to posting the notice of sale, the trustee must usually advertise for a period of time specified by law in a newspaper of general circulation in the county; the contents of the notice giving the time, date and place of the sale and terms in cash.

Between the time advertising starts and prior to the actual sale, the trustor may redeem the property, in most states, by paying the entire debt plus accrued interest and costs advanced by the mortgagee.

At the appointed time of sale, the mortgagee may bid the full amount due and apply it to the debt. All others must pay cash when successful in being highest bidder. The trustee will then issue a Trustee's Deed to the successful bidder giving him title to the property. The sale is final and absolute and the trustor may have no further rights to the property in most states.

Second Mortgages and Trust Deeds

Frequently it is necessary and/or advantageous to buyer and seller to create secondary financing in a real estate transaction, rather than to refinance and pay off existing loans or loan as the case may be.

Secondary financing security instruments such as mortgages and trust deeds are normally junior liens because of being recorded successive to other liens. The exception may be in the event a prior lien contains a subordination clause, which will be discussed later. A second mortgage or trust deed is a second because there is a first lien recorded ahead of it. A third mortgage or trust deed is such when there is a first and second mortgage instrument recorded ahead of it, etc.

In order for the lienholder to enjoy maximum protection, it is necessary that there is a sufficient equitable interest in the property based on market value over and above the total liens including the lien to be created. If the total mortgages or trust deeds exceed market value, there is a chance the mortgagor would walk away from the obligations and default because, in effect, he no longer owns an equitable interest.

Junior lienholders normally are advised to file a Request For Notices of Default and Sale with the county recorder. In the event of a default on a prior lien, the junior lienholder will receive a copy of the recorded Notice of Default filed by the prior lienholder. The junior lienholder may reinstate or redeem the prior lien and foreclose under terms and conditions of his own mortgage instrument.

If the security is insufficient and upon foreclosure, the junior lienholder suffers a loss in recovery of the full debt, he may recover from other assets of the borrower under certain circumstances. This, of course, will depend on

75

the laws of various states pertaining to deficiency judgments. Since there is such a great variance in the laws of most states in connection with deficiency judgments and procedures in obtaining them, it would be advisable to seek legal counsel in the matter prior to accepting any type of mortgage lien.

Subordination Clause

A subordination clause is often inserted into the terms and conditions of a mortgage, trust deed or land contract in the event of a real estate transaction involving future construction. In the purchase of a vacant lot, for example, the owner may carry a portion of the monies due him on a mortgage or trust deed or land contract and create a first lien. Construction funds are normally available only on the basis of a first lien so in order to become a first lien, the subordination clause in the existing mortgage instrument provides that the prior lien is to be subordinate to the construction loan lien and second in priority.

All terms, conditions and limitations of the subordination agreement are specified in the mortgage instrument at time of the original purchase of the property to the point of being unnecessary for further approval.

State laws may vary as to the form and phrasing to be contained in the agreement in order to be legal and valid. Therefore, the use of a subordination clause should be researched for full compliance with the law in the state in which the property is situated prior to utilizing it.

OTHER SECURITY INSTRUMENTS

Although mortgages and trust deeds are used predominately as security instruments throughout the nation, there are other forms of security in obligations preferred in use by some states. A few of the other forms are discussed here briefly.

Installment Contract of Sale

This device is utilized under a number of descriptive captions such as Installment Sales Contract, Land Sale Contract, Agreement to Convey, Agreement for Purchase and Sale, and many others. Regardless of the name in reference to the contract, the objectives are much the same in its utilization.

For various reasons, sellers may prefer to retain title to the property until some point in time. In some instances, the seller may own the property free and clear of all liens and encumbrances and prefer to carry the entire

76

loan balance as an investment without having to resort to conventional methods of foreclosure in the event of default. In other cases, it may be that when the seller receives all his equity between the sales price and existing loan, the buyer is to assume the existing loan obligations and will then receive a deed to the property.

When there are existing loans on the property, the purchaser normally will pay the seller a fixed amount of monthly payments with interest being charged on the full amount of debt, usually after a small down payment on the purchase price. The seller will use the funds received monthly from the purchaser to apply on existing loan payments, taxes, insurance and other obligations attached to the property. The balance of payments are then applied to interest and payment on the principal balance.

Terms and conditions of the contract provide for repossession upon default, transfer of title, etc., according to a meeting of the minds between the buyer and seller, which may vary according to circumstances and inducements of the purchase and sale. (*The Installment Contract of Sale* is also discussed in the chapter on sales contracts and in the chapter on financing.)

Absolute Deed

This type of security device may be an ordinary grant deed, bargain and sale deed, quitclaim deed or warranty deed given to the lender as security of repayment of the debt. It is considered a mortgage by the courts only when there is strong supporting evidence of that intent. Where there is sufficient proof that an absolute deed was given as security for the debt, the borrower may be entitled to pay the obligation and demand a reconveyance of title from the lender. However, if the debt is not paid, and it is proven that the deed was given as security, the grantee must foreclose as though it were a regular mortgage.

A well-written agreement in connection with this type of transaction and security instrument is essential in order to define whether it is given in security for a loan or intended as a sale. If an absolute deed transaction is used to defraud creditors, it may be set aside by them.

Conditional Sale

A conditional sale security transaction is more often utilized by corporations for business expansion purposes and/or for an income tax advantage. However, this arrangement is not always acceptable to the Internal Revenue Service as an income tax hedge.

77

This type of transaction is a procedure wherein the owner sells his property at full price and delivers title of ownership. In turn, the seller is given an option to repurchase the property at some point in time. The seller will retain possession of the property under a long term lease and may or may not be obligated to repurchase the property according to the terms of the option.

The lender has the advantage of a well-secured investment. The seller has a definite advantage in use of the funds without obligation to repay the loan or of becoming involved in a foreclosure suit, but can exercise his option to repurchase the property if he so desires.

Loan Deed to Secure a Debt

This type of deed provides on the face of it that it is being given to secure a debt. Title is passed to the grantor as security of the obligation, until the debt is satisfied.

When the loan is paid, title is reconveyed to the original grantor. If it is not paid and goes into default, the lender may take possession of the property by legal title of ownership as grantee in the deed.

Loan deeds are seldom used as security instruments except in two or three states. Operational procedures vary to some degree in the states that do use this type of mortgage security.

6

Security in Marketable Title

Prospective purchasers and lenders in real estate transactions are entitled to a maximum assurance of marketable title of ownership in the land or property in which investments are contemplated.

In the early times of our country's development, surveys were made, grants of land were either given or purchased on a relatively small scale and it was a simple operation to verify ownership of land through the public records.

The establishment of marketable title gradually became more difficult and complex with the growth of the nation, due to divisions and subdivisions of land into smaller parcels and the transfer of ownership from one party to another. As a result, title searches became a specialized occupation for some individuals who chose to do the work as a service to others for a fee. These specialists became known as "abstracters."

Eventually, abstracters began to accumulate their own sets of records as they prepared histories and summaries of abstracts of title on which their clients relied prior to completing real estate transactions. Until the advent of typewriters, abstracts of title were hand-written and, since it was necessary from the standpoint of legibility, abstracters generally developed a good hand in their own style of penmanship. Their notations were brief, but thorough, so that the "chain of title" and a history of recordings pertaining to a property could be easily followed in sequence.

ABSTRACT COMPANIES

The outgrowth of the abstracter's services ultimately developed into what are known today as abstract companies. In many instances, abstracters pooled their extensive files of abstracts and other data, including "lot books," which contained reference to all recorded documents, systematically arranged according to the property affected. In time, a general index, listing the landowners in alphabetical order, was accumulated.

The index now contains information concerning recordings that may have some effect on marketable title, including all persons with whom the recordings may have an effect on present or future marketable titles. These files and records became known as "title plants."

As a general rule, the operations of abstract companies are limited to the county in which they serve. They are usually located in the county seat, since their work is dependent on public records in the county courthouse and city hall.

ABSTRACTS OF TITLE

Abstracts of title begin with a full and complete description of the property followed by a recitation of all items the title search covers. It then sets out ownership of the property beginning at an undisputed time of origin. Each entry of recording is dated on the abstract and the book and page number of where the recording may be found is noted. The recordings reflect transfers of title, changes in the property, mortgages (not released), liens, encumbrances, a copy of the plat map and anything affecting good title to the property up to a specified date.

Certificate of Title

State laws vary as to the liabilities connected with the preparation and issuance of an abstract of title. In some states, the abstract company may issue a Certificate of Title, but makes no guarantees relevant to marketable title. The Certificate of Title merely certifies that the abstract is true and correct as of a certain date and may contain notations of exemption of certain items not shown in the abstract.

The abstract may then be given to the client's attorney to review and express an "opinion of good title." The attorney may accept or reject the abstract or clear up any notations he may deem necessary in order to provide marketable title for the present and future.

Guarantee of Title

In some states, the abstract companies issue a Guarantee of Title, whereby good marketable title is guaranteed to the owner of record, and he is indemnified against loss if the title should prove to be less than marketable. Abstract companies may carry liability insurance against errors and omissions in some localities.

It is customary in some sections of the country that the seller or

80

mortgagor is required to supply an abstract of title to the purchaser or lender, as the case may be. An attorney for the receiving parties may examine the abstract, deed and mortgage prior to delivery in escrow.

Considerable reliance is placed in an attorney's "opinion of good title" by buyers and lenders, and title insurance companies normally insist on the attorney's approval prior to issuing a policy of title insurance.

WARRANTY DEEDS

Warranty deeds contain express covenants of title, which are intended to assure the grantee and/or mortgagee good marketable title by the grantor. The covenants of title may differ, to some degree, according to local laws and customs. However, the following are generally included:

Covenant of Seizin: The grantor guarantees that he has good title to the land being conveyed. If it should be later proven that the grantor had less than good title, or only a life estate, the covenant would be in violation and the grantee may have cause for court action to recover plus damages resulting from the conveyance of title under those circumstances.

Covenant Against Encumbrances: When any encumbrances, including mortgages, liens, easements, restrictions or outstanding rights of others are not set forth and revealed to the grantee in the deed, the grantor may be held liable.

Covenant for Quiet Enjoyment: This covenant "runs with the land." If it should develop that the grantor did not have good title to the land and should the grantee or subsequent purchaser of the land suffer eviction at the hands of someone with better title than the grantor, the grantor may be held liable for any damages incurred as a result of the violation.

Special Warranty Deed: The special warranty deed is more limited in that it covenants only against lawful claims of all persons claiming by, through or under the grantor. The grantor may be held liable if the grantee should be disturbed by some claim arising through an act of the grantor himself. However, if the grantor had nothing to do with some claim that may arise, such as an outstanding title, he may not be held liable since it was not incurred while the property was under his control.

Use of the word "grant," as a conveyance such as grant deed, imports a covenant of special warranty. The words "warrant specially" in a deed may be sufficient to create a covenant of special warranty to a deed in some states.

81

TITLE INSURANCE

Title insurance companies normally function under the insurance code and laws of the states in which they operate. The primary purpose of a policy of title insurance is to indemnify owners of record and lenders against investment losses in real estate from the standpoint of good and marketable title. Their services are available in practically all states of the union and are used almost exclusively in a majority of the states as a guarantee of good title.

Abstract companies and title companies often work hand in hand from the standpoint of "title plants" and title insurance policies. The title company may utilize the services and facilities of an abstract company and their "title plant," while the abstract company may insure their abstracts through the facilities of the title insurance company in some localities.

In many instances, title companies may have their own "title plant" and abstracters, depending upon available business volume and individual state insurance laws under which they must operate.

Public records may sometimes be erroneous or incomplete. Certain "shortcomings" may have existed in recorded documents such as forgery, incompetency or a failure to comply with some legal requirement. In other instances, title defects may exist that were never made a matter of public record such as an error in surveying or some encroachment of property discovered only by a physical inspection and investigation. A title insurance policy, after its issuance, provides protection against loss for the insured under certain conditions and exceptions, according to the type of policy involved and the terms of it.

Standard Policy of Title Insurance

The standard policy of title insurance protects the purchaser against title defects of record. His protection extends normally to the purchase price and any legal costs that may be incurred in defending title to the property, whether successful or not. Although careful inspection of the public records is made, it is possible that some item is erroneous in content or may be overlooked altogether. In that event, the insured may be fully protected against loss.

If the buyer is aware of some title defect, but fails to disclose the facts to the title insurance company, he may lose benefit of protection in that particular instance. For example, if the buyer knew the deed of record was forged at the time of being insured but said nothing, he would have no protection. There is no protection against title defects such as liens, easements, claims and property rights of others, mining claims, water rights, encroachments, incorrect surveys, etc., not evidenced in the public records.

If the buyer should desire, he can obtain special endorsements or extended coverage for protection against most unrecorded title defects at an additional charge. The cost for extended coverage is often prohibitive, although it may depend on the risks involved as to the degree of charges for the policy.

A standard policy of title insurance is issued to protect only the owner of record. It is no longer in effect upon transfer of ownership of record. Therefore, it would be necessary to purchase another policy for a new owner if he is to enjoy the same protection afforded the former owner of record. In the event of death of the owner of record, the policy remains in effect and carries over to the heirs as long as title of ownership is with them.

American Land Title Association Policy of Title Insurance

This special type of title insurance was developed primarily for mortgage lenders who, in many cases, are not in a position to make a personal inspection of the property on which a new loan is being originated. Title insurance issued by the American Land Title Association is generally referred to as an A.L.T.A. policy of title insurance.

It is an extended coverage policy designed by the American Land Title Association to protect lenders against loss emanating from unrecorded title defects which are not normally covered by the standard policy of title insurance issued to an owner by title companies.

The A.L.T.A. policy of title insurance is issued through title companies, usually with the standard policy of title insurance being issued at the same time. However, it is not always the case, as there may be other circumstances in which an A.L.T.A. policy is issued.

This policy of title insurance is issued only after examination of an existing competent survey and a physical inspection of the property in question has been made by the issuing title company. When a new survey report is required, it is accomplished by an official surveyor who is paid directly for his services, in addition to the title insurance policy, by the buyer or seller as local custom may dictate.

The main objective of physical inspection of the property is to verify that there are no encroachments, that the description of the land is correct and that there are no rights of parties in physical possession of the property such as tenants or owners under unrecorded instruments.

Transfer of ownership has no effect on an A.L.T.A. lender's policy, as it remains in effect for the duration of the loan. However, when the loan is paid off, or otherwise no longer exists against the property, the policy expires and the coverage ceases. A similar extended coverage policy may be obtained by the purchaser at an increased cost for his protection, which would be effective as long as title is in his name.

In areas where warranty deeds are used and the seller gives a general warranty of good title, the seller may retain the protection of his owner's title policy as against future purchasers with recourse against him if a defect in title is later discovered. A policy issued under those circumstances may never terminate in liability as to the title insurance company, when and if the policy so provides.

TORRENS SYSTEM

Title insurance policies are issued by private insurance companies and, in many localities, are required to be purchased and supplied to purchasers and lenders. However, there are alternative methods of good title assurance acceptable in some states and localities.

One such alternative may be in the form of a Torrens Certificate of Title, which is issued by the Registrar of Titles, who is a public official, in localities utilizing the Torrens title system.

The Torrens system of land title registration, which originated in Australia, was molded from the system of registering title to ships at sea. Although the system prevails in other parts of the world, use of it is confined in the U.S.A. to those states that adopted it through legislation. With the exception of a few states and some of the metropolitan areas within those states, the Torrens system has never been exceptionally popular or extensively used.

Subdividers or builder-developers in areas such as Chicago, Boston and New York City, where the system is used, may often determine whether or not to use the Torrens system or a policy of title insurance or another method when the first sales are made and may favor the Torrens system. Individuals who own only one property may also have the same option.

It is accomplished through a lawsuit similar to a quiet title action against all persons named in an abstract and those which may be revealed through investigation of the premises to cloud title. When the court finds in favor of the owner-applicant, good title with the proven owner is registered by the Registrar of Titles. At that time the Registrar's Certificate of Title is issued and a duplicate of it is delivered to the owner by the Registrar.

From that time forward, mortgage liens or other documents affecting the owner's title must be registered and noted on the Certificate of Title by the Registrar in order to be effective. In the event of future conveyance by deed to another party, the deed must be examined and approved by the Registrar. A new Certificate of Title is then issued and a duplicate of it is delivered to the grantee. The deed does not pass title to the grantee until those steps have been taken, when the property is under the Torrens system of public records.

The Certificate of Title may contain certain exceptions and objections, as provided by the laws of the various state the same as other evidences of title. However, the Registrar is seldom, if ever, placed in a defensive position of litigation as to good title against the registered owner. The property owner normally defends title at his own expense and, if successful, without recourse against the Registrar for recovery of the expense of defending.

Consideration in title insurance rates is sometimes given by title companies when a Certificate of Title exists on the property to be insured. On the other hand, it is often less expensive to buy title insurance than to register under the Torrens system when a Certificate of Title does not already exist on the property.

Lenders sometimes require an American Land Title Association policy of title insurance to be purchased from a title company in spite of the fact the new loan is being placed on property registered under the Torrens system. The fact of such registration may not be sufficiently acceptable in some instances.

Since title protection costs for the lender are normally the buyer's expense, although it may be a matter of negotiation between buyer and seller, it is a subject with which the paying party should be thoroughly familiarized and agreed prior to signing an agreement of sale.

7

Voluntary Transfer of Title

DEEDS

Title of ownership to real property is normally transferred voluntarily from the owner (grantor) to another party (grantee) in the event of a sale, exchange or gift of the property.

The establishment of a voluntary transfer of title is when, of his own free will and accord, the grantor conveys title to the grantee through some type of deed.

Certain requirements may differ for the valid and legal effects of deeds in various states but, as a general rule, the basic essentials in content and provisions prevail throughout the country.

Must Be Written: All deeds intended to convey title of ownership must be in writing, not only to be valid, but also to establish intent and proof plus the essentials to be incorporated into the document.

Competent Grantor: The grantor must be competent to transfer title. Incompetents and minors may transfer title only through court jurisdiction or guardians, but may take title to property through gift or inheritance, although not in the usual manner of delivering or receiving title to the property.

Grantor and Grantee Described: A valid deed intended to transfer title must properly describe and identify the grantor and the grantee.

Description of the Land: Land description must be set out in a sufficient amount of clarity to establish true identity of the property being transferred.

Habendum Clause: The laws and customs in some states require the words "to have and to hold" inserted into deeds for validity. This is referred to as the Habendum Clause.

Recital of Consideration: A recital of consideration should be contained in all deeds. It is not necessary to state the actual price of the property; therefore, it is the custom in some localities for the deed to recite a consideration of $1.00 or $10.00 "and other good and valuable consideration." In other states, it is deemed sufficient to recite "for a valuable consideration."

The lack of consideration in a deed may affect the rights of the grantee as against the rights of certain third parties. For example, the act of a grantor, who is or will be rendered insolvent and transfers title without any or at least a fair consideration, may be fraudulent in the eyes of his creditors and the deed may be set aside by court action.

Words of Conveyance: A valid deed must contain some words of conveyance such as "convey and warrant," "grant," or "bargain and sell."

Covenants of Title: In some states, it is customary to set forth and "express" the covenants of title in deeds of certain form. These covenants may consist of certain warranties as to title. In other states, warranty covenants may be implied from the use of certain specified words of conveyance such as "grant," "bargain and sell" or "convey and warrant." Implied warranties are made effective by law, whether expressed or not.

Implied warranty covenants are that the grantor holds true title; that he has not conveyed title to anyone else; that easements, rights of way, building restrictions, etc. are included in the conveyance; that the land is free from encumbrances made or suffered by the grantor or any person claiming under him, including taxes, assessments or other liens.

Grantors' Signatures: The party or parties who are making the grant or conveyance must sign the deed themselves. It is sometimes a calculated risk for a deed to be signed in blank with no grantee written in and later filled in by an agent. The deed may later be held void in a court of law.

It is not necessary to have signatures to the deed acknowledged or to record the instrument in order to be valid, except in a few states. But, unless it is acknowledged by a notary public or others authorized to take acknowledgments, a deed can not be recorded in the grantee's name and made "constructive notice" of ownership in the public records.

Until a deed is recorded, it may be held ineffective and void so far as subsequent purchasers of the same property are concerned if the grantor should so act.

Delivery of the Deed: The deed is considered to be delivered when the grantor after signing it signifies by some act or word, his intention that the deed is to become effective and the grantee through some act or word, agrees to accept it. Delivery of the deed by the grantor must be accompanied by acceptance of the deed by the grantee in order to be a valid transfer of the property in ownership.

Statute of Frauds: The statute of frauds was adopted in England in 1677 and became a part of English common law. Subsequently, it was introduced and adopted in this country. The application, limitations and enforcement of the laws may vary in some states, but the essential purpose is to prevent perjury, forgery and dishonest conduct by unscrupulous people in proving the existence and terms of certain important types of contracts.

The statute provides that certain contracts are invalid unless the contract, or some note or memorandum thereof, is in writing and subscribed (signed) by the party to be charged or by his agent.

Because deeds must be in writing and are connected to some degree with contracts, or may in themselves create a contract, violations of the law in conveyancing may well be instituted under the statute of frauds under which certain conditions and circumstances a deed may be held voidable or invalid.

For example, it may be a violation when a deed is signed as the result of undue influence by the taking of unfair advantage of another's weakness of mind, necessities, or distress. This might be done by someone in whom full confidence has been placed or by someone who holds apparent authority over the other.

Menace or threat of physical injury or character injury to a grantor's well being as well as duress to compel someone to execute a deed could be a violation. Misrepresentation of facts are often characteristic of unscrupulous persons and their acts may cause a deed to be held voidable or invalid, depending upon the degree of damages created and other considerations.

WARRANTY DEEDS

In some states, warranty deeds may serve as a conveyance and also guarantee marketable title protection by the grantor to the grantee and/or mortgagee in a real estate transaction.

This type of deed contains express covenants of title, with certain possible exceptions, through mutual agreement between grantor, grantee or mortgagee. The degree of guarantee may vary in different localities according to the laws, customs and conditions peculiar to the transaction. However, the basic concept is that the grantor is or may be held liable in the event title is not as he represented it to be in the deed.

In many localities, the warranty deed and its contents and covenants of title are the only assurance of good title extended to the purchaser or mortgagee. In the event of a title defect, it is incumbent on the grantee to sue the grantor in a court of law for remedy.

The covenants of title expressed in a warranty deed may differ to some degree from state to state, but generally the covenants as set forth under warranty deeds in the chapter *Security in Marketable Title* are included in this type of conveyance.

Special Warranty Deed

The special warranty deed is more limited in scope since it covenants only against lawful claims of all persons claiming by, through or under the grantor. More specifically, the grantor may be held liable in the event the grantee is later disturbed by some claim arising through an act of the grantor himself. On the other hand, if the grantor was not in control of the property at the time of creation of the claim and/or otherwise had nothing to do with such claim such as an outstanding title, he may not be held liable.

Use of the word "grant," as a conveyance, imparts a covenant of special warranty. The words "warrant specially" in a deed may be sufficient to create a covenant of special warranty in some states. The choice of words and phrasing in connection with special warranty is strictly a matter of individual state's laws and customs.

GRANT DEEDS

Grant deeds are used extensively in the west coast states such as California. Bargain and sale deeds are used on the east coast in states such as New York. Grant, bargain and sell deeds are used in the state of Nevada.

The warranties in a grant deed are not written into the form, as they are in the bargain and sale deeds. The word "grant" expresses implied warranties, which are effective by law regardless of not being written.

The grantor warrants that he holds true title; that he has not conveyed title to anyone else and that title is free from encumbrances done, made or suffered by the grantor or any persons claiming under him, including taxes, assessments, or other liens. The grant also includes easements, rights of way and building restrictions. It also applies to appurtenances and the usual rights of a property owner, unless otherwise reserved in the deed and or provided for in a sales contract.

The grant deed also conveys after acquired title, which means that in the event he does not have full and complete title at the time of executing the deed but afterward, through inheritance or some other means, the grantor should acquire title, such title will automatically pass to the grantee without the necessity of an additional deed of conveyance.

While the warranty includes encumbrances made or done by him during his possession of the property, it does not include any other such as the occurrence of title defects prior to the grantor's acquiring title to the property.

BARGAIN AND SALE DEED

The bargain and sale deed, as previously stated, contains written warranties. In general, the written warranties are basically the same as the "implied warranties" expressed in a grant deed by virtue of the word "grant." The exception may be from the standpoint of "after acquired title." The words "to have and to hold," are always included in this deed.

This type of deed may be in two different forms. One form is the "Bargain and Sale Deed—With Covenant Against Grantor's Acts." This deed would contain the following written covenant:

And the party of the first part covenants that the party of the first part has not done or suffered anything whereby the said premises have been encumbered in any way whatever, except as aforesaid.

The other form of this type deed is the "Bargain and Sale Deed—Without Covenant Against Grantor's Acts." In this form, the above covenant is omitted.

It is customary in most states that the contract of sale or sales agreement is to specify the form of deed to be given to the purchaser. This would apply largely to those states in which the warranties are written into the form.

Essentially, all deeds of conveyance are intended to provide the buyer with good marketable title. From that point on it is a matter of the degree of guarantee of good marketable title the seller is willing and able to provide.

To specify in the contract of sale that the purchaser is to receive a policy of title insurance is not always the protection a buyer desires, because a policy of title insurance may be issued in which a great many exceptions are provided. For example, there may be restrictions as to mineral rights, building and zoning. Buyers should have prior knowledge of such matters.

QUITCLAIM DEEDS

Normal use of a quitclaim deed is when the grantor relinquishes any right or claim he may have in the property, regardless of what it may be. It is frequently used in community property settlements or in situations wherein there may be a potential claim under community property laws. It is also often used to clear up some "title cloud," which may prevent the property status of being absolutely perfect in title.

Quitclaim deeds carry no guarantees or warranties, implied or expressed, nor do they indicate guaranteed ownership or what specific interest, if any, is being relinquished by the grantor. The general effect is the granting of a future silence as to rights or claims to the property on the part of the grantor. The instrument does not convey any after acquired title.

GIFT DEEDS

A grantor may make a gift of property to a grantee through the use of a gift deed. However, if the conveyance is made in the performance of defrauding the grantor's creditors, the deed may be voided by them.

In accordance with the laws and customs of the state in which the property lies the deed may or may not be required to specify some consideration such as love and affection or for valuable consideration. In some states it is customary to set forth in the deed a nominal consideration of from $1.00 to $10.00. The words "love and affection" are sometimes specified in a gift deed, although it is not usually necessary.

DEED OF RECONVEYANCE

A deed of reconveyance is issued by the trustee, designated in a trust deed, to convey legal title back to the owner upon full payment of the mortgage debt secured by a note and trust deed.

The parties to a trust deed consist of the trustor (borrower), the beneficiary (lender) and the trustee (third party) to whom "naked legal title" is given by the trustor to hold until full payment of the obligation is accomplished. The trustee has no other interests in the property unless in the event of default, the beneficiary may instruct the trustee to exercise foreclosure proceedings and power of sale.

Although the trustor retains equitable title and is the owner of record in possession of the property, he is not the legal owner entirely until the obligation is satisfied and discharged.

Satisfaction in payment of the debt will cause the beneficiary to instruct the trustee to reconvey legal ownership to the owner of record. Upon being so instructed, the trustee will issue a Deed of Reconveyance to the owner of record (trustor) who is responsible for recording of the instrument in order to remove the mortgage lien from against the property.

Involuntary Transfer of Title

TRUSTEE'S DEED

In the event a borrower (trustor) defaults in the terms and conditions specified under a note and trust deed, the lender (beneficiary) may instruct the trustee (third party holder of legal title) to commence foreclosure proceedings. When the necessary procedures of law have been accomplished, the trustee may exercise the power of sale vested in him.

When the sale is made, usually on the courthouse steps in the county in which the property lies, it is normally a final sale, with no further redemption rights accorded to the trustor. Under those circumstances, the trustee will issue a Trustee's Deed to the purchaser of the foreclosed property.

Upon delivery of the deed, the purchaser is entitled to immediate possession. Title to the property is the same as that which existed at the time of the execution of the trust deed and note plus any after acquired title.

With the exception of tax, assessment and mechanic's liens, any liens recorded subsequent to the trust deed may be eliminated as being against the foreclosed property.

SHERIFF'S DEED

Mortgage foreclosure procedures through court action may differ from state to state but, as a general rule, the county sheriff is the appointed official in charge of enforcing the sale of real property to satisfy a lien judgment. Upon court approval or confirmation of the sale to a successful bidder, a Sheriff's Deed is issued to the purchaser immediately in some states. In other states, the purchaser may be issued a certificate of sale until after the redemption period provided by law has expired. At that time the deed is delivered. This type of deed conveys only that title that was acquired under judgment suit and carries no warranties or representations whatsoever.

WRIT OF ATTACHMENT

A writ of attachment does not convey title to property. It merely prevents anyone having an interest in it from transferring title, or otherwise disposing of the property until a court decision is rendered. In effect, certain rights of ownership are placed in suspension as assurance for the availability of the property should it be necessary to sell to satisfy the plaintiff, who may be successful in a judgment suit against the owner of record. This may extend to any property he owns and also that which is his but is of record under the name of someone else.

WRIT OF EXECUTION

If, in a judgment suit, it is necessary to sell the property to satisfy a judgment in favor of the plaintiff, the court may issue a Writ of Execution directing the county sheriff, or some official, to proceed with the sale for the purpose of obtaining satisfaction of the debt.

In order for the sheriff, or designated official, to sell the property under a writ of execution, he must post a written notice in a public place such as the court house, for at least the number of days required by law in the various localities. Such notice will normally state the time and place of the sale and will include a complete description of the property to be sold. The notice, most usually, must be published in a newspaper of general circulation at least once each week during the legally required number of days. A copy of the notice is normally mailed to any person who has recorded a request for a copy of it. The sale is usually required to be held in the county in which the property lies and at a public auction to the highest bidder for cash.

CERTIFICATE OF SALE

The successful bidder at a public auction of real property being sold under a writ of execution is issued a certificate of sale by the sheriff or other official in charge of the sale and a copy of it is recorded in the public records.

The certificate of sale is the purchaser's only title to the property until after the redemption period as provided by law has expired. However, it is an assignable instrument. Redemption of the property by the defendant may normally be accomplished by paying the holder of the certificate an amount equal to the sale price plus any interest and advancements for the expenses of taxes, maintenance, insurance, repairs, assessments or other costs. In the event redemption is made, a certificate of redemption is recorded by the person receiving payment.

TAX DEED

When property taxes and assessments are delinquent for a certain period of time, according to the laws of the state in which the property is situated, the property is subject to a tax sale. Methods of tax sales and redemption periods will vary to some extent in the different states but, in all cases, the objective is to recover the deliquencies due to the city, county or state in which the property is located.

Upon the completion of a tax sale, the appointed official in charge of selling the property will issue a tax deed to the successful bidder. In most states, the former owner has no further rights of redemption after a tax sale has been completed. In other states, the former owner may have a certain period of time in which to redeem the property under certain conditions even though a tax deed has been issued to a new owner.

Procedures in Closing Title

Real estate laws vary from one state to another and the customs and procedures in processing transactions prior to closing title and after the recording of documents differ to a great extent in the different sections of the country. Therefore, the knowledge of such procedures is imperative to acquire in application to the locality in which the property lies.

In some of the smaller communities in certain localities, where the principals to a transaction are well known to each other, the entire transaction from beginning to end may be a matter of simplicity from the standpoint of procedure. It is sometimes merely a matter of agreement as to terms and conditions, the drawing and exchanging of the necessary documents and monies and finally the recording as constructive notice of transferring title. Under such circumstances, there is ordinarily no third party interests to be considered such as mortgages, liens, etc. existing prior to the transfer of ownership.

The employment of legal counsel may be only for the purpose of drawing legal documents and, in isolated cases, examining title for possible defects. The buyer or his attorney may not bother to search the public records for title defects because they trust the seller's ability to deliver good title. This may be particularly true where the seller conveys ownership through the issuance of a warranty deed with full covenants, which is described under the heading of Warranty Deeds in the chapter *Security in Marketable Title.*

Upon receiving the described warranty deed, if for some reason title to the property should later prove to be defective, the buyer may have recourse against the seller and cause of action for a suit in a court of law.

A judgment in favor of the buyer is one thing, but full recovery of sustained losses may be another. For that reason, buyers in most sections of the country require a more refined measure of protection in good marketable title and place less reliance on the seller's apparent abilities and integrity. In many instances, the seller may not be aware of defective title to the property.

Consequently, the buyer may specify in the purchase and sale agreement that the seller is to furnish an abstract or other evidence of title setting forth the condition of the seller's ownership, including any existing liens, encumbrances and restrictions connected thereto. In addition, the type of deed of conveyance is usually specified in the original agreement.

The buyer may then engage the services of an attorney at law to review the abstract of title for an opinion of good title to the property. The attorney may also be requested to search the public records for any existing or pending liens, judgments or other conditions against the seller whereby a "title cloud" exists.

If any defects appear as to the property or the seller, the facts are so noted and the buyer is advised accordingly. In most cases, upon the attorney's advice, such defects must be remedied, or removed, prior to the title transfer. Thus the buyer is protected to the extent of the findings.

In most localities, it is a common practice for real estate brokers and/or attorneys to hold deposit monies in their own "trust accounts" or "escrow accounts." Such funds are then turned in or credited to the buyer's account upon final settlement of the transaction. Brokers and attorneys will represent their clients and guide them along or assist them in the gathering of necessary documents, loan funds and other matters pertinent to the closing of title.

Where title insurance is purchased, whereby the buyer is insured against loss due to certain title defects, the examination of title and a perusal of the "general index" in addition to a search of the public records, is normally left to the insuring title company. (See chapters on closing costs.)

ESCROW HOLDER

When monies and documents are handed to a disinterested third party by one principal for delivery to the other upon the happening of certain events or conditions an escrow has been created. For example, a seller may hand a deed conveying title of ownership of a property to a "stake-holder" or "escrow holder" and instruct him to deliver the instrument to the buyer upon the collection of certain funds. The buyer will deposit the funds with the escrow holder and instruct him to deliver the funds to the seller in exchange for the deed.

Escrows are not always required in connection with real estate transactions. In the sale, leasing or construction of real property, it is not unusual for the principals involved to pass legal documents and monies to one another without benefit of a responsible third party delivering these instruments for them. In most localities, it may be considered that the principals are dealing at "arms length" and their protection from loss may be after the fact through the statute of frauds. Without a third disinterested party acting as a "stake-holder," there is no escrow.

An escrow holder is often essential to a real estate transaction. Under the circumstances of a new loan being granted to the purchaser by an absentee lender, reliance is placed on the escrow holder to obtain the mortgagor's signatures on the mortgage instruments prior to the funding of the loan. Subsequently, the mortgage instruments are recorded in the public records by the escrow holder, thereby securing the lender's investment even though absent at the time of signing final settlement papers.

The same situation may apply in the event an existing loan, held by an absentee lender, is to be paid off. In some instances, the seller may be required to remove any mortgages, liens or other existing conditions that prevent delivering clear title to the buyer, prior to receiving any funds from the buyer. This may be possible in some cases but, ordinarily sellers rely on the receipt of such funds in order to clear title of the property.

Obviously, the buyer would not want to advance the required funds directly to the seller for the purpose of clearing title without complete protection and assurance that the proper steps are taken prior to the time title of ownership is transferred. Therefore, the escrow holder is instructed by the buyer that his earnest money deposits and/or new loan funds may be delivered to the seller at a time when it is possible for the seller to deliver good title. In turn, the seller will instruct the escrow holder to pay off or otherwise remove the necessary mortgage liens or other liens from his proceeds in the sale in order that he may deliver good title to the buyer. The escrow holder will then pay off any lienholders, record title of ownership to the buyer and then record any new mortgage liens contracted by the buyer.

Lienholders will ordinarily release any security instruments only to professional or reliable escrow holders with instructions to record a deed of reconveyance or satisfaction of mortgage only when the escrow holder has received the necessary funds with which to pay. Judgment lienholders include the same instructions when submitting releases to the escrow holder in exchange for payment.

Escrow instructions, often referred to as "escrow agreements," generally act as a supplement to the terms and conditions of the original contract. However, in the event of mutually agreed contract revisions being placed in the escrow instructions and signed by all principals, such instructions may constitute a later contract and prevail over the original.

Conditions may be changed by mutual consent of all parties to the escrow or either party may change his own instructions at any time, prior to recording, provided the changes are not detrimental to the other party.

In the states where stringent escrow laws are in effect, an escrow holder is ordinarily obligated to proceed with the necessary recordings of instruments and the disbursement of funds, or otherwise make delivery when all terms and conditions of all contract instructions have been completed, unless notified in writing by either party not to proceed. Such written notice should be submitted through the channels of legal counsel, as the act could lead to litigation in a court of law, since a legal binding contract exists in connection with the escrow.

INFORMATION REQUIRED

The accomplishment of a real estate agent bringing a buyer and seller together into a meeting of the minds to the point of a signing of the contract of sale does not necessarily relieve him of further responsibilities, since commissions are usually paid from proceeds of the completed transaction. It is, therefore, necessary for the agent to assist his client in any way possible in the process of closing in order ultimately to receive any compensation due him.

Regardless of whether the closing of title is to be processed by a professional escrow agent or an attorney who specializes in such work, the following information is essential in the hands of the processor:

1. Correct property address and legal description
2. Sellers' full names and address
3. Buyers' full names and address
4. The manner in which buyers are to take title to the property
5. Exact terms and conditions of the transaction
6. Financial arrangements—
   a. If new loan is to be obtained—how and where
   b. If loan assumption—cash requirements
   c. If secondary financing—specified special clauses to be included in mortgage instruments
   d. Personal property included in sale—Bill of Sale
   e. Names and addresses of existing mortgage lienholders
   f. Disposition of other liens and encumbrances
   g. Proration data
   h. Hazard insurance information—new policy or prorate old policy
7. Amount of earnest money deposited and if to be increased

8. When and where final settlement meeting to be held—if to be
9. Provide any available records and documents regarding property
   a. Deed—shows exact title and property location
   b. Existing hazard insurance policy
   c. Most recent loan statement from mortgage holders
   d. Existing policy of title insurance—if available
   e. Any paid receipts affecting property title

The above information provides a nucleus from which matters of record may be examined in connection with the property, seller and buyer. The time required in the processing of title may vary from a few days to several weeks, depending upon the nature of the transaction. Where there are no third party interests such as existing mortgages or other liens, and new loan funds are not to be obtained, it may take only a short period of time. Otherwise the processing time may be extended with the involvement of third party interests.

Title Search

One of the first steps taken, under normal circumstances, is a title search in order to verify that the seller does possess good marketable title to the subject property. Title defects such as liens, judgments, divorce suits, probate and other legal actions may prevent delivery of marketable title from seller to buyer. The same defects as to the buyer may attach to any property he may acquire. Therefore, if title insurance is involved, the title company may require the removal of title defects connected to the seller or buyer. Title companies will ordinarily issue a preliminary title report revealing the property description, status of title, any existing recorded liens and title defects.

Abstract of Title

When title defects are brought to light, it is usually possible to clear them up during the processing of other matters concerned with the transaction. Such defects may be discovered in an abstract of title which is a brief history of a specified parcel of land. It discloses the chain of title to the property from an undisputed point in time of past ownership through subsequent ownership up to and including the present owner as of a specified current date.

Recorded documents that affect ownership and title are also revealed or noted in the abstract of title. The information is normally obtained from an accumulation of files and records pertaining to each parcel of land in the county of operation which are called "title plants." These "title plants" may be owned by an abstract company or a title company and in many instances, ownership may be one and the same and operate under the name of XYZ Abstract and Title Company or simply the XYZ Title Company.

General Index

Abstract and/or title companies also maintain an alphabetical listing of all landowners together with any recorded information concerning them that may tend to affect title of ownership. They also maintain an index of liens, judgments and legal proceedings recorded against all individuals in the local public records which may have some effect of attachment or "title cloud" on property owned presently or in the future.

The card file may disclose some sort of court action against the buyer or seller that would have an effect, or provide a cloud on the title, if and when title to real property is taken in the buyer's name or sold by the seller.

Statement of Identity

Where title insurance is to be provided, the title company may require a Statement of Identity form to be filled out in the event someone known by the same name as the buyer or seller appears to have some legal action against them according to the index file. Information regarding past employment, addresses and marital status is usually requested in order that it may be compared with the information indicated on the index card file. In most cases, proof is established that the two parties are not one and the same, but it is sometimes determined that it is the same party.

A complete reliance is not placed in the "general index" files. In order to make certain that some item of record against the seller, buyer or property owned by either party has not been overlooked, further investigation is made with various public agencies, some of which are as follows:

County Tax Collector: Tax records are checked to determine the status of tax liens pertaining to the property. Any delinquencies are noted along with tax lien dates, the amount of installments paid or due and any other pertinent information connected with personal and real property taxes against the subject property.

County Recorder: A survey of the records is made to determine existing mortgage liens or other liens and encumbrances. Any recorded releases are also noted as they may apply to prior liens.

County Treasurer: The treasurer's office records are examined for any existing improvement or special assessment bonds. Bond balances, interest and prepayment conditions are noted.

U.S. District Court: If the buyer or seller have any federal tax liens against them, or soon will have, the information is noted.

County Clerk of Superior Court: Records are checked in this office for recordings of incompetency, guardianships, etc., which may affect good title for the buyer or seller.

City Offices: Where property is located in larger cities and where records of city property are maintained separately from county records pertaining to taxes, bonds, and other items affecting property title, such records are also studied.

A Report of the Findings

When an investigation of the public records is completed, the abstracters or title examiners submit a report of their findings to the processing attorney for an "opinion of title." In some instances, the attorney may be a full-time employee of the abstract or title company. In reviewing the report the attorney may discover certain items affecting good title that will either have to be remedied or eliminated altogether before he will express an opinion of marketable title, for guarantee or insurance, if title insurance is required.

In localities where individual attorneys specialize in the processing of title closing, the processing attorney must pass on an opinion of good title and will take the proper course of action prior to transfer of title.

Clear Up Notations on Title Examination Reports

When title defects appear as a result of title examination or from information contained in the "general index" records, the real estate agent is frequently contacted for assistance in removing certain "title clouds." Such defects may range from the necessity of obtaining a quit claim deed from a party who may have an unrecorded future interest in the property to the locating of an unrecorded mortgage release.

Lienholder's Statement or Demand

It is customary in some sections of the country that the seller is responsible to contact personally the mortgagee of an existing mortgage loan on the property for a statement of the status and condition of the loan. In most localities, either the escrow holder or the attorney processing the transaction will contact the lender as a part of their services. For this reason, it is important to supply the correct loan number, mortgagors' names and the lender's name and address.

In a "loan assumption" type of transaction, where the loan is to remain on the property, a mortgagee's loan statement is requested if the loan is secured by a regular mortgage. If the loan is secured by a note and deed of trust, a beneficiary's statement is requested from the lender. In either case, general reference is made as to an "off-set statement."

Where the loan is to be paid off, the holder of a regular mortgage is requested to forward the statement along with a "mortgagee's demand." The holder of a note and deed of trust is requested to forward a statement along with a "reconveyance."

In the event of other liens such as judgments, bonds, taxes, etc. the lienholder is requested to submit a demand for payment in full in exchange for a release of the lien. The same request is made of a lienholder against the buyer, if such is necessary to be paid off prior to the buyer taking title.

The "off-set statements" will indicate the exact principal loan balance, due date, the amount of interest, impound (trust fund) balances, monthly payments and if current or delinquent, insurance coverage and other information pertinent to the loan. The demands submitted by other lienholders will normally contain only the outstanding balance plus any interest and penalties connected with the lien.

When the sale contract specifies that any improvement bonds or special assessment bonds are to be paid off by either party, a statement for full payment is requested and should be in written form—not oral. However, if the bonds are to be assumed by the buyer, the amounts disclosed in title search and verification thereof are usually acceptable.

Broker's Demand for Commissions

The broker's commission is usually provided for in the sale contract agreement. However, it is customary that the broker place his demand for commissions at the time of the settlement meeting that he attends. In some instances, the seller may pay the broker directly after the closing of title, but usually the broker is paid from disbursement funds withheld from the seller's proceeds by the title processor that have been authorized by the seller. In many localities, where the entire transaction is processed by an escrow agent, or an attorney specializing in escrow work, the broker's demand may be submitted in the early stages of processing title.

Hazard Insurance

When the existing hazard insurance on the property is to be prorated to the buyer, it will be necessary to notify the insurance company of the transfer of title. In addition to the new owners' names and address, the company should be notified as to a "loss payable" clause to any third party interests. For example, if the seller is to carry a portion of the purchase price in some form of secondary financing, he should be named in the policy along with the holder of the first mortgage in a loss payable clause for protection of his interests.

If the buyer is purchasing a new hazard insurance policy and the former policy is to be canceled, the buyer should arrange for such coverage far in advance of title transfer. In the event a new loan is involved, most lenders have certain requirements as to the classification of the insurance company and will normally require the original and a copy of the new policy prior to funding the loan.

Pest Control Inspection

In many localities, lending institutions and/or government insuring agencies will require a pest control inspection report and a "clearance report" certifying there are no wood-destroying organisms or fungus growths in or about the premises.

This matter should be attended to immediately upon the signing of the purchase and sale contract agreement in order that any defects may be remedied far in advance of final settlement. Local laws and customs vary from state to state as to which party is to provide inspection and clearance reports. The Veterans Administration will not permit a buyer to pay for an inspection when obtaining a new G.I. loan.

Rent Statement

In the event a transaction involves some form of rental property, the seller should prepare a statement as to the names of tenants, amount of rents, due dates, advance security payments, cleanup and damage deposits, etc. prior to final settlement. This statement is the basis on which accurate rent prorations may be computed and deposits credited to the purchaser.

105

Bill of Sale

When personal property is involved with the transaction, the seller should provide a Bill of Sale, which itemizes all the personal properties being transferred to the buyer.

Assignment of Lease

In the event there is an existing lease, or leases, on the property, the seller should assign all his rights, title and interests of such to the buyer. An example of a lease assignment is as follows:

ASSIGNMENT OF LEASE

For a valuable consideration, the receipt whereof is hereby acknowledged, the undersigned does hereby sell, transfer, assign and set over unto _____ all right, title and interest in and to that certain lease made and entered into the _____ day of _____ by and between _____ Lessor, and _____ Lessee, covering the premises commonly known and designated as _____.

Dated this_____day of_____19

_____

_____

FINAL SETTLEMENT

In a few states, attorneys are seldom required in the drawing of real estate contracts or in the processing of closing title. The real estate broker, or an agent under his supervision, will ordinarily draw up the agreement of sale and purchase contract and will employ a professional escrow agent to gather all the necessary monies and documents. Such escrow holders may be employed by a title company or a lending institution or they may specialize only in processing escrows.

As a general rule, real estate transactions in these states use title companies to insure good marketable title. Title companies employ attorneys on a full time basis for the purpose of expressing an "opinion of title" prior to the insuring of title. These companies also employ "title examiners" who search the records for title defects as to the property and also to check for recordings that may be adverse to present or future good title against the buyer and seller.

When all the facts are verified, the escrow agent will draw instructions, as directed by the broker and will have gathered the necessary documents for signatures of the principals. At the time of signing, the buyer will deposit the balance of any funds due in the transaction, including his share of the closing costs and escrow expenses. The seller signs any documents that convey title at the time of signing escrow instructions. The escrow agent records the necessary documents and disburses authorized payments from the seller's proceeds and the buyer's funds that have been paid in. The escrow agent then distributes a final closing statement, or accounting of the transaction, to the buyer, seller and broker, as the statment applies to each. Some of the larger real estate firms maintain their own escrow departments.

An "escrow fee" is charged for the services employed and may be charged to the buyer in some localities or charged to the seller in other areas. The fee may be split between buyer and seller in some places. It is simply a matter of established local custom in this connection with the exception that the Veterans Administration will not permit buyers using new G.I. loans to pay escrow fees.

In most sections of the country, however, it is customary to establish a date, place and time for the signing of final settlement papers and predetermine the proration dates for taxes and insurance, etc., in the original sales agreement.

The meeting is generally held in the offices of the attorney who is in charge of processing the closing of title, although in some instances, where new loan funds are involved in the transaction, the new lender may insist on the meeting being held in his offices.

Those normally attending the meeting include the buyer, seller, real estate agent and attorney for both parties, the lenders, who may have an interest in the transaction and a representative of the title company insuring the loan, if such is the case. Other parties having an interest in the property may also attend for release of such interests in exchange for payment or other considerations as the case may be.

At this time, final settlement papers are signed by buyer and seller and the demands of various parties with an interest in the proceeds are properly authorized for payment by the appropriate principal to the transaction.

As a general rule, the escrow agent and/or title processing attorney will have the necessary documents prepared prior to the meeting from the information provided at the beginning of processing. The seller's deed, in the form specified in the original sale contract, verification of ownership and the necessary documents pertaining to the mortgages and other liens will be ready for signatures of the principals. However, the procedure may vary somewhat in different localities. Therefore, the real estate agent may have to direct and assist his clients in providing any required receipts, documents and

107

statements not previously mentioned. It is frequently advisable for the purchaser to bring a certified check or cashier's check to such meetings for the amount of funds needed to complete closing.

After closing of title in these meetings it is the seller's responsibility to record all documents necessary to place good title in position to transfer. It is the buyer's responsibility to record all documents establishing ownership and all new mortgage instruments. These recordings may be a part of the services performed by the escrow agent or the processing attorney in some sections of the country. In other localities, such recordings may be left up to the principals. In such case the recording of mortgage documents would be the lender's responsibility.

10

Property Taxes

Although tax dates vary from state to state and, in some instances, special assessment dates may vary according to laws of localities within different states, the fundamentals in property tax collection are generally the same throughout the country.

The date of assessment is a fixed time of possession of real and personal property at which time it becomes a lien against the real property involved. In most states, personal property is imposed and where no real property is involved, the tax obligation is of an individual nature. For example, the household and personal property of an individual party who may be renting a home is assessed and separate billing may be received from the official county tax collector, or city tax collector, as the case may be.

In instances where personal property is included as a separate item in the tax bill for real property, the personal property portion of the bill is not normally prorated in a real estate transaction, unless a material amount of personal property is included in the sale. In such case, the purchaser may be expected to pay his proportionate share of personal property tax.

Prorations of personal and real property taxes are of no concern to the tax collector, as the taxes are assessed become a lien and are due and payable regardless of who may own the property at the time. Prorations are, therefore, strictly a matter of mutual agreement between buyer and seller in the sales agreement.

ASSESSMENT DATE

Property taxes become a lien as of a fixed assessment date on which property is in possession of the owner of record. The assessed value of personal and real property may be on the basis of from twenty percent of market value to full market value, depending on established laws and customs in the various states.

TAX RATES

The due date for taxes is usually on the beginning of the fiscal tax year that commences a few months after the date of assessment. Although taxes may be due, they are not payable until a tax rate has been established by the appropriate state or county governing board. This board is normally made up of elected public officials who analyze the assessed tax roll and weigh the potential revenue against anticipated costs to operate local government for the coming year. The tax rate is then established on the basis of their findings. In most instances, the tax rate is a certain number of dollars, per hundred, of the assessed value. For example, $10 per hundred against a property with an assessed value of $4,000 would equal $400.

After the tax rate has been established and made known to local taxpayers, a period of time is set aside for the governing tax board to hear complaints of taxpayers who may feel they are being unjustly taxed on the assessed value of their property or on some other basis. Tax adjustments are frequently allowed, or ordered, by the governing board when complaints are proven or justified.

When the allotted time for complaints has expired, the official assessed tax values and established rates are turned over to the tax collector for tabulation and billing.

DUE AND PAYABLE DATE

In most localities, property taxes are considered as being due and payable upon the property owner's receiving the tax bill. If the owner of record or a lender who is to pay the tax bill from the owner's impound account, should fail to receive such billing for one reason or another, it is that party's responsibility to investigate and arrange for payment.

A certain period of time, usually thirty to forty days, is allowed for payment before taxes become delinquent. The taxpayer may have the option of paying property tax bills in two or more installments, depending upon local laws and customs, or of paying the entire bill at one time.

Holders of trust deeds or mortgages against a property frequently require the owner to make monthly payments into a tax and insurance reserve account and when bills for these two items of expense become due and payable, they are mailed direct to the mortgage lienholder for payment.

The tax reserve portion of an owner's impound account is usually based on previous tax bills or anticipated amounts of property taxes. In periods of rising taxes, it is a common occurrence for a deficiency to exist in the owner's tax reserve.

Through failure to collect a sufficient amount in monthly tax reserve payments from the mortgagor with which to pay the tax bill, some lenders may advance the necessary funds and request the deficiency from the mortgagor in a lump sum. Monthly payments are subsequently increased for future tax reserves according to the deficiency.

Some lenders may not demand the current deficiency in one payment, but will increase monthly tax reserve payments in amount sufficient to collect the deficiency and to provide ample reserves for future tax bills. In either case, the lender's objective is to prevent tax bills from becoming delinquent.

DELINQUENT DATE

When taxes are not paid on, or before, the stipulated deadline for payment, certain delinquency charges are added to the amount due. These charges are usually based on a percentage of the past due installment plus other charges, according to local laws and customs. Tax payments are ordinarily credited to current due and payable bills and any excess may be applied to the most recent delinquent taxes and penalties.

PRORATION OF TAXES

Tax bills are normally mailed out by the tax collector according to special instructions. In lieu of special instructions, the collector will mail tax bills to the owner of record at the time of mailing. When ownership to real property has been recorded only a short time prior to the mailing of tax bills, the former owner or lender, as the case may be, may receive the tax bill. In such cases, the bill should be forwarded to the new owner of record, since the former owner has normally paid his prorated share of taxes to the new owner.

Prorations are based on the time of possession during the fiscal tax year. When taxes are due, but not yet payable, and the former owner was in possession of the property for a period of time between the beginning of the tax year and prior to paying the tax bill, he will pay the new owner for his share of the taxes. The new owner will be held responsible for payment of the entire bill when taxes become due and payable.

Conversely, if the former owner has paid taxes for a period in advance of recorded transfer of ownership date, the new owner will pay the former owner for taxes paid in advance from the date of recording.

In any case, prorations are provided through escrow between buyer and seller, as real property taxes are a lien against the real property and the tax collector looks to the owner of record for payment.

111

11

Closing Costs–
New Loans–Seller's Costs

When a property is being purchased on the basis of the buyer's paying all cash or obtaining a new loan with which to purchase, the seller may be obligated to certain additional expenses that would not otherwise exist if the transaction involved the assumption of existing loans and liens.

Where existing loans and liens are to be paid off, it is advisable to determine the seller's position, from the standpoint of sufficient equity, after all extra charges in that connection are considered. Such prior determination may be expedient in the event a buyer, with limited funds, offers to purchase on the basis of obtaining a new loan or when it may be otherwise necessary to refinance in order to consummate a sale of the property. The demand for a seller's property, as well as the current money market and other economic conditions, may usually govern what buyers and sellers are willing to do and what is prudent for them to do.

FIRST TRUST DEED OR MORTGAGE

In transactions involving refinancing, lenders normally require all prior security liens to be removed as against the property. This would mean the first trust deed or mortgage must be paid off if the new loan is to be in the position of a first security lien.

The exception could be in the event an existing prior recorded mortgage contains a subordination clause which is a written agreement to the effect that the existing lien is to become subordinate to a later recorded mortgage lien. This frequently is the case where a lot is purchased on a trust deed or mortgage which is to become subordinate to a new construction loan. The loan may be granted without necessity of paying off the original or prior security lien when it is to become a junior lien.

113

How to Determine Correct Balance

At the end of each year, most institutional lenders mail a loan statement to the mortgagor, as required by law in many states. This statement will indicate the loan number, principal balance, interest paid and property taxes paid the preceeding calendar year. It will give an accounting of the monthly payments and a breakdown of what portion of the payments apply to impound account reserves, the amount applied to principal and interest and the interest rate.

The principal balance and the impound balance of an existing loan may be determined at any time during the year from information contained in the loan statement by taking the following steps:

1. Compute the interest for one month on the indicated principal balance of the loan, using the rate of interest shown on the statement.
2. Note the amount of principal and interest payment indicated.
3. Deduct the interest from the principal and interest payment and find the amount that would be applied to the principal balance.
4. Determine the number of months for which principal payments were made after the statement was issued and multiply the principal payments by that number. The total amount applied to principal is then determined.
5. Deduct the total payments made from the principal balance shown on the statement. The difference will be the approximate current principal balance. Since principal payments increase a few cents each month, the computed balance may differ by a dollar or so from the actual balance, but will be close enough.
6. The impound balance (trust fund) may be calculated by adding the additional payments for impounds to the balance shown on the loan statement.
7. Deduct any tax and insurance payments from the total impound balance and payments into it that were made after the loan statement was issued. The difference will be the current balance. In knowing the due and payable dates for tax payments in a particular area and by looking at the fire insurance policy, payments out of the impound account may be determined. On F.H.A. loans, the Mutual Mortgage Insurance premiums are paid on the anniversary date of the loan origination. This should also be considered as an accumulated obligation to be paid to F.H.A. as it is earned.

The annual loan statement is an important tool to use in calculating

114

balances and also for the information revealed when listing a home or at the time of presenting an offer to purchase the home. Sellers are sometimes prone to believe their loan balance to be lower than it actually is. When there is a material difference between the actual balance and what it was thought to be, it may be impossible to close escrow.

In the event the mortgagor never receives a loan statement from the lender to provide the above information, or if the mortgagor has misplaced the statement he received, the lender should be contacted and the information requested. (A form letter to use for this purpose is illustrated as Exhibit 2-2 in a previous chapter concerning listing contracts.)

JUNIOR MORTGAGE LIENS

Mortgage security instruments normally become first, second, third, etc., according to the priority date of recording, unless a subordination agreement is contained in a prior lien. When a new loan is to be secured by a first trust deed or mortgage, it is usually necessary to pay off all junior and prior mortgage liens existing against the subject property.

Holders of junior mortgage liens do not always provide annual loan statements to the mortgagor. However, payment books, amortization schedules, or other forms of records of payments are normally available from which loan balances may be determined. When such records are not in the hands of the mortgagor, the lienholder should be contacted in order to receive accurate information in writing.

ASSESSMENT AND IMPROVEMENT BONDS

When a new first loan is being considered for a property buyer, the lender will often reduce the available loan amount commensurable to the existing bond balances or will require such bond balances to be paid off.

In the case of a new F.H.A. loan, the loan commitment for insurance is usually issued on the basis of there being no bond balances existing against resale properties. If there is an existing bond balance, insurance for the loan may be reduced accordingly. For example, if an F.H.A. insured loan commitment is issued for $25,000 and there is a bond balance of $500, the commitment may be reduced to $24,500 unless the bond balance is eliminated.

The buyer may either pay the bond off or pay the difference in down payment and assume the bond obligation. As a general rule, the seller is asked to eliminate the bond in order that the buyer's investment of cash is kept at a minimum. Provisions for disposition of existing bond and assessment balances are normally set forth in the original sales agreement.

When the buyer is applying for a new G.I. loan, the Veterans Administration will allow the bond balance to be assumed provided the total sales price plus the bond balance does not exceed appraisal value indicated on the certificate of reasonable value.

If the purchase price exceeds appraisal value under any circumstances, which would include the additional obligation of bonds, the veteran will be required to sign a statement certifying that he is aware of the fact and that payment for the excess purchase price will be accomplished from his own cash resources.

Bond Prepayment Penalty

When improvement and assessment bonds are paid in full, prior to maturity, there is usually some sort of penalty involved. It may be based on a percentage of the balance or on the basis of a certain amount of unearned interest.

Bond Interest

The interest on bonds is normally paid every six months. An interest-only payment may be made in the spring, for example, and payment on principal and interest is paid in the fall of the year.

Verification of Information

It is normally advisable to verify the exact conditions of bond balances, interest earned and what, if any, prepayment penalties may be imposed immediately upon placing a property on the market for sale. This may be accomplished by contacting the appropriate public agency where principal and interest payments are collected. In most instances, the city or county treasurer keeps records in this connection.

The seller may have receipts and current records regarding balances, interest and principal payments and all the necessary information, but it would be a rare set of circumstances. In many instances, where there is an existing loan on the property, the lender makes bond payments from a reserve maintained in the borrower's impound account.

Special assessments are often imposed in districts for paving streets, curbs, sidewalks, street lighting and sewer installation or other construction projects. The completed work is usually apparent, but in the case of sewer installation, there may be no definite evidence of sewer connection to the property. When there is some reason to believe the sewer was never "hooked up" and the property may be on a septic tank and a "dry well" or "leach lines," verification should be made. It is always possible that property owners failed to obtain verification of sewer connection when purchasing the property from previous owners.

OTHER LIENS

Since liens against a property reduce the seller's equitable interest, any judgment liens, or other liens that must be paid off prior to the transfer of property, should be considered at the time of placing the property for sale on the market or prior to entering into a contract of sale agreement.

PREPAYMENT PENALTIES

Most conventional lenders provide in their mortgage instruments some form of prepayment penalty if the obligation is paid off at some future time prior to maturity of the note and trust deed or mortgage or other type of security instrument.

An exception to this may be with the mortgage instruments involved in conventional loans granted under the F.N.M.A. Conventional Loan Program initiated on February 14, 1972. Prepayment penalties are not provided for in this program.

Exception may also be in the case of a seller who carries back some form of secondary financing, but would rather have the cash than the paper. In any case, the mortgagee has a contractual right to keep his money invested and earning the stipulated interest, unless he agrees to waive this right within the terms of the security instrument.

When mortgage instruments provide that the debt is payable "on or before" the due date, or that the debt is payable in a specified monthly payment, or more, for example, "$50 per month, or more," the mortgagee (lender) has agreed to allow the debt to be paid off at any time without penalty. This is commonly referred to as a "prepayment privilege."

With each loan to be processed, the lender experiences a varied degree of expenses. If the loan is paid off in advance of the investor's projected yield, he is faced with the same expenses again in order to keep his money working for him. Therefore, the normal device to offset extra expenses and loss of yield is in the form of a prepayment penalty. Mortgage instruments concerning G.I. loans may be paid off at any time prior to maturity.

Effective May 1, 1972, the prepayment penalty of 1 percent on F.H.A.

117

loans when paid off in less than 120 payments was eliminated even though the mortgage instruments may provide for it.

Conventional Lenders

Since conventional lenders are constantly revising their policies as to terms and conditions of the loans they grant according to current money markets, there is no exact pattern to follow in anticipation of specified prepayment penalties.

Individual lenders should be contacted regarding penalties for prepayment of loans granted currently. The holder of an existing mortgage should also be contacted in this connection in the event the property is to be sold. Sellers frequently receive some consideration in costs when a new loan is placed with the lender who holds an existing mortgage.

Savings and Loan Associations

Savings and loan associations prepayment penalties may vary from two percent of the loan balance to three percent of the original loan amount. The penalty is frequently based on an amount equal to three to six months' unearned interest.

Commercial Banks

Commercial banks are often more lenient than savings and loan associations concerning prepayment penalties. The cost may be two percent the first year and will decline one-half percent per year until there is no penalty after five years.

Insurance Companies

Insurance companies often charge as much as five percent penalty if the loan is paid off within two years. It will normally decline each year until after five years there is no penalty.

Private Investors and Syndicates

Investment syndicates and private investors normally demand the most severe prepayment penalties. This may be particularly true in the case of a secondary equity loan being secured by a note and trust deed or mortgage.

UNEARNED INTEREST

Unearned interest is that which the lender may collect to envelop a certain period of time after the loan ceases to earn interest. It is a form of penalty charged when a loan is paid off prematurely.

Since interest feeds the yield on a real estate loan investment, it is essential to the lender that his money constantly earns maximum interest. Accredited lenders for F.H.A. and V.A. loans are permitted to charge an unearned interest penalty for a period of sixty days after a loan has been paid off. However, when the lender is notified at least thirty days prior to the first of the next month following, as to an approximate date he may expect the existing loan to be paid in full, the unearned interest penalty may be reduced to thirty days. In receiving such advance notice, the lender will have an opportunity to project the funds into another investment with no loss of time on earned interest.

Professional escrow agents, real estate brokers and attorneys who have attained a certain degree of experience in such matters are usually familiar with various lender's policies in connection with unearned interest penalties. (A form letter, illustrated as Exhibit 2-2, will be found in the chapter on listing contracts, which will provide a format for requesting the desired information.)

EARNED INTEREST

Interest on real estate loans is ordinarily not paid until it has been earned, except when used as a basis for a prepayment penalty and in the case of the first month prepaid interest on a new loan as discussed in the chapter on buyer's closing costs.

It is often a mistaken impression by the borrower that when he pays a regular monthly payment, interest is being paid in advance. Very few, if any, lenders collect interest in advance of its being earned, although the situation may prevail in some form of conventional loan.

Regular monthly payments of principal and interest on real estate loans reduce the principal balance of the debt and pay the interest earned in the previous month. Therefore, earned interest is that which has accrued subsequent to the last regular monthly payment of principal and interest.

Since earned interest is an expense connected with paying off the loan and because in most cases it is impossible to pick an exact date for the loan to be paid off, it is advisable to anticipate a full month of earned interest in estimating the seller's costs. When less than a full month's interest is actually

119

paid the seller is that much ahead, but he was at least prepared to pay more if necessary.

FORWARDING FEE

When an existing loan is to be paid off a request is made of the mortgagee to prepare a statement of the condition of the loan concerning principal balance, impound account balance, interest due, prepayment penalties and other demands for full payment of the obligation. Mortgage release instruments and instructions to the escrow holder will normally accompany the statement when the lender forwards it.

Under normal circumstances, the lender will charge the mortgagor, or someone, a nominal fee for the preparation of the documents and refer to it as a "forwarding fee."

As a general rule, the mortgagee will expect payment of the forwarding fee whether the loan is subsequently paid off or not. Therefore, it would be advisable to request a loan statement only when the transaction is certain to be completed in escrow.

RECONVEYANCE FEE

In the event an existing loan is secured by a note and trust deed, the trustee to the mortgage instrument must issue a Deed of Reconveyance to the mortgagor when the debt is fully paid. The charge for this service is often referred to as a reconveyance fee or a trustee's fee. The charge for the deed of reconveyance and services connected to it may vary from $15 upward, depending upon the individual policies of the trustee and any legal limitations prevailing in different localities.

SATISFACTION OF MORTGAGE

When a regular mortgage is paid off it is necessary to have an instrument drawn and recorded to remove the lien from the public records. This is often performed by the mortgagee or his attorney. Some state laws require all legal documents to be prepared by legal counsel. In other states, a release form may be filled in by anyone and signed by the mortgagee. Other states, South Carolina for example, merely require a sentence upon the mortgage document signed by the mortgagee that the mortgage has been satisfied. In Massachusetts, the statutory form contains only four lines to the effect that the mortgage has been satisfied.

The usual form used in this connection is referred to as a Satisfaction of Mortgage in some localities or a Discharge of Mortgage in other areas. The charges for preparation of the document by others may vary according to the amount of work involved in individual cases.

ACKNOWLEDGMENTS

The recording laws of most states provide that any instrument that conveys or transfers ownership of real property must be acknowledged prior to delivery and recording. An acknowledgment is a formal declaration made before a qualified public official by the person delivering an instrument that such delivery is his own act and deed.

When a Notary Public or other designated public offical is satisfied that the signature is genuine he will affix his seal on a Certificate of Acknowledgment and attach it to the instrument unless the certificate is printed on the form as a convenience. Acknowledgment fees are relatively small and in many instances they are included in the services of escrow holders who perform the work themselves.

RECORDING FEES

The seller customarily pays the recording fees of any instruments deemed necessary to remove liens and encumbrances from against the property or himself in order to deliver real property on a basis of marketable title. This may include the recordation of mortgage satisfactions, releases or deeds necessary to provide good title to the purchaser.

TRUE EQUITY

When consideration has been given to the payment of all liens and encumbrances and the expenses involved therein, the total is deducted from the sales price. This will establish the seller's true equity balance with which to pay actual selling costs, escrow expenses and prorations involved with a new loan type of transaction.

COMMISSIONS

Ordinarily, when a licensed real estate agent has negotiated a transaction to the point of a complete meeting of the minds between buyer and seller and the transaction is reduced to writing in a contract of sale agreement and signed by all parties, a commission has been earned. Under normal circumstances, the broker agrees to waive payment of the earned commission until completion of the sale and the close of escrow. The commission is then paid from the seller's proceeds.

The agent's responsibility does not usually end with the signing of the sales agreement even though his commission has been earned. There are a great many details involved in a transaction from the time of sale and the close of escrow. The agent's full cooperation may become necessary on several occasions in assisting the escrow holder and client to the completion and close of escrow.

NEW LOAN DISCOUNT POINTS

Investors who fund real estate loans consider money as a commodity to be rented out to others for a profit. Such profit is commonly referred to as "yield." These lenders constantly consider the factors of interest rates, term of the investment and the risk involved when determining investments in real estate loans as opposed to other avenues of investment. Their prime objective is to realize the highest possible yield with the lowest possible risk.

Consideration of Other Investments

Consideration may be given to an investment in, for example, state and municipal bonds, which are essentially risk-free with repayment amortized over a period of fifteen years. Interest rates are normally lower on this type of an investment than they are on real estate loans, but the yield may be tax-free, which is an important factor. The same situation may prevail in short term government treasury notes. Further consideration is given to the fact that the expenses of servicing and record keeping are relatively small in bond and treasury note investments in comparison to these costs involved with real estate loans.

Considerations in Real Estate Loans

Interest rates on real estate loans vary according to current money markets, which are controlled by supply and demand as is any commodity. When the demand for money is higher than the supply, interest rates increase. Conversely, when there is a surplus of money on deposit in savings accounts, interest rates decrease because there is less demand.

The term of real estate loans is normally twenty to thirty years, which means that the investor is potentially "locked in" on interest yield for that period of time. Should inflationary forces increase interest rates during the term of the loan in order to liquidate the investor may be forced to sell the note and mortgage instrument at a discount. With the exception of F.H.A. insured loans and the Veterans Administration guaranteed loans, there is always a certain element of risk involved with real estate loans.

122

Equalize Yield

Discount points are imposed only for the purpose of equalizing the investor's yield on real estate loans in comparison to the projected yield in other available investments. The number of "points" demanded may fluctuate with interest rates, down payments and term of the loan.

Application of Discount Points

A "point" is equal to one percent. Therefore, a quotation of three discount points means that the loan will be discounted three percent. For example, if a buyer is granted a $20,000 loan he will sign a note and trust deed or mortgage for that amount, but in discounting three percent of $20,000, which is $600, the lender will advance only $19,400 to the seller's account in escrow.

There is a distinct difference between "discount points" and "loan origination fees." A mortgage broker who takes the loan application and packages and processes the loan, may receive a loan origination fee for the service. However, the investor who actually provides loan funds will withhold discount points in the disbursement of funds to the seller's account in escrow.

Discount Points on Government-sponsored Loans

As a general rule, discount points are applied more predominately on F.H.A. and V.A. loans because of limited interest rates allowed by these two government agencies. F.H.A. and V.A. regulations prohibit the buyer from paying discount points. Therefore, the seller must bear the expense of this item if the purchaser intends to purchase by obtaining a new F.H.A. or G.I. loan.

Discuss with Clients

It is essential at the time of listing a home for sale that the seller thoroughly understands his obligation to pay discount points in connection with government-sponsored loans for a prospective purchaser. It is not advisable for the agent to guarantee a specified quotation of discount points to the seller, nor is it advisable to allow the seller to specify a limited number of points in the listing. Justification in this respect would depend largely on the seller's equity and his motivation in placing the property for sale on the market.

No one individual will have any control over developments occurring in the money market and this, of course, is the determining factor in the required amount of discount points to be paid. Quotations fluctuate from time to time and may change over night. However, loan agents are often in a position to protect clients for a limited time and will, when possible, give the real estate agent a written statement of guarantee for a specified time on an individual loan basis.

ABSTRACT OF TITLE AND EXAMINATION

The costs of an abstract of title may vary in the different states and localities where this form of title history and summary document is used. The charge may be based on the number of entries to be accounted for or it may be levied according to property value or sale price.

In some areas, an abstract of title may be used merely as a document to be reviewed by an attorney for the issuance of an "opinion of title" or subsequent title insurance. Other states utilize the document as an accepted form in evidence of marketable title by buyers and lenders without the necessity of title insurance. Charges for the service may be paid by the seller or buyer according to agreement between them or it may be a matter of local custom as to which party pays for it.

TITLE INSURANCE PREMIUM

This type of marketable title protection is available in practically all states and is used as a matter of course in most of them. Charges for a policy of title insurance normally includes the title search.

The standard coverage policy of title insurance is commonly used to protect ownership of the described property and the validity and priority of liens such as trust deeds and mortgages that may be recorded against the property. Coverage of the policy normally includes all items of record plus certain title defects not of record such as forged instruments, acts of minors and incompetents and undisclosed rights of others. It is issued by private insurance companies specializing in title insurance and they will defend the owner against anyone who may challenge the insured as to rights of ownership.

Since this insurance coverage applies only to an insured owner of record, when title of ownership is transferred the policy is no longer in effect. Therefore, it becomes necessary to obtain a new policy of title insurance for a new purchaser under a lender's normal requirements.

The laws and customs vary in most states, as well as in some areas within certain states, as to whether the buyer or seller pays for this

124

protection. In areas where it is customary for the seller to provide a standard policy of title insurance, the expense is not considered in the closing costs for the buyer in computing maximum F.H.A. loans. Where it is customary for the buyer to pay the cost, F.H.A. will consider it in arriving at the maximum loan figure. (This factor is discussed further in the chapter on F.H.A. loans.)

ESCROW FEE

An escrow fee is charged by professional escrow agents or holders who gather the necessary information concerning a transaction and, after recording the legal documents, disperse funds to those who are entitled to them.

Escrow fees may seldom be charged in some states, but escrow agents, real estate brokers and attorneys do charge for this service in other states. The amount charged will usually depend on the amount of work involved or the fee may be based according to the dollar amount involved in various transactions.

In some instances, attorneys may include the charge for escrow services in with a flat fee for all services rendered in connection with a transaction. In many localities, the fee is included into the cost of a policy of title insurance when escrow is handled by title companies. In other areas, a separation of escrow fees and title insurance premiums is customary and, in some instances, mandatory.

It is the custom for sellers to pay escrow fees in some areas, while it may be customary for the buyer or the buyer and seller to pay the cost in other localities.

The Veterans Administration will not permit G.I. loan applicant-purchasers to pay escrow fees in some areas such as California, although that government agency does allow the buyer to pay for a policy of title insurance.

ATTORNEY FEES

As a general rule, the services of an attorney at law are employed in a real estate transaction either directly or indirectly and to varied degrees throughout the country. The nature of an attorney's services may depend largely on the laws and customs connected with real estate transactions in different states. In some areas, the services may be limited to merely expressing an "opinion of title" as a full time employee of an abstract or title company. The laws of some states make it mandatory for all legal

125

documents, including printed forms, to be drawn by an attorney. In other states, printed forms may be filled in by anyone.

In some localities, the entire transaction is normally processed by an attorney including searching the records, processing escrow, preparing all legal documents, negotiating in a sales agreement and handling final settlement between buyer and seller in his office. The charges, in any case, may depend on the amount of services rendered and based on a flat fee or on the dollar amount involved in the transaction. Regardless of location, prudent real estate agents and escrow agents are careful not to be placed in the compromising position of practicing law by word or act.

PROPERTY SURVEY

Lenders frequently require an official property survey document to be submitted by a registered or professional land surveyor. This may be particularly true when metes and bounds are included in the property description. The purpose is for the assurance of correct property measurements, the establishment of lines and boundaries and to make certain there are no encroachments attached to the property.

A less complete investigation is usually required on smaller properties that have been subdivided and current plat maps are on file in the public records concerning the subdivision. Such requirement may be in the form of a purchase of an extended coverage title insurance policy issued by the American Land Title Association through title companies and is normally referred to as an A.L.T.A. policy of title insurance.

An A.L.T.A. policy coverage is in addition to the standard policy of title insurance, issued to an owner of record as protection for good title against items of record that may be defective. The extended coverage protects the lender against title defects not of record for the term of the loan with some few exceptions. It involves a physical inspection of the property measurements, lines, boundaries and encroachments, but does not include an official survey report. Inspections are normally performed by someone employed by the issuing title company.

The cost of an A.L.T.A. policy may be nominal in some localities and very expensive in other areas when issued to lenders, but an owner's policy for like coverage may be proportionately much more expensive depending on the involved risks. This item of expense is normally paid by the buyer, but current economic conditions may be considered, at time of sale, if the buyer is short of funds.

126

DRAWING FEES

The party who is expected to furnish a legal instrument is normally the one who pays for the drawing of it. From the seller's standpoint, this may include any form of deed to be delivered in conveying ownership and title of the property to another party. It may also involve some form of a release of a lien or encumbrance to place the property into a transferable position. A bill of sale, as an example, is often required in real estate transactions.

Drawing fees may vary for different types of instruments and may differ in various localities. Under normal circumstances, the fees are seldom included in with escrow fees. Therefore, an additional charge may be imposed for drawing documents.

TRANSFER TAX

Several different states and localities impose some form of a sales or transfer tax when a change of ownership and property title occurs. The basis of such tax and the methods of collection are varied in many instances, but the documentary stamp method is most widely utilized.

The form of taxation was first inaugurated by the federal government for revenue to aid the financing of the Civil War in the 1860s. It was eliminated shortly after that war ended, but was reactivated in 1940 and continued until January 1, 1968 at which time the federal government again abandoned it. As a federal revenue tax, regular tax stamps were affixed to the deed or the appropriate instrument that conveyed title of real property in the public records.

When the federal government ceased to require the tax most states, or counties within those states, continued the method of taxation for local revenue. Documentation by use of a rubber stamp on the conveyance document is the general accepted form, rather than tax stamps used previously for indicating the amount of tax paid.

Originally, in the event of an "all-cash" type of sale, including refinancing to a new loan, the seller's tax was based on the full sales price at $1.10 per thousand dollars or 55 cents for each $500 or fraction thereof. The tax on a $20,000 sales price would, therefore, be 20 X $1.10 to equal $22.

Where the sale was based on a loan assumption, the tax applied would be on the amount of equity, which is the difference between the sales price and the loan balance assumed. Thus, the tax on a $20,000 sale, where an existing loan of $15,000 was assumed, would be based on the $5,000 equity and the tax would be 5 X $1.10 to equal $5.50. The tax rate of $1.10 per thousand dollars still prevails in many localities. However, it would be advisable to check state and local jurisdictions for variations in the normal rate, as it may differ in some areas.

EARNED MUTUAL MORTGAGE INSURANCE

F.H.A. mutual mortgage insurance is based on one-half percent of the loan balance on the anniversary date of the loan origination and divided into twelve equal monthly payments. These monthly premium payments are held in the borrower's impound account by the lender and paid to F.H.A. in one payment on the next anniversary date. Since mutual mortgage insurance premiums are collected and paid on an accumulative basis from the reserves in that portion of the impound account the seller will probably be obligated for a few months of earned premiums when the loan is paid off prematurely.

TRUTH IN LENDING STATEMENT FEE

Virtually all new real estate mortgage loans are governed under the procedures of Regulation Z, of the Federal Consumer Credit Protection Act, Public Law 90-321; 82 Stat. 146, which became effective July 1, 1969.

There may be some few exceptions, but it may be advisable to anticipate the expense of a truth in lending statement, which is otherwise known as a disclosure statement of loan for the consumer's benefit of analysis. Since the procedure of making up this statement is more or less complex, mortgage lenders ordinarily request a fee of $20 to $35 to cover expenses for the time involved in its preparation.

Either the buyer or the seller may pay this cost in the event of a conventional type of loan as it can be a matter of negotiation. However, if the purchaser is obtaining a new F.H.A. or G.I. loan, he is not permitted to pay this item of expense under the rules and regulations of these two government agencies.

PHOTO AND INSPECTION FEE

When a new loan is being processed on a property, lenders will frequently require their representatives or correspondents to inspect the premises and submit a report as to the general condition of the improvements and neighborhood. At the same time they may request a photograph or two of the neighborhood and the subject property.

The cost for these photographs and property inspection may vary from $10 to $25 depending on the amount of work involved. Although the cost may be paid by either the buyer or seller when the loan is of a conventional nature, the F.H.A. or Veterans Administration will not allow the purchaser to pay this item of expense. Therefore, it is the seller's cost for the latter two types of government backed loans.

Lenders and mortgage brokers often include the service in their loan fees and do not require reimbursement. However, it should be anticipated in estimating the seller's costs.

TERMITE INSPECTION FEE

When a new loan is to be insured by F.H.A. or guaranteed by the Veterans Administration, a termite and dry rot inspection and clearance report is normally required from a licensed pest control company. In the case of a new conventional loan, the lender usually imposes such a requirement. The purpose of an inspection is to determine whether or not the improvements, such as the house, garage or other buildings, are infested with wood-destroying insects or fungus.

Inspection fees are widely varied throughout the country and may cost from $20 upwards, depending upon the rate schedules of the trade for the service in different localities. It is often a matter of custom or negotiation between buyer and seller as to which party pays the cost. A purchaser in obtaining a new G.I. loan is not permitted to pay for a termite inspection under the Veterans Administration rules and regulations. Therefore, it would automatically become a seller's cost.

It is often advisable for a purchaser to condition his offer to purchase on the basis of receiving a certified pest control inspection and clearance report from a licensed pest control operator that the improvements are free from damage or infestation by termites, fungus or other wood-destroying organisms. It should be specified as one of the conditions of the purchase even though it may not be required by a lender or government agency.

Buyers, lenders and government agencies frequently neglect to require a termite, pest and dry rot fungus clearance report when a home is constructed on a cement slab type of flooring. Termites and other wood-destroying organisms are not always restricted to a subterranian entrance—therefore, damage may occur in other areas of a structure. Leaking pipe connections in the interior walls may cause a dry rot condition. New homes have been found to have some sort of a built-in problem that was discovered by a licensed pest control operator.

If such inspection and clearance reports are not required by the buyer, lender or government agency, it may be advisable for the agent to have a "waiver" signed by all parties. An example of the waiver may be as follows.

This is to certify that I have thoroughly inspected the property located at (address) and that I am satisfied to purchase said property in its present condition and without requiring a structural pest control inspection and clearance reports. As purchaser of the subject property, I hereby declare and agree that neither the real estate agent, broker nor seller shall be held responsible or liable to me for any structural pest damage or other condition of the said property that might have been discovered in an inspection by a licensed pest control inspector.

TERMITE REPAIRS

In the event an inspection report reveals an infestation of some variety of wood-destroying insects or fungus on about the premises, the lender or government agency involved will normally require such conditions to be corrected prior to granting a loan. In some instances, when the inspection report indicates preventive work is necessary, the corrections may be extended to include all recommendations.

The laws and customs may differ in the various localities, but as a general rule it is customary for the buyer to pay for the inspection report and the seller to pay for any necessary repairs. One exception would be in the case of a G.I. loan where the Veterans Administration will not permit a new loan applicant to pay for termite inspections.

It is usually advisable for a seller to order an inspection and clearance report from a licensed pest control operator at the time of listing a home for sale on the market. In doing so, he may be aware of the costs of making any necessary corrections and repairs prior to accepting a lower offer for the property than the listed price and take the extra cost into consideration. To accept a lower offer to purchase and then discover the extra expense could be disastrous to anticipated net proceeds from the sale. Some sections of the country may not generally encounter these conditions in which case, of course, an inspection and clearance report may not be required.

APPRAISAL FEE

Ordinarily, prior to the creation of a new mortgage loan, lenders will require an appraisal report of the property. In the case of a new mortgage loan being sponsored by the F.H.A. or the Veterans Administration, the appraisals and commitments of these two government agencies may be sufficient.

With a conventional type of loan, the lenders normally do not issue a firm appraisal and commitment on homes until there is a definite sale and the application for a loan on the property is being processed. An appraisal is then made and the results are considered along with the sales price and the buyer's capabilities for repayment of a loan that may be granted.

When a buyer finds it necessary to obtain a new loan with which to purchase a home, the appraisal fee is usually paid to the lender at the time of making application for the loan, regardless of whether the new loan is to be a conventional type or an F.H.A. or G.I. loan. The charge for an F.H.A. appraisal and commitment for an insured loan is $40 and the cost of the Veterans Administration Certificate of Reasonable Value is $40. It is customary in most localities for the buyer to pay for appraisal fees, but it may be a matter of negotiation between buyer and seller as to which party is to pay the cost. The paying party should be specified in the sales agreement at the time of offer and acceptance.

In areas where F.H.A. loans are the predominate source of financing, it is frequently advisable for an owner to place application for an F.H.A. commitment through an accredited F.H.A. lender at the time of listing his home for sale on the market. The owner may then be prepared for the buyer who may be inclined to rely on an F.H.A. appraisal as assurance of market value. A commitment obtained prior to sale of a home is a "conditional commitment." It becomes the property of the lender who submitted the application after processing it for the owner. However, the commitment is assignable and most lenders assign it upon request when preference is given to another lender for loan application.

When there is no existing F.H.A. commitment on a home that is being sold on the basis of a buyer obtaining a new F.H.A. loan with which to purchase, an appraisal and "firm commitment" is applied for.

Veterans who intend to purchase under their G.I. entitlement apply for a C.R.V. (Certificate of Reasonable Value) at the time of making application for their loan and normally pay the appraisal fee then.

In either case, of an F.H.A. or G.I. loan, certain statements are to be signed by the applicant in connection with the appraisal being for a lesser amount than the sales price. These statements are normally provided by the lender at the time of loan application.

PRORATION OF TAXES

The property owner of record is normally responsible for payment of tax liens when they become due and payable. Therefore, the local tax collector will send the billing for such payments due to the owner of record, or lender, according to instructions.

Tax prorations and whether the seller pays or receives them is a matter of possession during the fiscal tax year and also depends on whether the taxes have been accumulating or have been paid ahead by him. In most states, there is a period of time between the beginning of the fiscal tax year and the dates on which tax liens become due and payable. If the seller has possession during this period of accumulating taxes, which are not yet paid, the seller will pay prorated taxes to the buyer. The buyer will then be obligated to pay the entire tax bill when it becomes due and payable and will do so, in part, with funds received from the seller for his share of the tax bill by virtue of possession.

On the other hand, if the seller has paid taxes ahead, but is giving possession prior to the end of the period for which he has paid, the buyer will reimburse the seller for the unused portion of time. Each party is normally expected to pay for the time in possession and use of the property. Therefore, most contracts of sale state that taxes are to be prorated from date of closing.

PRORATION OF WATER BILLS

When the water supply is on a meter, as it normally is with other utilities, the user is charged according to the amount consumed. If a new consumer is to take responsibility for payment of the water bill, the water company will read the meter as of possession date and charge the responsible parties accordingly. In many localities, the water is not on a meter, and therefore, the charge to the consumer is based on a flat rate and billing may be made on a monthly, bimonthly, quarterly, semi-annually or annual basis.

Water Districts

When the source of water is supplied by a water district, the billing may be on a monthly or bi-monthly basis. Advance payment for all or a portion of the water bill may be required. In the event the seller has paid any portion of the water bill in advance, the buyer would be expected to reimburse him for the unused period of advanced payment.

If the seller has not paid in advance and the bill is in an accumulative period, he would be expected to prorate and pay the buyer for water used between the beginning of the billing period and the date of possession. The buyer will then pay the entire bill for the period when it is received.

Water district offices will normally forward a bill to escrow upon request when given a proration date for which to charge the seller. Payment for the seller's share is then paid from his proceeds out of escrow.

Municipal Water

If water is supplied by the city, billing for it is frequently on a quarterly basis. Payment may not be required in advance, but is due at the end of each three months and, in most instances, becomes a lien on the property, the same as taxes. The seller is usually expected to pay his prorated share of accumulated usage as a credit to the buyer in escrow.

Irrigation Districts

Water supplied through the facilities of an irrigation district is usually paid for semi-annually. Such water bills when due and payable usually become a lien against the property and the owner of record is held responsible for payment. In most instances, as it is with property tax bills, a portion of the water bills have accumulated for payment in usage and a portion may be in advance to a specified date.

Contact with the irrigation district office is often advisable in order to establish the status of due dates and payment made thereon. It would not be unusual to discover the water bill to be a matter of record against the property in a title search. Buyers and sellers normally pay their proportionate share of the lien through escrow when the bill is due and payable.

PRORATION OF RENTS

In the event the property being sold is partially or altogether occupied by tenants, the escrow agent should be furnished with a statement of rents in order that the proper prorations may be computed.

Such a statement would identify the rental unit with the tenant and provide information concerning the monthly rent, advance payment dates and the amount of security deposits held by the seller. It is normally a more satisfactory arrangement when rents are prorated and deposits are turned over to the purchaser through escrow.

OTHER PRORATIONS

Where there is a supply of consumable personal property such as coal, fuel oil or propane gas, payment for these items may be arranged through escrow or handled on a personal basis. The prorated costs should be based on actual date of possession in all fairness to the purchaser. A mutual understanding should be expressed in the sales agreement in connection with all personal property.

IMPOUND OR ESCROW ACCOUNT

A seller's impound account, which may be also referred to as an "escrow account," "trust account," "reserve account" or "trust fund" by different lenders in various localities, consists of monies accumulated through monthly payments in addition to principal and interest payments.

133

The account is maintained at a sufficient level and held by the lender for payment of taxes, insurances, assessments, water, etc., when such bills become due and payable.

Upon full payment of the loan, such funds, held by the lender, are refunded to the owner. Methods of refund may differ with various lenders according to their own policies pertaining to such matters.

Some lenders may credit the account balance towards the principal balance. Others may treat it as a separate refund in their escrow and demand instructions. In many instances, refund is made direct to the owner three or four weeks after close of escrow and the lender is satisfied that all obligations, including mutual mortgage insurance premiums, have been met.

Since the owner will ultimately receive refund of the account, it is not an expense under normal circumstances. Therefore, as a credit on the work sheet, it would reflect additional funds to the seller when determining his net proceeds. In instances of a serious delinquency in payments on the subject property, the account may be depleted.

Lenders normally provide an annual loan statement in January of each year, which will indicate the account balance as of the previous December 1st payment. By adding subsequent payments to that balance and deducting any tax, insurance, etc., payments that would have been paid, the current balance of the account may be closely estimated.

CANCELLATION OF HAZARD INSURANCE

In establishing a new loan when purchasing a property, the buyer will usually purchase a new fire and hazard insurance policy for one reason or another. When insurance is handled in this manner it becomes a matter of cancelling the seller's existing policy. Refund of the unused portion of the policy is normally based on a "short rate" cancellation, by the insurance company, which may mean approximately ten percent less than if the buyer assumed the policy and prorated the unused portion to the seller accordingly. Therefore, it is more economical for the seller if the buyer keeps the existing policy in force.

Since cancellation of a policy is not often effective until the date of recording the transfer of ownership, refund is made directly to the owner from the insurance company. This item may, as a result, be treated as a credit in determining the seller's net proceeds on the work sheet, although it will not appear as such on final closing statements. Insurance companies usually make cash refunds within thirty days when policies have been cancelled.

In the event the buyer assumes an existing policy, the seller would be credited in escrow on a prorated basis and such proration would appear on the final closing statement.

Exhibit 11-1 may be utilized as a checklist with which to estimate the seller's costs when a property sells on the basis of refinancing to a new loan.

CLOSING COSTS—CHECKLIST

Seller's (Estimated) Expenses—NEW LOAN

Property Address . . . . Sales Price $_____

PAY-OFF EXPENSES—EXISTING LOANS—LIENS—ENCUMBRANCES:

1st Trust Deed or Mortgage Balance	$. . . . . .
2nd " " " " "	. . . . . .
Other " " " " "	. . . . . .
Assessment & Improvement Bond Balance	. . . . . .
Bond Prepayment Penalty	. . . . . .
Bond Interest Earned	. . . . . .
Other Liens	. . . . . .
Prepayment Penalties	. . . . . .
Unearned Interest Penalty	. . . . . .
Earned Interest	. . . . . .
Forwarding Fee (Lender's Statement)	. . . . . .
Reconveyance Fee	. . . . . .
Satisfaction of Mortgage or Lien	. . . . . .
Acknowledgments	. . . . . .
Recording Fees	. . . . . .

DEDUCT—TOTAL PAY-OFF EXPENSES . . . . $. . . . .

**BALANCE—SELLER'S TRUE EQUITY (est.) $. . . . .

**Use in determining Seller's position after paying selling and escrow costs. Carry balance forward to next page.

EXHIBIT 11-1

BALANCE—SELLER'S TRUE EQUITY—BROUGHT FORWARD . . $		
Selling Costs—Escrow Expenses—Prorations	DEBIT	CREDIT
Real Estate Fee (Commission)		
New Loan Discount Points		
Abstract of Title & Examination		
Title Insurance Premium		
Escrow Fee		
Attorney Fee		
Property Survey		
Drawing Fees		
Transfer Tax		
Earned Mutual Mortgage Insurance		
Truth In Lending Fee		
Photo & Inspection Fee		
Termite Inspection Fee		
Termite & Dry Rot Repair		
Appraisal Fee		
Prorations—Taxes		
Water		
Rents		
Other		
Impound Account Credit		
Cancellation—Hazard Insurance		
TOTAL DEBITS and CREDITS		

*ADD TOTAL CREDITS TO (Estimated) TRUE EQUITY $ . . . . . .

TOTAL . . . . $ . . . . . .

**DEDUCT TOTAL DEBITS . . . . $ . . . . . .

ESTIMATED NET PROCEEDS TO SELLER . . . $ . . . . . .

*Seller receives credits
**Seller pays debits

EXHIBIT 11-1 CONT.

12

Closing Costs—
New Loans—Buyer's Costs

When property is purchased under conditions whereby the buyer is to pay all cash through his ability to obtain new financing and loan funds, certain additional expenses will be encountered, which do not occur in a loan assumption type of transaction. It is extremely important for the purchaser to acquire a knowledge and understanding of the costs to which he will be subjected, in order that he may anticipate the required amount of cash resources for completion of his purchase.

In addition to the required cash investment as a down payment in securing a new loan, the buyer's costs may generally be classified into two categories which are, nonrecurring closing costs and recurring closing costs.

Nonrecurring costs are those expenses that occur only once and are paid at the time of originating a new loan. They do not have to be paid again in connection with that loan.

Recurring costs are items of expense necessary to pay at the time of the loan origination and will normally continue until the loan is paid in full.

NONRECURRING COSTS

Loan Origination Fee

Origination fees involved with conventional types of loans may vary according to individual lending policies and current money markets. Commercial banks and insurance companies may charge the borrower a flat fee of $50 to $100 or possibly one to two percent of the loan amount. Savings and loan associations and mortgage brokers more often base the fee on a percentage of the loan only, or the entire charge may be regarded as "discount points," and withheld from the loan funds. Either the buyer or

139

seller may pay discount points on conventional loans, but buyers are restricted from paying discount points charged on government-sponsored loans such as those insured by the F.H.A. or loans guaranteed by the Veterans Administration.

In the case of new loans backed by F.H.A. or V.A., lenders may charge buyers one percent of the loan amount as a loan origination fee, but are not permitted to charge buyers any "discount points" as a media of equalizing investment yields.

The one percent loan origination fee may be imposed on the buyer by an approved lender or mortgage broker for F.H.A. and V.A. loans for processing the loan papers and packaging the loan. However, the lender, who actually provides the funds, normally will withhold discount point monies at the time of funding. A "discount point" is one percent. Five points would amount to five percent of the loan amount. Lenders have always charged the one percent loan origination fee, even at a time when loan funds are granted at par, with no discount points being withheld.

The Veterans Administration, under Public Law 91-506, effective October 23, 1970, terminated a one-half percent funding fee previously charged to post Korean conflict veterans under the Cold War veterans loan program.

American Land Title Association—Standard Policy

As a condition of granting a loan, most lenders require more security in marketable title than that offered in other forms of protective measures and devices.

A lender's extended coverage policy was designed and is issued by the American Land Title Association through title companies as protection against all but a very few title defects that do not appear in the public records. In instances where this type of coverage is required, the buyer normally provides it at his expense for the lender and the policy is in effect for the term of the loan or for as long as the loan exists, regardless of subsequent ownership of the property, after issuance of the policy. It is normally referred to as an A.L.T.A. policy of title insurance.

The coverage in an A.L.T.A. policy insures the lender of having a valid and enforceable lien, subject only to the exclusions from coverage and such defects, liens and encumbrances on the title as are shown therein. In addition, the policy expressly includes priority insurance to cover mechanics' liens and assessments for street improvements and that the land has a right of access and is not landlocked.

A physical inspection of the property, normally made by the title company, is to make certain the land is as described and that there are no encroachments connected with the property. Inspection may also be made as some degree of assurance that others do not have prior rights to the property.

If some title defect should appear during the term of the loan, the title company may either remedy, defend title or otherwise protect the lender from loss. In some instances, an inspection fee may be charged for physical inspections in addition to costs of the policy. When an official survey report is required from a licensed surveyor, direct billing is made for the service.

American Land Title Association—Owner's Policy

This extended coverage policy provides essentially the same protection for an owner, with some few possible exceptions, such as the A.L.T.A. lender's policy. It is effective as to protection for the owner of the fee or other interest in the land such as a lessee or sublessee, for the term of ownership, or lease, as the case may be.

The cost for this type of owner's insurance is frequently prohibitive to the average owner or lessee since it is normally about double the amount of the owner's standard coverage policy of title insurance. In some instances, the cost may be still higher depending on the amount of risks that may have an effect on good title.

In most instances, the borrower may still be obligated to furnish the lender an A.L.T.A. loan policy, even though the borrower may purchase an A.L.T.A. owner's policy for himself.

Standard Coverage Policy of Title Insurance

A standard coverage policy of title insurance is normally designed to insure good title according to the laws and customs of the various localities in which it is used. The cost of this type of title insurance, for a new owner, may also be paid according to custom of the area in which the property lies, or through mutual agreement between buyer and seller. It is customary, in some areas, for the seller to furnish evidence of good title and insure it. In other localities, it is a buyer's expense or the cost may be divided between buyer and seller. The charge is normally based on the land value or purchase price in the case of an owner's standard policy as opposed to the loan amount on a policy to protect the lender.

It is called an owner's policy when insurance is limited to the owner. If protection is for a lender only, it is called a loan policy. When the policy covers the owner and the lender, it is a joint protection policy. A policy of

141

standard coverage insures ownership of the estate or interest in the described land and the priority and validity of the lien upon the estate or interest of the insured mortgage.

Protection is generally considered to be as against title defects which are matters of public record. It could also be stated that protection is provided as to defective instruments recorded in the public records since an insured is protected against title defects pertaining to forged instruments in the chain of title; acts of minors and incompetents, whose incapabilities were not revealed in the public records; undisclosed rights of others; voided attorney-in-fact recorded documents and other defects in recorded instruments. This policy normally contains certain exclusions that in turn may be covered under the American Land Title Association policies.

Torrens Certificate

The Torrens system of registration whereby the Registrar of Titles issues a Certificate of Title to the property owner is in use in some states and localities, as well as throughout many parts of the world.

When property is registered and the seller possesses a Torrens Certificate, it may be advisable to continue the registration. In such cases, the cost of registration is nominal and if the new owner desires the added protection of a policy of title insurance, the cost for such policy is often less. On the other hand, if the property is not registered under the Torrens system, his costs for such registration will normally exceed those charged for a policy of title insurance.

Some lenders may require an American Land Title Association lender's policy of title insurance, even though the subject property is registered under the Torrens system, as they may feel the protection of such registration to be inadequate to their lending policies. (The Torrens system is more fully discussed in the chapter *Security in Marketable Title.*)

Property Survey

Lenders often require a survey be made of a property by a licensed or registered surveyor as a condition to granting a loan on it, particularly when the land description is of a metes and bounds nature. Where the land description may be easily identified, an American Land Title Association lender's policy of title insurance may be sufficient and an official survey report may not be requested.

The primary purpose of an official survey report is to determine or verify the correct measurements, boundaries and "setback" and lot lines of

142

the subject property. It is also to make certain there are no encroachments by or against the adjoining properties.

Escrow Fees

New loans being granted on real property normally require the services of professional escrow agents or attorneys acting in that capacity. The charge for such services, which include gathering and processing necessary documents and information, is called an escrow fee.

The charge is not always set forth as a separate item of cost in some localities—however, it is often included in with the charge for a policy of title insurance by title companies or it may be a portion of the flat fee charged by attorneys who perform escrow processing services.

Escrow fees are shown as separate items in some localities and may vary in amount according to degree of work involved in the escrow or charged according to the dollar amount of the sale. The Veterans Administration will not allow new loan applicants to pay escrow fees in some areas, although they are permitted to pay for a policy of title insurance.

Attorney Fees

The laws and customs of some localities require the services of an attorney in connection with real estate transactions. Each party to the transaction may employ his own legal counsel, or the same attorney may represent both parties on a split-fee basis. A schedule of charges may be provided by some attorneys who specialize in real estate for clients.

In many states it is not necessary to employ an attorney unless unusual legal circumstances prevail in some sort of a transaction. (A more detailed discussion will be found in the chapter *New Loans—Seller's Costs*.)

State Tax

In addition to the transfer tax normally paid by the seller, a few states impose a tax on deeds prior to the recording of them. Where the laws and customs of various localities provide that the buyer must pay some form of transfer or recording tax the expense should be considered.

Tax Service

Tax service companies perform invaluable services to lenders and borrowers in connection with property taxes, improvement bonds and other liens that may affect the status of a mortgage loan after it has been recorded against the property. These companies procure city and county tax bills and special district tax and improvement bond bills each year for the lender and verify the taxing description with the loan identification. Notices of any new liens affecting the property on which the loan exists are also provided.

In the event of some sort of a tax delinquency, the lender is notified in order that the situation may be remedied prior to a tax sale that might otherwise result. For example, it could be a case in which the lender mailed tax payments to the tax collector, who in turn applied payment to the wrong parcel of land. The tax service company would, no doubt, catch the error from published tax-delinquent properties.

Another service is in notifying the lender of any new improvement bonds not included in the tax levy. In such case, the lender may require the borrower to establish an additional reserve in his impound account to provide funds for payment when the bill becomes due and payable.

These services are available to lenders in most states and a majority of lenders subscribe to the service on a continuing annual basis. However, the initial cost of from $15 to $25 is normally required to be paid by the borrower.

Credit Report

A favorable credit rating is essential in qualifying for a new loan. At the time applications for loans are submitted, lenders normally require applicants to prepare a financial statement and a statement of credit history and references. This statement is submitted to a local credit reporting association for verification and for a written credit history as to the manner in which the applicant has paid past obligations. The report is of a confidential nature, but in the event it is unfavorable there is a possibility of error and the applicant may clear the matter up through personal contact with the reporting agency.

Applicants for F.H.A. or G.I. loans may be disqualified by a derogatory credit rating even though some lenders would be willing to go along with such a rating. On the other hand, in the case of conventional type loans, lenders may compensate the risk of an unfavorable credit history by requiring more down payment and increased interest rate. It would depend on current lending policies and on the credit rating.

Fees for credit reports may differ in all communities and there may be additional charges for out of town credit verifications. Applicants are usually required to pay the necessary costs at the time of applying for a new real estate loan.

Appraisal Fee

Another important factor considered along with the credit report by the lender is an appraisal report on the property. An evaluation of the property and loan applicant are usually reviewed by the lender's loan committee at the same time prior to granting or rejecting a loan application.

In the event there is an existing F.H.A. conditional commitment or a V.A. Certificate of Reasonable Value, the buyer frequently escapes the expense of obtaining another appraisal for an F.H.A. or G.I. loan. However, if no such commitments exist, the buyer is normally required to pay for an appropriate firm commitment at the time of loan application. Appraisal fees are collected at the time lenders submit applications for government loan commitments.

Conventional loan appraisal fees may be included in the lender's loan origination fee when a staff appraiser is employed to make appraisals of properties on which a loan is being considered. Lender's policies differ throughout the country with conventional loans. Therefore, it may be advisable to determine local customs.

Photo and Inspection Fee

In addition to an appraisal report on a property being considered for a new loan, lenders normally require photographs of the property and the immediate neighborhood. They may also request their representatives, or agents, to prepare a report as to internal and external conditions of the buildings and grounds. The photographs and report of inspection are kept with the loan files.

Photo and inspection fees are often absorbed in the loan origination fee, but it is frequently a separate charge of from $10 to $25. F.H.A. and G.I. loan applicants may be prohibited from paying this expense item.

Termite Inspection Fee

A termite and dry rot inspection and a subsequent clearance report, from a licensed pest control company, is a normal requirement of lenders prior to granting a new loan. When some sort of infestation exists upon inspection, it will be necessary for corrections to be made prior to the delivery of loan funds.

The laws and customs may differ in various sections of the country, but, as a general rule, the buyer pays for the inspection and the seller pays for the corrections outlined in an inspection report.

F.H.A. and the Veterans Administration normally condition their commitments on a termite and dry rot inspection and clearance report. In any case, it may be advisable for the buyer to provide for it in the sales agreement. It should be noted, however, that effective May 15, 1967, the Veterans Administration issued a directive that prohibits new G.I. loan applicants from paying for an inspection.

(See also *Termite Inspection* and *Termite Repairs* in the chapter *New Loans—Seller's Costs.*)

Drawing Fees

As a matter of general practice, the lender making the loan will draw the necessary notes and trust deeds or mortgages plus other instruments pertaining to loan funds. In most cases, the charge is absorbed by the lender who prepares documents on his own forms or the prescribed Federal Housing Administration and Veterans Administration forms. There may be certain circumstances in which the work is accomplished by an outside attorney or others and the buyer may have to pay the drawing fees.

Acknowledgments

In order for documents such as mortgage liens to be in a position of recording into the public records, it is necessary for them to be acknowledged before a notary public or some other designated public official according to local law.

An acknowledgment is a formal declaration made before a designated public official by the person delivering the instrument that it was his own act and deed in signing the instrument to be recorded. The official may attach his certificate to the instrument or fill in the form provided on most instruments to be recorded. This is called a Certificate of Acknowledgment and is signed by the designated official. This cost is relatively small and, in many instances, it is included in the escrow fees as a part of the service.

Recording Fees

The responsibility for payment of fees for recording instruments pertaining to ownership of real property is normally that of the buyer. This would include deeds, trust deeds, mortgages or any document that proves ownership or voluntary obligations.

RECURRING COSTS

Interest, taxes and insurance are often referred to as continuing expenses attributed to ownership rather than as being closing costs. Regardless of what these expense items may be designated as in description, the fact remains that buyers are expected to pay them in order to complete escrow. Therefore, these expenses are called recurring costs since they are continual as opposed to nonrecurring costs, which are paid only once upon loan origination, but not again in connection with that particular loan.

Recurring costs may be placed into two classifications. Those items that are to establish an impound account and are subsequently collected each month to maintain the necessary balances for payment of taxes and insurance, are called "prepaids." Prorated taxes paid to the seller and prepaid interest paid to the lender for a portion of the month in which the mortgage instrument is recorded, do not go into the impound account; therefore, are not considered as "prepaids" in the context of usage in some of the F.H.A. programs.

"Prepaids"—Impound Account

Impound accounts are variously called "trust account," "trust fund," "escrow account," or "reserve account." The account consists of a tax and insurance reserve deposited with the lender. It is maintained at a sufficient level of funds, collected in monthly payments, for the lender to pay property taxes and insurance premiums when the bills for those items become due and payable. The funds are collected along with monthly principal and interest payments.

The impound account system was initiated by F.H.A. as a requirement for lenders to follow as insurance that borrowers would not be faced with large tax and insurance payments with no funds to pay them when due. The system was adopted by the Veterans Administration for G.I. loans and through the years has become a policy for most lenders on conventional type loans.

"Prepaids," as they apply to the establishment of an impound account, must be paid only by the purchaser on new F.H.A. loans. However, in some of the F.H.A. loan programs, a limited amount of "prepaids" may be included into the computations of maximum loans to help reduce the buyer's required total cash outlay in escrow.

Tax Reserve

The amount of tax reserve to be established in the impound account will depend mainly on the time of year in which the loan is to originate and, to a large degree, on the lender's policy as to the method of paying tax bills.

Property taxes may be paid on a quarterly basis in some states or on a

Month Recorded	1st Payment Due		Est. Tax Reserve	Status of Taxes
January	March	1	5 Months	1st Installment Paid
February	April	1	1 Month	Both Installments Paid
March	May	1	1 Month	Both Installments Paid
April	June	1	2 Months	Both Installments Paid
May	July	1	3 Months	Both Installments Paid
June	August	1	4 Months	Both Installments Paid
July	September	1	5 Months	Paid thru June 30th
August	October	1	6 Months	Paid thru June 30th
September	November	1	7 Months	Paid thru June 30th
October	December	1	8 Months	— or 2 Months if 1st Inst. Paid
November	January	1	3 Months	1st Installment Paid
December	February	1	4 Months	1st Installment Paid

EXHIBIT 12-1 SCHEDULE OF TAX RESERVES ESTIMATED TO BE REQUIRED BY LENDERS*

*NOTE: The above schedule is based on semi-annual payment of taxes by lenders. For lenders who pay tax bills only on a full annual basis once each year, add approximately five additional months to the estimated tax reserve, which is indicated above.

semi-annual or annual basis in other states. Since there is a certain amount of expense involved each time tax payments are made, the lender may choose to pay taxes only once each year. Accordingly, the tax reserve account must be sufficient from the beginning so that subsequent monthly payments, equivalent to one-twelfth of annual taxes, added to the reserve, will provide sufficient funds to pay property taxes when due and payable.

Exhibit 12-1 will reflect the approximate tax reserve required by lenders who pay tax bills semi-annually out of the mortgagor's tax reserve portion of the impound account. The information will be based on a fiscal tax year beginning July 1st and ending June 30th of the following year. Other fiscal tax years may be interpolated in the chart.

An example of how the schedule may be used is, if a transaction should record on July 1st, the amount of tax reserve required would be an amount equal to five months taxes when paid on a semi-annual basis.

When a transaction closes on July 1st, the borrower will pay prepaid

*Illustrated form courtesy of Wolcotts, 214 So. Spring St., Los Angeles

interest for the month of July and his regular monthly payment will not become due until September 1st, which will pay interest earned during the month of August. (A more detailed explanation of this will be found in this chapter under *Prepaid Interest.*)

Since the first regular monthly payment, which includes a tax-reserve payment, is not made until September 1st, the lender will have received September 1st, October 1st and November 1st tax-reserve payments by the time the first installment of taxes becomes due and payable in November.

The three monthly tax-reserve payments received, plus the five months prepaid to establish the tax-reserve account, equals eight months reserve balance. Sometime in November, the lender will pay the first installment of taxes from the impound account which will leave only two months in the tax reserve. The first installment is to pay taxes from July 1st through December 31st.

After the December 1st, January 1st, February 1st and March 1st tax-reserve payments have been received, and added to the two months left after payment of the first installment, the lender will have six months' taxes in reserve. The second installment is due and payable on or before February 1st and delinquent after April 10th, but by receiving monthly payments through March 1st, the lender is in position to pay the second installment of six months' taxes for the period of January 1st through June 30th, which ends the tax year.

The process will start over again with the April 1st payment and by the time the first installment is due again in November, the lender will have eight months tax reserve with which to pay six months' taxes.

Under the same set of circumstances, if the lender's policy is to pay the tax bill only once each year, the borrower may be required to establish a tax-reserve account equal to ten months' taxes. This reserve plus the addition of the September and October payments would provide a reserve sufficient to pay the full tax bill in November for both installments.

Since real estate transactions may record at any time during the year, tax-reserve requirements at a new loan origination will vary. However, the purchaser may have to pay tax prorations to the seller or he may receive payment of tax prorations from the seller. Therefore, the overall situation must be considered as to the month of recording documents. (Tax prorations are more fully discussed later in this chapter.)

Fire and Hazard Insurance

All lenders require fire and hazard insurance to be purchased by the borrower prior to funding a loan. The minimum coverage is for the full amount of the loan and the policy must be of a broad form or extended coverage type. The lender is to be named as the recipient of "loss payable" in the event of partial or total destruction of the property on which the mortgage exists unless the insurance company restores the property to its original condition prior to the loss sustained.

Most insurance companies write hazard insurance policies for a period of three years and provide for deferred annual payments, whereby the insured is to pay premiums only one year in advance. The amount of the premium may vary according to additional coverage such as a homeowner's policy and the district in which the property is located.

Although some lenders may allow "binders" for insurance coverage at the time of funding a loan, the greater majority will require the original and one or two copies of a policy along with a one-year "paid receipt," to be deposited in escrow prior to forwarding loan funds.

Payment may be made directly to the insurance agent, for which a "paid receipt" should be attached or the required premium amount may be deposited in escrow for payment of the policy upon recording documents of ownership. It is important for the borrower to arrange for insurance far in advance of the date escrow is anticipated to close.

Fire and Hazard Insurance Reserve

The normal requirement for an insurance reserve account to be established by the borrower of a new loan is an amount equal to two months of the policy premium. Although the buyer is required to pay at least one year's premium in advance, the lender must have sufficient funds in the insurance reserve account to pay the premium when it becomes due one year later.

One of the two months reserve is to provide for the time lapse between the effective date of the policy, which is usually date of recording, and date of the first payment into the reserve account, which is included in the regular monthly loan payment. (See *Prepaid Interest* in this chapter.)

The other month of the initial insurance reserve is to provide for at least thirty days time in which the lender may receive billing from the insurance company and make payment thereof, prior to the expiration date.

Mutual Mortgage Insurance Reserve—F.H.A.

Mutual mortgage insurance premiums are paid to the Federal Housing Administration on each anniversary date of the loan origination. Such payments are made in arrears rather than in advance, as in the case of hazard insurance. Therefore the premium obligation is on an accrual basis. M.M.I.

premiums reduce to a lower amount each year, as they are computed by taking one-half percent of the loan balance and divided into twelve equal payments collected monthly, with the loan principal and interest payments to be placed in reserve in the impound account held by the lender. The premium funds are used by F.H.A. to insure lenders against losses on loans in the event of default and foreclosure. There is no benefit to the borrower other than the fact that if lenders were not insured against loss, loan interest rates may be considerably higher than those available on F.H.A. loan programs.

At the time an F.H.A. loan is originated, the borrower is required to establish a mutual mortgage insurance reserve account, along with tax and hazard insurance accounts, in an amount equal to one months' premium based on one-half percent of the loan amount being granted. Upon the accumulation of twelve M.M.I. premium payments, the lender will forward the reserve funds to F.H.A. for the accrued obligation.

In the event of default on a loan, the lender must follow the necessary reporting procedures, in that connection, to F.H.A. The lender may have the option of retaining title to the property and foregoing mutual mortgage insurance benefits. However, if the lender is to receive M.M.I. benefits, he must convey title of ownership to F.H.A. within thirty days of foreclosure and apply for debentures of the mutual mortgage insurance fund.

In effect, these debentures are government bonds, which may carry varied interest rates and maturity dates, established in the policy of insurance, and are normally in an amount to cover loan balances, earned interest and advancements of funds involved in foreclosure proceedings. The debentures are negotiable and may be sold on the market or used at face value to offset any obligations to F.H.A. incurred by the lender.

Tax Prorations

Under normal circumstances, a purchaser should be prepared to pay five or six months' taxes when applying for a new loan, either in establishing a tax reserve in an impound account, in prorations of prepaid taxes or in a portion of each.

Property tax prorations are usually computed as of recording date and if the seller retains possession past that date, he will pay rent to the buyer for the period between recording date and actual possession date or time of vacating the property. However, tax prorations are sometimes based on the date of vacating the property, but it is not an equitable arrangement, since the buyer's expenses on the property involve much more than taxes, and thus he should be compensated accordingly.

151

If the seller has paid taxes in advance of recording date, he should be reimbursed for the portion that he will not have use of the property. If the property tax obligation is in a period of accumulation, but has not yet become due and payable, the seller should pay the buyer for the time the seller had possession of the property during the accumulative period.

Prorations are normally processed through debits and credits to each party in escrow settlement papers. Prorated taxes, paid to the seller, are not considered as "prepaids" in the context of F.H.A. terms for some of the loan programs, since they are not paid into the impound account. They are, however, considered as recurring costs, since they are in the category of continuing expenses.

Prepaid Interest

Upon the origination of a new real estate loan, lenders will frequently instruct escrow agents to collect prepaid interest from the date of recording to the end of the month in which escrow is closed. In some instances when the recording date is near the end of a month, the lender may collect prepaid interest for the few remaining days of that month plus prepaid interest for the following month. This is normally the only time interest is paid in advance on a real estate loan. In this situation, however, interest is not collected again on the loan until after it has been earned and paid with the regular monthly payment sixty days later.

Interest payment, at the inception of a new loan, is required to be prepaid in order to provide sufficient time after recording for the lender to process loan documents, prepare loan payment devices and mail the necessary material to the borrower before the first regular monthly payment becomes due. Otherwise the first payment may become delinquent before the borrower knows where to pay it and the exact amount to pay.

As an example in this connection: If a transaction recorded on April 28th, the lender may request prepaid interest for the two remaining days of April plus prepaid interest through May 31st. Earned interest would commence on June 1st and accumulate through June 30th. The regular monthly payment would be due on July 1st, which would pay interest earned in June plus a principal payment and impound account payments. Subsequent payments pay interest earned the previous month until the loan is fully paid.

When the recording of a transaction occurs on the first of a month to about the twenty first day, the lender may require less prepaid interest. For example, if recording should be on the 15th of April, the lender would require prepaid interest from the 15th through the 30th of April. Earned interest would begin on May 1st and accumulate through the 31st. The first regular monthly payment would be due on June 1st, which would pay the interest earned in May plus payment on the principal loan balance and payments into the impound account. The lender would have ample time to notify the borrower concerning the amount of monthly payments and where to pay them.

Payments on government-sponsored loans such as F.H.A. and G.I. are always due on the first day of each month and are delinquent after the fifteenth of the month. Most conventional lenders follow the same pattern of payments becoming due on the first day of each month, but the delinquency date may be sooner than that of government sponsored loans.

Private Mortgage Insurance

Private mortgage insurance, similar to the F.H.A. mutual mortgage insurance, is frequently used by lenders in most states when granting conventional loans. This insurance is often required by such lenders as protection against foreclosure losses in case of default in payment of the loan. With such insurance, the lender may provide better interest rates, lower down payment requirements and other relaxed terms and conditions normally imposed in the conventional type loans.

The cost of private mortgage insurance is similar to that of F.H.A. mutual mortgage insurance, but the borrower may be required to prepay the first years' premium and establish a reserve account with monthly payments for the payment of future premiums when they become due.

This type of insurance is available to approved lenders by the insurance companies issuing such coverage, such as savings and loan associations, banks, mortgage bankers and life insurance companies.

Life Insurance

Low-cost term insurance is usually available to purchasers who have a mortgage on their homes. Most life insurance companies offer policies to provide protection on declining mortgage balances and, in case of the mortgagor's death, will pay off the loan balance existing at that time.

There are also disability policies available whereby the mortgagor's mortgage payments are paid by the insurance company in the event of physical disability due to illness or accident. In some instances, such insurance may be arranged through lenders with a possible benefit of lower "group rates" on premiums.

Lenders do not ordinarily require life and disability insurance coverage, but the purchaser may want to consider such insurance for personal protection.

Other Expenses

There may be other items of costs and expenses charged to the buyer, not discussed in this chapter, but which do exist in different sectors of the country. In such instances, it would be advisable to anticipate them along with those mentioned herein where they apply. The purchaser should be prepared to meet his total obligations necessary to complete escrow.

Exhibit 12-2 may be utilized for the purpose of estimating the buyer's costs when the transaction is conditioned upon the buyer obtaining a new loan.

CLOSING COSTS—CHECKLIST

Buyer's (Estimated) Expenses—NEW LOAN

Property Address .... Purchase Price $_____

NONRECURRING CLOSING COSTS:

Loan Origination Fee (1%—loan amount F.H.A. & G.I.) $ ....

A.L.T.A. Loan Policy of Title Insurance ....

A.L.T.A. Owner's Policy of Title Insurance ....

Standard Coverage Policy of Title Insurance ....

Torrens Certificate ....

Property Survey ....

Escrow Fee ....

Attorney's Fee ....

State Tax ....

Tax Service ....

Credit Report ....

Appraisal Fee ....

Photo and Inspection Fee ....

Termite Inspection Fee ....

Drawing Fees ....

Acknowledgments ....

Recording Fees ....

TOTAL NONRECURRING COSTS $_____

Note: These costs are paid at time of originating a new loan. Buyer normally does
not have to pay them again in connection with loan after origination. Laws
and customs prevailing in various areas are determining factors as to which
items of costs are paid by buyers and sellers.

EXHIBIT 12-2

CLOSING COSTS—CHECKLIST

Buyer's (Estimated) Expenses—NEW LOAN (cont'd.)

Property Address . . . . Purchase Price $_____

RECURRING CLOSING COSTS:	DEBITS	CREDITS
*Tax Reserve (see chart)	$.	$. . . . .
*Fire and Hazard Insurance (1 Yr. Minimum)		
*Fire and Hazard Insurance Reserve (2 Mo.)		
*Mutual Mortgage Insurance—F.H.A. (1 Mo.)		
Tax Prorations		
Prepaid Interest (est. 1 Mo.)		
Private Mortgage Insurance		
Life Insurance Premium		
Other Expenses		

TOTAL DEBITS & CREDITS . . . . $ $

DEDUCT CREDITS . . . . $_____

BALANCE TOTAL RECURRING COSTS . $_____

BUYER'S (Estimated) TOTAL CASH OUTLAY:

ADD:

Purchase Price . . . . $

Nonrecurring Costs . . . . $

Recurring Costs . . . . $_____

TOTAL COSTS $

DEDUCT:

MAXIMUM LOAN AMOUNT . . . . $_____

ESTIMATED TOTAL CASH OUTLAY . . $

*These items establish Buyer's Impound Account and are referred as "prepaids" in the computations of maximum loans in some F.H.A. programs. Only the buyer is allowed to pay these items in F.H.A. loan programs.

EXHIBIT 12-2 CONT.

13

Closing Costs–
Loan Assumption–Seller's Costs

When a real estate transaction is conditioned upon the buyer's assuming existing financing and paying the seller for his equity difference between purchase price and existing loans, it is a loan assumption type of transaction.

The purchaser is taking full responsibility of existing obligations when it is specified in the sales agreement that he is assuming the loan. If he is not to be responsible for payment of any deficiencies, which may arise through foreclosure, it must be written into the sales agreement that he is purchasing "subject to the loan." In either case, the processing of this type of transaction is the same.

The seller's costs and expenses in this kind of sale are considerably less than when a new purchase money trust deed or mortgage is originated and existing financing is eliminated. However, when existing financing is of a conventional nature rather than under a government-sponsored program, it may be advisable to make certain that a loan assumption is possible as there may be some restrictive conditions for assumption contained in the mortgage instruments.

F.H.A. and G.I. loans are normally assumable under the regulations and provisions of these two government agencies but in some instances, the seller may be justified in insisting on certain conditions of his own. (See *F.H.A. and V.A. Loans* in chapters on financing.)

COMMISSION

A real estate fee or commission is normally earned by virtue of bringing a buyer and seller together, resulting in a meeting of the minds, which is reduced to writing in a signed contract. The same rate of commission normally applies regardless of the financial arrangements.

Loan assumptions often require as much and often more work than a new loan transaction. Agent's commissions are normally received from the seller's proceeds, after recording of the documents, when disbursements are distributed by the escrow agent.

ABSTRACT OF TITLE AND EXAMINATION

An abstract of title is a complete history of ownership, liens, encumbrances, judgments and releases dating back from the original owner to current ownership.

The laws and customs in the various states and localities differ in the provision of an abstract of title and the examination of it by attorneys or other specialists in the field. In some areas, the buyer may customarily pay the cost for this service while in other sectors, the seller may pay for it or the expense may be divided between the two parties. It may also be dependent on negotiations at the time of signing the sales agreement.

TITLE INSURANCE PREMIUM

In certain sections of the country, a standard policy of title insurance is customarily provided to the buyer for insurance of good title as to items of public record. The policy may contain some exceptions.

Although the seller may have such protection, the policy and coverage is no longer effective upon transfer of ownership. The exception to this is that, when an owner dies, the coverage carries over to his heirs. If a buyer is to be provided the same protection a former owner had, it is necessary to purchase a new policy of title insurance.

There is ordinarily no law regarding which party to the transaction is to pay the expense of a standard policy of title insurance, but the customs prevailing in different localities will normally dictate whether it is a buyer's or seller's expense or if the cost is divided between them. In many instances, it may be a matter of negotiation as to which party is to pay.

Title insurance companies do not ordinarily insure good title when a search of the public records reveals title defects as against the property or owner of the property. A policy may not be issued to a new owner when a potential title defect would attach to the property at the minute of recording ownership in his name. In some instances, an exception to coverage may be noted as a condition of the policy.

Prior to the issuance of a title policy, it may be necessary to examine title and run an abstract of the property. Property records and files are normally maintained on a current basis in "title plants" owned by the title company, or by an abstract company specializing in this type of work.

In addition to a title search in connection with the property, an examination of the "general index" is conducted for recordings made in the public records pertaining to the individual seller and buyer. The public records are also searched in this connection. This work may be performed by title company employees, an attorney, a professional abstracter, or by private companies that specialize in title examination and maintain records and files.

When all pertinent information has been assembled, it is usually submitted to an attorney for examination and an "opinion of title." Although the attorney's opinion of title is not necessarily a guarantee of good title, it may be the foundation of reliance on which a title company will issue the standard policy of title insurance to the new owner. From that time forward, it is incumbent upon the title company to remedy or defend good title as against any claims arising from title defects of recorded instruments appearing in the public records at the time new ownership is recorded.

In some states and localities, title insurance costs may include escrow fees and, in some instances, recording fees. It may be customary in other areas to charge separately for the cost of title insurance, attorney fees, escrow fees, recordings and other services connected with insuring good title.

When existing financing is assumed on real property, the original American Land Title Association loan policy, which protects lenders against title defects, remains in force even though property ownership is transferred from one party to another. It is not necessary to purchase a new A.L.T.A. policy unless a new loan is being originated.

ESCROW FEES

Escrow fees are charged for services performed by an attorney or an escrow agent qualified to process escrow functions. The amount of the charges may vary according to the services required and the complexities involved in the transactions.

In some areas, according to the laws and customs therein, most real estate transactions may be handled by attorneys from the beginning through close of escrow. They may represent either the buyer or seller or both parties and charge a flat fee to include escrow services along with the other work.

The laws and customs in other sectors of the country may not ordinarily require the services of an attorney in any way with the possible exception of the examination of title prior to the issuance of a policy of title insurance. In such localities, escrows are normally processed by the insuring title company's escrow department or by independent escrow companies

159

which specialize in this type of work. The printed legal forms, required in real estate transactions, may be filled in by anyone and this is usually done by the escrow agent.

It is customary for the seller to pay for a new policy of title insurance for the buyer in some areas and the escrow fees may be included in the title insurance cost. In other sections, the entire cost may customarily be paid by the buyer for a policy of title insurance, which would include escrow fees. The expense of title insurance and escrow fees may be divided equally between buyer and seller in some parts of the country, or the expense may be a matter of negotiation in the purchase and sale. As a general rule, the escrow agent will fix the charge according to practices in local custom unless notified and otherwise instructed.

DRAWING FEES

Ordinarily, there will be very few legal instruments to be drawn in the case of a loan assumption. Necessary documents normally consist of a deed and possibly a bill of sale for personal property in some instances. Since the seller is the delivering party, he usually is charged for the drawing of these papers, unless the purchaser agrees to do so in the sales agreement and escrow instructions. When secondary financing is involved such as a note and second trust deed or mortgage, the buyer is the delivering party and normally is charged for the drawing of these instruments.

In all instances, an attorney should be employed to draw up any complex agreements such as an installment contract of sale. It is advisable for the buyer and seller to reach an understanding as to which party is to pay for the preparation of complex documents, since the cost may be relatively higher.

ATTORNEY FEES

In some states, the services of an attorney are not necessary when the real estate transaction involves a simple loan assumption. However, the laws and customs of many states and localities necessitate the employment of an attorney regardless of the type of transaction involved. It is customary, in some areas, for an attorney to handle the entire transaction, after the real estate agent brings a buyer and seller together, while in other localities the attorney may only prepare documents and more or less act in an advisory capacity.

It is an accepted practice, in some states, whereby the layman, or escrow agent may fill in the blank spaces of most printed legal forms such as

160

deeds, notes and trust deeds or mortgages, etc., but even so, this should be performed by experts in this type of work. Under all circumstances, complex transactions and installment contracts should be examined and prepared by a competent attorney who specializes in real estate procedures.

TERMITE INSPECTION FEE

It is often advisable for a property owner to obtain an official pest control inspection report at the time of placing his property for sale on the market. By doing so, the owner may be aware of existing conditions on or about the structures on the land, which may need corrective or preventive repair work. Consideration may then be given to the costs for such work in the event an offer lower than listed price is received from a buyer who conditions his offer on the basis of a clear pest control report.

Infestations of pests such as, termites, beetles, roaches, etc., may prevail in different sectors of the country, or a leaking water pipe connection or shower pan may cause extensive "dry rot," or fungus damage. Continual dampness will eventually destroy wood in walls and subflooring in virtually all parts of the country.

The laws and customs of various states and localities may differ on the point of responsibility as to corrective and preventive pest control inspections and repairs, but such an inspection is often excellent insurance for all parties concerned.

TERMITE REPAIRS

When an inspection of the property by a professional pest control operator reveals the existence of some insects, or other wood-destroying organisms around the structures, corrective work should be performed immediately. Additionally, when a situation exists where there is a good chance for development of a serious condition of pests or dry rot, it should be corrected without delay.

In a majority of the states and localities, it is common practice for the buyer to condition his offer to purchase on the basis of a clearance report to be issued by a licensed pest control company. The laws and customs may differ in various parts of the country in this connection, but as a general rule the buyer will pay for the inspection cost and the seller will pay for repairs. It may also be a matter of negotiation between buyer and seller as to which party is to pay. (See *New Loan* chapters for buyer and seller costs.)

TRANSFER TAX

Prior to January 1, 1968, a transfer tax known as documentary stamps, which were affixed to deeds pertaining to real property sales, was a form of federal taxation. The federal government discontinued the tax on that date, but most states and counties continued it as a form of local tax revenue.

In a loan assumption type of transaction, the transfer tax is based only on the amount of equity between sales price and existing loan balances. The rate is $1.10 per thousand dollars of equity or 55 cents for each $500 or fraction thereof. For example, if a property should sell for $20,000 cash to an existing loan of $15,000, the tax would be $1.10 for each thousand of the $5,000 equity to equal a total transfer tax of $5.50. A documentary stamp is imprinted on the deed and the appropriate amount of tax is filled in. If the same property should sell for $20,000 cash or new financing replaced the existing $15,000 loan, the tax would be 20 x $1.10 or $22.00.

Several states use other methods of taxation on real estate transactions in addition to this form of revenue. A determination with respect to tax on real estate involving change of ownership should be based and anticipated according to laws and customs applied in the area in which the property lies.

ASSESSMENT AND IMPROVEMENT BONDS

When there is an existing assessment or improvement bond lien against a property for sale, buyers frequently condition their offers on the basis of the bonds being paid off and eliminated. In effect, the buyer's actual cost of the property is increased by the amount of existing bonds if he assumes liability for payment of the obligation.

Disposition of existing bond balances may be a matter of negotiation between buyer and seller. Therefore, it is advisable to consider such liens within the framework of establishing a market value and listing price.

Bond payments are normally amortized to pay out over a predetermined period of fifteen years with interest payments to be paid semi-annually.

Bond Prepayment Penalty

When assessment and improvement bonds are paid in full, prior to maturity, there is usually some sort of penalty involved. It may be based on a percentage of the balance or on the basis of a certain amount of unearned interest.

Bond Interest

Under normal circumstances, assessment and improvement bonds

162

require two annual payments. One payment is of interest only and another payment, approximately six months later, will include principal plus interest earned since last paid. Regardless of whether the bond balance is to be paid off or assumed by the purchaser the earned interest should be considered in the seller's costs and paid by him. This is normally accomplished through debits and credits contained in escrow instructions and final settlement papers.

Verification of Information

Immediately upon placing a property on the market for sale, it may be advisable for the real estate agent to verify all information concerning existing bonds, supplied by the seller. This may be accomplished through contacting the appropriate public agency where bond principal and interest payments are collected.

The exact bond balance, interest earned, rate of interest and prepayment penalty should be examined in order to pass the correct information on to prospective purchasers. Details of what the bond was assessed for should be determined and, in the event it was for a sewer line, it should also be determined whether or not the property is connected to the sewer line. The owner may not be aware of pre-existing conditions prior to purchasing the property and may have the wrong information to pass on to a new owner.

OTHER LIENS

In order to deliver marketable title to the purchaser, it may become necessary to clear up any other matters such as judgment liens, secondary financing or some other obligation which the buyer has not agreed to assume. Consideration should be given for the payment of any such obligations or debts that may deter transfer of good title.

MONTHLY PAYMENT—NEXT DUE

Lenders frequently instruct escrow holders to collect the next monthly payment due on an existing loan being assumed by a new purchaser. These instructions normally accompany the lender's off-set statements and are effective in the event escrow is to close after a specified date in the month of anticipated recording. The date specified is usually any time after the twentieth day of the month.

It does not ordinarily matter to the lender whether the next payment

163

coming due is collected from the seller or buyer, but it must be done. The request is made in order that lenders may have sufficient time, after transfer of ownership, to change their records and mail the necessary payment cards or other information to the new owner prior to the payment's becoming delinquent.

In some instances, sellers may not understand and will object to making a loan payment in escrow ten days before it is due and particularly when they may not own the property by that time. In the last analysis, the seller would be paying only his prorated share of expenses during his possession of the property. In making such payment, the seller would be decreasing his principal loan balance, increasing his impound account balance and would receive credit from the buyer in escrow for the buyer's prorated share of interest from closing date to the end of the month.

Exhibit 13-1 is an example of this type of situation and the mechanics of how it works out.

EARNED MUTUAL MORTGAGE INSURANCE

Mutual mortgage insurance is earned at the end of each month and is collected along with other reserve monies included into the regular monthly loan payment. The premium is paid from the mutual mortgage insurance reserve account held by the lender upon the anniversary date of the loan origination on F.H.A. insured loans. The premium is based on one-half percent of the loan balance on the anniversary date and divided into twelve equal payments.

Since the M.M.I. reserve is included in the impound balance, which the buyer will replace, consideration should be given to the fact that earned premiums, which have accumulated but not paid, are the seller's obligation.

For example, the seller's impound account may reflect ten months' M.M.I. premiums in reserve, which the buyer will replace, but since the seller had possession of the property for that ten months, he should credit the buyer for that amount. The buyer, in turn, will have a full twelve months' premium paid out of the reserve account two months later. On the basis of the monthly M.M.I. premium being $10, if ten months have been collected, it would amount to $100 to be credited to the purchaser.

PRORATION OF TAXES

If the seller has paid property taxes ahead to the end of an installment period, but possession of the property is given to the purchaser before the end of that period, the seller should receive credit from the buyer, in escrow, for the unused portion of such prepaid taxes.

Monthly Payment Next Due On Loan

When Seller Pays

Assumption — Cash to Loan:

When Lender's Instructions Call For Loan Payment Next Due

Example

Sales Price $25,000	Trust Fund ....$ 450	
Loan Balance 20,000		
$ 5,000	Normal amount of cash to loan if lender did not ask for Loan Payment Next Due.	

Escrow to close (recording date) 10-25-7_.

Lender requests escrow officer to collect payment due 11-1-7_ in amount of $165.

Amount Applied to Interest................$100

Amount Applied to Principal................ 25

Amount Applied to Trust Fund................ 40

$165

Effect If Seller Pays:

Interest for 31 Days $100

Earned Interest — 25 Days .... 80.65   (Seller would have to pay in any event.)

$ 19.35   (Buyer credits back to Seller for 6 days.)

Loan Balance $20,000

Applied to Principal 25

$19,975   (Reduced loan balance.)

Trust Fund Balance $450

Amount of Increase by Payment................ 40

$490   (Buyer now pays $490 instead of $450.)

Seller Receives ....$ 25   More equity.

Seller Receives 40   More Trust Fund

Seller Receives .... 19.35   Credit from Buyer for 6 days interest.

$ 84.35   Seller receives back from $165 monthly payment if made by him.

80.65   Earned Interest Seller would have to pay in any event.

$165

EXHIBIT 13-1 LOAN PAYMENT NEXT DUE—SELLER PAYS

On the other hand, if escrow should close during a period when property tax bills are in an accumulative stage, but not yet due and payable, the seller should credit the buyer in escrow for the time of possession between the beginning of the period and close of escrow.

Personal property included into the real property tax bill should also be credited to the buyer unless such personal property is to be transferred to the buyer as a part of the transaction. (See the chapter, *New Loans—Seller's Costs.*)

PRORATION OF INTEREST

Interest on real estate loans is not collected until after it has been earned, under ordinary circumstances. For example, a loan payment due on the first day of a month is to pay for interest earned on the loan the preceding month.

When escrow closes during any given month, interest is being earned from the first day. In prorating interest, the seller will be charged from the first day to the day transfer of ownership is recorded to the purchaser's name.

Since it is not always possible, at the time of signing a sales agreement, to be certain of the exact date of recording, it may be advisable to anticipate a full month earned interest for the month of closing when estimating the seller's costs.

(See the chapter *New Loans—Seller's Costs.*)

PRORATION OF INSURANCE

Since fire and hazard insurance is normally paid in advance, this item will not be a seller's expense, but rather will appear as a credit from the buyer for the unused portion of prepaid premiums if the buyer assumes the existing insurance coverage on a prorated basis.

In many instances, the buyer may prefer not to assume the present coverage and will purchase a policy better suited to his needs. In that case, the seller's insurance may be transferred to his next residence or it may be cancelled out on a short-rate basis upon request. Short rate cancellation of a policy usually involves an approximate ten percent loss of returned premium on prepaid hazard insurance and the refund will be made directly from the insuring company to the seller.

PRORATION OF WATER BILL

When water is on a meter, it is a simple matter for the water company to "read out" the buyer. Billing for the amount used by the seller is mailed directly to him.

Water sources are often municipally owned and billing is frequently made on a quarterly or semi-annual basis. The bill may be only for water used in the past specified period or it may be a partially advance payment.

Water districts owned by stockholder may require all or a portion of their water bills to be paid in advance.

Irrigation districts may be county owned and billing for water becomes a lien against the property much the same as property tax bills when they become due and payable. Billing is often on a semi-annual basis.

When the seller has paid in advance for water, he should receive credit from the buyer, in escrow, for the prepaid but unused portion of the bill. Conversely, if he has not received billing, but the water bill is on an accumulative basis, the seller should credit the buyer, in escrow, for that portion of the bill in which he was in possession of the property.

PRORATION OF RENTS

In the event all or a portion of the property is occupied by tenants on a monthly rental or lease basis, the rents are normally collected in advance by the owner. With a lease, the tenant may have paid the first and last month, or first and last two months rent in advance. Most tenants are also required to deposit a certain sum of money with the owner for cleanup or damages which may be incurred as a result of the tenancy.

Any rents, paid in advance of recording date, and security deposits held by the seller should be credited to the buyer's account in escrow or paid to him through escrow by separate funds.

A statement of rents should also be submitted to the escrow agent and a copy of it submitted to the purchaser, in order that there is a complete understanding in connection with prorations, deposits and tenant status.

OTHER PRORATIONS

Other prorations may consist of consumable personal property such as a supply of coal, fuel oil or propane gas. The seller should be compensated on the basis of cost and the supply on hand at the time of giving possession to the buyer.

Payment for personal items that are consumed daily is frequently made directly from buyer to seller as of the date of possession, although, it may be possible to provide for payment through escrow on an estimated basis of prorations.

167

There may also be certain taxes or other expenses to be paid on a prorated basis, in some localities, that are not mentioned here. All items of expense in a real estate transaction as they apply in the various sectors of the country should be considered and appropriately prorated to buyer and seller.

IMPOUND OR ESCROW ACCOUNT

The impound account consists of monies accumulated by the seller on a monthly basis and paid as a portion of regular monthly loan payments. The funds are held by the lender for the payment of taxes, insurance, assessment bonds and other liens as they become due and payable. In effect, the impound account is a noninterest bearing savings account.

When property is purchased on the basis of a loan assumption, the buyer normally replaces it by paying the seller an amount equal to the impound account balance. Replacement of such funds is accomplished through escrow and will appear as a credit to the seller on the final closing statement and not as an expense. Lenders do not refund impound accounts unless the loan is paid in full. On a loan assumption, lenders transfer ownership of the funds by having an authorization signed by seller, and in some instances, the buyer must also sign for receipt of it. Exhibit 13-2 is a checklist for sellers' costs in a loan assumption type of transaction.

168

CLOSING COSTS—CHECKLIST

Seller's (Estimated) Expenses—LOAN ASSUMPTION

Property Address . . . . Sales Price $		
Selling Costs—Escrow Expenses—Prorations:	DEBITS	CREDITS
Real Estate Fee (Commission)	$_____	$_____
Abstract of Title and Examination	_____	_____
Title Insurance Premium	_____	_____
Escrow Fee	_____	_____
Drawing Fee	_____	_____
Attorney's Fee	_____	_____
Termite Inspection Fee	_____	_____
Termite Repairs	_____	_____
Transfer Tax	_____	_____
Assessment and Improvement Bonds . . .	_____	_____
Bond Prepayment Penalty	_____	_____
Bond Interest	_____	_____
Other Liens	_____	_____
Monthly Payment—Next Due	_____	_____
Earned Mutual Mortgage Insurance	_____	_____
Prorations: Taxes	_____	_____
Interest	_____	_____
Insurance	_____	_____
Water Bill	_____	_____
Rents	_____	_____
Other	_____	_____
Impound Account (credit if buyer replaces)	_____	_____
TOTAL DEBITS & CREDITS	$_____	$_____
TO DETERMINE SELLER'S NET PROCEEDS:		
Sales Price	$.	
Deduct Existing Loan Balance	$.	
Seller's Net Equity	$.	
Deduct Total Debits	$_____	
Seller's Gross Proceeds	$.	
Add Total Credits.	$_____	
Seller's Net Proceeds	$.	

EXHIBIT 13-2

14

Closing Costs–
Loan Assumption–Buyer's Costs

When a buyer pays the difference between sales price and existing loan or loans and assumes payment thereof, it is a loan assumption purchase.

If the sales agreement and subsequent documents provide for the purchaser to assume and pay the existing loan, he is assuming responsibility of the obligation and may be held liable for any deficiency judgments arising as a result of foreclosure losses. However, when the sales agreement and subsequent documents specify that the purchase is "subject to" existing financing, the buyer agrees to make loan payments, but assumes no liability for any deficiencies resulting from foreclosure losses. The purchaser's losses are, therefore, confined to his original investment and subsequent monthly payments paid to the lender. In such case, the seller remains liable to the mortgagee for any such deficiencies.

The mortgagee may look first to the owner of record and then to the prior owner for liability and may go back to the original mortgagor for a deficiency judgment, if it should become necessary. Some states have abolished deficiency judgments on purchase money trust deeds or mortgages under ordinary circumstances, but the laws of many states continue to provide such protection to the mortgagee.

In the event of conventional and private loans, it may be advisable to establish whether or not assumption of existing financing is possible. Most conventional and private loan trust deeds and mortgages contain special clauses that provide that the entire loan balance is to become due and payable if the mortgagor should transfer any of his interests in the property to another party. In most instances, the lender will allow the loan to be assumed upon written request, but may negotiate an increased interest rate or other forms of compensation in the form of assumption fees.

If the loan is insured by F.H.A. or guaranteed by the Veterans

171

Administration, there are no present restrictions connected with loan assumptions. At the present time, anyone may assume government sponsored loans without permission or penalty, other than a nominal statement and assumption fee.

There are a great many advantages to be realized in assuming a loan rather than in obtaining new financing. The main advantage, to buyer and seller, is a material reduction in expenses involved in an assumption.

REPLACE SELLER'S IMPOUND ACCOUNT

With the exception of the cash investment in the seller's equity, and in some instances tax prorations, the largest item of cash outlay for the purchaser is to replace the seller's impound account.

This account consists of property taxes and insurance reserves plus reserves for special assessments accumulated in monthly payments and held by the lender. When bills for these items become due, the lender pays them from the appropriate reserve account, which is a portion of the impound account.

The lender does not refund impound account monies to the seller and collect them from the buyer when a loan is being assumed. Therefore, it is up to the seller to collect an amount equal to the funds from the buyer, in escrow, and authorize transfer of ownership of the funds to the buyer. Lenders normally supply a form to the escrow agents for signature and authorization. Since the buyer pays the deposits directly to the seller, it is called "replacing" the impound account.

NEW HAZARD INSURANCE

When a loan is being assumed, there is normally a fire and hazard insurance policy existing for protection of the property, but in many cases it may not be satisfactory coverage for the purchaser. Most such policies may be extended or increased, but the buyer may prefer to have the seller cancel an existing policy and will arrange for new coverage.

Since a homeowner's policy is effective only for owner-occupants, if the purchaser does not intend to live in the home he is purchasing, he would not have use for the policy. If the purchaser does intend to live in the home he purchases and a homeowner's type of policy does not exist on the property, the buyer may either increase the coverage on the existing policy or purchase new coverage.

In the event an existing policy is cancelled and replaced with a new one, the lender may charge a $5.00 cancellation fee for making the change in the borrower's loan records. In some instances, the insurance reserve portion of the impound account may contain sufficient funds with which to pay for a new policy after the impounds have been transferred to the new owner. If there are not sufficient funds in reserve, the buyer will have to supply the first year premium for a paid up policy before the lender will allow the existing policy to be cancelled.

Any difference in insurance premiums may reflect in the insurance reserve and a subsequent adjustment may be made accordingly in the regular monthly loan payments.

It should be noted that it is possible for tenants to purchase a homeowner's—tenant's policy, which has essentially the same coverage as the homeowner's policy except for coverage on real property and personal property owned by the landlord.

LENDER'S ASSUMPTION FEES

In a loan assumption type of transaction, it is necessary to notify the lender and request an off-set statement to establish the condition of the loan according to the lender's records. When the transaction is being processed by an escrow agent, the lender will instruct that agent to collect a statement fee for preparing the statement and an assumption fee for changing the loan records. If the transaction is being processed by the buyer and seller only, the lender will demand these fees in advance of complying with the request.

There may be some differences in charges by various lenders for these services depending upon lending policies, basis of computations and whether or not the trust deed or mortgage contains special clauses as to loan assumption.

Conventional and private lenders may base their charges on a flat rate, a small percentage of the loan balance, or an amount equal to two to six months' unearned interest. It may be advisable to verify the lender's assumption fees when the facts are unknown, prior to signing an agreement of sale.

In the case of an F.H.A. or V.A. sponsored loan being assumed, the lender may charge a $15.00 assumption fee and a $25.00 statement fee; however, this could vary to some extent according to lenders and locality of the properties in question.

ESCROW FEES

Escrow fees are charged by escrow agents, attorneys and title companies for handling the details of information, documents and funds concerning a real estate transaction. Whether the buyer or seller is to pay the fees will depend on the laws and customs prevailing in the locality.

In some instances, escrow fees are included in the cost of a policy of title insurance, but in other localities the charge may be separate. It may also be a matter of negotiation in other sections of the country in which the property is located.

ATTORNEY FEES

The laws and customs of many states require the services of an attorney to some degree in the processing of real estate transactions. Charges for the service may depend on the type of transaction involved and the amount of work to be performed. Attorney's services are not required in some states for real estate transactions.

ABSTRACT OF TITLE FEES

Assurance of good title is as important to the purchaser on a loan assumption transaction as it is in the event of new financing. It is usually advisable for the buyer to insist on an abstract of title and an "opinion of title" from a competent attorney in areas where abstracts are ordinarily used instead of title insurance.

The cost may vary in different localities as some abstract companies charge a flat rate, while others may base their charges on the number of entries on the abstract or on the amount of work and services requested. Local custom normally prevails as to which party pays the costs, but it may be a matter of negotiation in the sales agreement.

TITLE INSURANCE PREMIUM

The standard policy of title insurance, which protects owners against recorded title defects, normally will expire upon transfer of ownership. If the purchaser is to have the same protection as the seller had, it will be necessary to obtain a new policy of title insurance. It is not necessary to purchase another A.L.T.A. policy for the lender's protection, when a loan is being assumed, because that policy was purchased at the time of originating the loan and will remain in effect for as long as the loan exists.

The cost of title insurance and which party is to bear the expense may depend on local custom or negotiation between buyer and seller.

TORRENS CERTIFICATE

Where the Torrens system of registered ownership of property is available and the property in question is so recorded with the Registrar of Titles, the buyer may be wise to continue registration.

The cost is usually nominal, after the first registration, and the possession of a Torrens Certificate of Title may enhance sale of the property to a future purchaser. In the event a title insurance policy is also desired, the title companies frequently issue the policy at a reduced rate to the purchaser when a Torrens Certificate of Title exists on the property.

TERMITE INSPECTION FEE

Some states' laws provide protective legislation concerning a pest control inspection and clearance report being made available to the purchaser prior to the transfer of ownership. Such reports are to be issued by licensed pest control operators. In most instances, the burden of proof rests with the purchaser in the event of a dispute or litigation.

The F.H.A. and V.A., along with a majority of lenders, require a termite inspection and clearance report prior to the origination of a new loan. Unfortunately, when the loan is subsequently assumed, there are no requirements to be considered by anyone other than the purchaser. Therefore, it is the purchaser's responsibility to make certain that the property he is buying is free of infestations of termites, beetles and other wood-destroying insects, as well as cellulose-destroying fungus caused by dampness and often referred to as "dry rot." The purchaser should also subscribe to preventive measures against damage by such infestations in the future.

Since some condition of insects or fungus may occur at any time, too much reliance should not be placed in pest control reports more than three to six months old.

Homes constructed on cement slab floors should not be exempted from an inspection report, because insects may attack through the roof, attic or walls when conditions are right for them. Leaking water pipes and connections inside the walls could eventually develop into a fungus condition on any wood contacted and spread to extended areas.

It is customary, in most sections of the country, to construct homes with full basements. However, this type of construction may not be practiced in other localities due to costs and soil conditions and the home is built on a concrete foundation with about two feet clearance between the subflooring and the ground. In such construction, builders frequently leave blocks of sawed off subflooring lying on the ground where they have fallen. These wood blocks constitute the hazard of an infestation of the sub-terranean termite. Improper drainage, or water seepage, may be other hazards under the structure unless the conditions are corrected.

As a general rule in a loan assumption purchase, the buyer pays for the inspection fee and the seller pays for any repairs or corrections. However, the laws and customs prevailing in various localities may differ or it may be a matter of negotiation between buyer and seller at the time of signing the sales agreement as to which party is to pay for the possible termite inspection and repairs. (In the event the buyer is willing to waive an inspection and take the property on an "as is" basis, phrasing for such a waiver will be found in the chapter pertaining to buyer's and seller's costs in new loans.)

DRAWING FEES

A charge for drawing documents involving property ownership is normally assessed in addition to escrow fees. In the case of a loan assumption, the buyer is not generally faced with drawing fees unless secondary financing is involved in the transaction. This may consist of the drawing of notes, trust deeds or mortgages and any special contracts or agreements being delivered to the seller. The cost of drawing documents may depend largely on the amount of work connected with preparing them.

STATE TAX

Under ordinary circumstances in most states, the seller pays the expense of a sales or transfer tax based on equity or sales price, as the case may be, but in a few states there is another tax charged in connection with the buyer's recording of the deed. Depending on the laws and customs of those localities, the cost may be nominal and paid according to negotiations between buyer and seller.

ACKNOWLEDGMENTS

Acknowledgments are not usually necessary for the buyer in a loan assumption transaction unless he is delivering some instrument of property ownership to the seller for recording in the public records. This may involve instruments pertaining to secondary financing or some other agreement to be recorded by the seller.

The expense is often included in the escrow agent's fee or an attorney's fee unless the acknowledgment is taken by an outside notary public or other designated official.

RECORDING FEES

In the usual case of a loan assumption, the buyer's expenses for recording fees are limited to those documents affecting his own recording of ownership and title to the property such as deeds.

TRUTH IN LENDING FEE

This item of expense is normally confined to the new loan type of transaction and not considered in a loan assumption. However, it is not unusual for a buyer to borrow funds through various sources with which to make the loan assumption possible.

In the event of that situation, it may be necessary for the buyer to be provided with a truth in lending statement, depending on the source of funds and whether or not the law applies to that source.

Where a lender or originator is required by law to prepare a truth in lending statement for the borrower's signature, a fee for the preparation may be levied against the purchaser. The amount may vary according to the individual lender's policies.

MONTHLY PAYMENT—NEXT DUE

It is a normal procedure for lenders to instruct escrow agents to collect the next monthly payment due on a loan if escrow is to close in the latter part of a month. Lenders make this request only for the purpose of allowing ample time to transfer and change their records over to the new owner's name and to issue payment instructions to the new owner prior to the date on which the regular monthly payment becomes due. Without this provision for time, the new owner may not know where to mail his first payment until after it has become delinquent.

Lenders are not usually concerned as to whether the seller or the buyer provides the next monthly payment due, but it is dependent upon one or the other to do so if escrow is to be placed in position to close. When provision is made for this payment in the sales agreement, it could save delay and embarrassment when final closing papers are to be signed.

The situation is often difficult for the average layman to understand and the buyer may feel that he is paying something that he should not pay. The most simple explanation to him is that he would be required to pay it anyway within a few days, but unless it is paid through escrow, he may not know where to send his check for proper credit for the payment.

When the buyer pays it instead of the seller, he is assuming a higher loan balance and replacing a lower impound account balance. In addition, the buyer will receive a credit for earned interest from the seller for the seller's share of prorated interest during his possession of the property. In

177

the last analysis, the buyer is paying only his own prorated share of earned interest. Once the payment is provided, it does not become due again for thirty days after the first of the following month.

Exhibit 14-1 is an example of the situation and how it works for a better understanding of the results.

PRORATION OF TAXES

When the seller has paid property taxes in advance to the end of an installment period, but possession of the property is given to the purchaser before the end of that period, the seller is entitled to receive credit from the buyer in escrow for the unused portion of such prepaid taxes.

On the other hand, if escrow should close during a period when property taxes are in an accumulative state, but the tax bill is not yet due and payable, the buyer should receive credit from the seller for the time taxes accumulated prior to close of escrow, which would be recording date.

Tax prorations should not include personal property taxes, which are often included in with the real property tax bills, unless that personal property is also being transferred free to the purchaser as a condition of the sale and purchase. (More details on property taxes will be found in the new loan chapters for buyers and sellers.)

PRORATION OF INTEREST

Interest payments on mortgage loans are normally paid after the interest has been earned. When the seller is in possession of the property during that portion of a month in which interest is earned and escrow is closed, it is an accumulated seller's expense. The expense is normally paid by the seller in the form of a credit, in an amount equal to earned interest, given to the purchaser's account in escrow and deducted, or debited, on the seller's escrow account and closing statement.

The new owner will then pay the next monthly payment due which will include all the interest earned during that month. Therefore, each party is paying his prorated share of earned interest. (See also chapters on New Loans.)

PRORATION OF INSURANCE

It is often the case whereby an existing hazard insurance policy provides more and better coverage than could be purchased in a new policy. In such instances, the purchaser may desire to continue the existing coverage

Monthly Payment Next Due On Loan
When Buyer Pays

Assumption — Cash to Loan:

When Lender's Instructions Call For Loan Payment Next Due

Example

Sales Price	$25,000	Trust Fund	$ 450
Loan Balance	20,000		
	$ 5,000	Normal amount of cash to loan if lender did not ask for Loan Payment Next Due.	

Escrow to close (recording date) 10-25-7_.

Lender requests escrow officer to collect payment due 11-1-7_ in amount of $165.

Amount Applied to Interest	$100
Amount Applied to Principal	25
Amount Applied to Trust Fund	40
	$165

Effect If Buyer Pays:

Amount Applied to Interest	$100
Amount Applied to Principal	25
Amount Applied to Trust Fund	40

Loan Balance	$20,000	
Amount to Principal	25	
	$19,975	Loan balance reduced by $25. (Same would happen if Seller pays and is due within a week anyway.)

Trust Fund	$450	
Increased by Payment	40	
	$490	Trust Fund increased by $40. (Same would happen if Seller pays and is due within a week anyway.)

Interest 31 Days	$100	
Earned Interest, 6 Days	19.35	(Would have to be paid to Seller if he pays — or otherwise in escrow).
	$ 80.65	Credit received from Seller for his portion of earned interest.

Buyer Receives:		
Reduced Loan Balance	$ 25	
Credit to Trust Fund	40	
Credit Interest from Seller	80.65	
	$145.65	Total Credit.
	19.35	Buyer's actual cost for 6 days interest to be paid anyway if Seller made payment.
	$165	

Buyer is actually making a payment due within a few days anyway. No more payments due until 12-1-7_.

EXHIBIT 14-1 MONTHLY PAYMENT NEXT DUE—BUYER PAYS

and pay the seller for the unused portion of the hazard insurance policy in a loan assumption transaction rather than to replace the policy.

Hazard insurance is normally prepaid for a period of from one to three years. If a policy premium has been paid in advance for three years and the seller has used only one year, the buyer will reimburse the seller for the remaining two years through prorations in escrow. This would involve a debit cost to the buyer and a credit receipt to the seller, if the policy is continued.

PRORATION OF WATER BILLS

In some localities, water bills are paid much the same as property tax bills. In some cases, the bill is not paid until sometime after the charges for water have commenced and when the bill is issued it may include a period into the future.

When the seller has paid in advance for water the buyer should reimburse him for the unused portion of the bill from the date of recording to the date of such advance payment.

On the other hand, if the seller has not prepaid the water bill, but charges have accumulated, he should pay his proportionate share to the buyer in escrow. The buyer will then pay for the entire billing period when the bill is due and payable.

Billing for water is processed differently in various localities and, in many instances, it is a simple matter of reading a meter or flat rate monthly charges. In such instances, the water company may send the closing bill directly to the seller, or to escrow, to collect as of a certain date with the buyer's obligation commencing on that date.

PRORATION OF RENTS

When a property being sold involves some type of rental units, the buyer ordinarily will receive credit, in escrow, from the seller for any prepaid rents and security deposits paid by the tenants and held by the seller. Such credit for rents would be from recording date of the transaction through the end of the prepaid rent period.

In the event leases are involved, it is a normal procedure for the tenant to pay the last one or two months rent in advance along with the first months' rent. Such advance payments should also be turned over to the purchaser in escrow.

There may be "cleanup" and "damage" deposits that belong to the tenants and held by the seller to be refunded to the tenant when the unit is

180

vacated. Any such deposits are usually credited to the purchaser in the escrow settlement papers.

The seller should provide a signed rental statement to the buyer, which will identify the rental units with tenants, the amount of rent each tenant pays, an inventory of furnishings owned by the seller and included in the sale, the amount of prepaid rents and rental periods and any deposit monies held in each tenant's account.

Immediately after close of escrow the new owner should contact the tenants, deliver new instructions as to where future rents are to be paid and inform the tenants of any rental policy revisions.

PRORATION OF ASSESSMENT BOND INTEREST

Interest on assessment bond balances is usually paid every six months after it has been earned and principal payments are normally paid on an annual basis along with one of the interest payments. In most instances, there will be a certain amount of earned interest accumulated. Such accumulated interest, as a general rule, is credited to the buyer in escrow when the assessment bond is to be assumed for payment by the buyer through mutual agreement.

It is a safe practice to verify the exact amount of bond balances, the interest rate, when interest was last paid and when the next principal and interest payment will become due and payable prior to the purchaser's agreement to assume the bond obligation. The city or county auditor, or some other official who maintains assessment bond records will normally supply such information upon request.

PRORATION OF MUTUAL MORTGAGE INSURANCE

F.H.A. mutual mortgage insurance premiums are accumulated each month along with regular monthly payments on insured loans and held by the lender in a M.M.I. reserve account, as a portion of the impound account. The mutual mortgage insurance premiums are paid from the reserve account each year on the anniversary of the loan origination They are paid in arrears after they have been earned and accumulated on that basis in the impound account.

Since the buyer, in replacing the seller's impound account, will be obligated to pay the entire M.M.I. premium amount when it becomes due, he should receive credit in escrow from the seller for the amount of premium

181

earned while the seller had possession of the property, or was responsible for paying the monthly loan payments.

OTHER PRORATIONS

There may be other items of costs and expenses to be prorated, but not mentioned herein. However, those items should be considered according to the laws and customs prevailing in various sections of the country. In some areas, stored heating fuel, bought and paid for by the seller, will remain on the property after the seller vacates. In such circumstances, the seller would be entitled to a prorated credit based on his costs.

Prorations are based on each party's paying his proportionate share of expenses according to prepaid expenses, accumulated expenses not yet paid, possession and usage.

Exhibit 14-2 is a checklist to use in estimating the buyer's costs in a loan assumption type of transaction.

CLOSING COSTS—CHECKLIST

Buyer's (Estimated) Expenses—LOAN ASSUMPTION

Property Address . . . . .Purchase Price $_____

	DEBITS	CREDITS
Replace Seller's Impound Account	$ _____	_____
New Hazard Insurance	_____	_____
Lender's Assumption Fees	_____	_____
Escrow Fee	_____	_____
Attorney's Fee	_____	_____
Abstract of Title Fee	_____	_____
Title Insurance Premium	_____	_____
Torrens Certificate	_____	_____
Termite Inspection Fee	_____	_____
Drawing Fees	_____	_____
State Tax	_____	_____
Acknowledgments	_____	_____
Recording Fees	_____	_____
Truth in Lending Fee		
(for "hard money" loan)	_____	_____
Monthly Payment—Next Due	_____	_____
Prorations: Taxes	_____	_____
Interest	_____	_____
Insurance	_____	_____
Water Bill	_____	_____
Rents	_____	_____
Bond Interest	_____	_____
Mutual Mortgage Insurance	_____	_____
Other	_____	_____
Total DEBITS & CREDITS	$_____	$_____

EXHIBIT 14-2

To Determine Buyer's (estimated) Total Cash Outlay:

	Purchase Price	$. . . . . .
ADD:	Total Debits	$. . . . . .
	Total Acquisition Cost	$. . . . . .
DEDUCT:	Existing Loan Balance	$_____
	Gross—Balance Due	$. . . . . .
DEDUCT:	Total Credits	$_____
	Buyer's Total Cash Outlay	$. . . . . .

EXHIBIT 14-2 CONT.

15

Financing in General

Real estate financing is a prime factor to be considered in the sale and purchase of properties. Its importance may be attributed largely to the fact that most prospective purchasers are unable to accumulate the full amount of cash required by sellers. In some instances, for varied reasons, it is a monetary advantage for a purchaser to obtain the highest possible loan on a property he is buying even though he may be in a financial position to pay the full price in cash.

There are two types of financing. One is conventional loans wherein the lender takes all the risks in granting mortgage loans. In taking such risks, lenders are normally more demanding of higher interest rates and other terms from the mortgagor than is required on government sponsored insured or guaranteed loans.

The other type of financing is sponsored by the government whereby the lender is either insured by F.H.A. or guaranteed by the V.A. to receive payment of the loan balance in the event the mortgagor allows the secured property to go into foreclosure. Thus, the lender's risk is reduced which in turn lowers the requirements on interest rates and other conditions of the loan.

Due to a mass desire for individual homeownership, mortgage lenders invest in real estate loans with varying degrees of risk according to their lending policies, current money markets, the property and the borrower. Some lenders prefer higher risk mortgage loans because of a higher yield on their investments. Others confine their investments to government sponsored mortgage loans with less risk and lower interest rates. However, institutional lenders generally engage in both categories of loans in order to diversify their investment portfolios.

Mortgage markets are generally classified as "primary" and "secondary." The primary market is sustained mainly by lenders who grant mortgage loans to borrowers and retain possession of the mortgage until the debt is discharged.

The secondary market consists of lenders who purchase existing mortgages on the basis of a competitive yield after considering the potential to be gained in other avenues of investment. The majority of mortgage lenders deal in both markets.

The Federal National Mortgage Association, funded by the federal government, was formed in 1938 to provide an outlet for lenders to sell their loans on a secondary market basis. Subsequent Federal Housing Acts have continued to provide funds for that purpose through the organization which is commonly referred to as "Fannie Mae." It is now a government sponsored private corporation with an ultimate goal of becoming self sustaining.

Lenders, who sell their mortgages to F.N.M.A., are required to buy capital stock in the corporation based on a small percentage of the mortgage amount sold.

The Housing and Urban Development Act of 1968 provided for the formation of a new corporation known as the Government National Mortgage Association, which is known as "Ginnie Mae." This new organization now operates the special assistance, management and liquidating functions of federal housing programs to relieve Fannie Mae of such responsibilities. Conventional loans entered into the operations of F.N.M.A. on February 14, 1972. New standard mortgage documents must be used for this market in order that investors, who submit bids for the purchase of mortgages from F.N.M.A., will know exactly what terms and conditions are contained in the mortgage instruments. The most significant factor in the standardized mortgage forms is that the borrower may repay the loan prior to maturity without penalty.

The secondary mortgage market normally involves discounted prices based on available competitive offerings. The degree of risk, term of the loan and interest rate most usually govern the amount of discount taken on the principal balance of a mortgage at the time of sale to establish the lender's projected yield.

Many of the large institutional lenders will commit "blocks" of loan funds to a mortgage broker at specified rates of discount on loans the broker may originate and process. The loan is then sold to the lender, who has commited funds, and the originating broker is normally appointed to service the collection and handle other details involving payment of the loan for a small percentage fee.

Mortgage loan funds are a commodity, from the investor's viewpoint, and if private individuals and lending institutions were not willing to make this commodity available to real estate transactions, the industry would suffer.

INSTITUTIONAL LENDERS

The principal source of loan funds throughout the nation is made available by institutional lenders. This category of lenders consists primarily of life insurance companies, savings and loan associations, commercial banks, mutual savings banks and mortgage companies.

Each institution operates under state and federal regulations and its individual established lending policies.

Life Insurance Companies

As a general rule, insurance companies are prone to diversify their lending practices to include conventional loans on all types of real estate investments. However, preference is normally confined to the larger units of investment projects. For example, most insurance companies are more interested in lending on large tracts of home development or commercial projects such as shopping centers, industrial properties, apartment houses, hotels and motels. Others are in the market for funding loans on large farm operations. In some instances, loans are granted on a basis whereby the insurance company shares the funding of loans with other lenders or on a participation of ownership and profits with the borrower.

A great number of insurance companies deal in the "primary" and "secondary" loan market of government sponsored programs. Loan funds are normally placed through mortgage companies, who are appointed correspondents for the lender; however, there may be some exceptions to the rule.

Insurance companies are regulated in their operations by the state in which they are incorporated as well as by the states in which they operate. Lending policies vary to some extent between individual companies from the standpoint of the types of loans, terms of loans and other considered factors.

Conventional loans are more often restricted to 75 percent of company appraised market value. Terms of the loan may be for a period of twenty-five to thirty years with the borrower using his own assets for the down payment. Interest rates fluctuate according to current money markets and the availability of funds, outstanding investments and general practices. Loans are normally granted on a sound investment basis from the factors of risk, "prime" properties and "prime" borrowers.

The usual prepayment penalty on insurance company conventional loans is relatively high if paid off within the first two years, but may decline to the point of being no penalty after five years from the date of originating the loan. As a general rule, the borrower may be allowed to pay off 20 percent of the original loan annually without a prepayment penalty.

Savings and Loan Associations

Lending policies and restrictions of savings and loan associations are normally applied within the framework of state and federal laws.

Although there is a definite distinction between Federal chartered and state chartered associations, from the standpoint of regulatory agencies, the difference is hardly apparent to a borrower under ordinary circumstances, as their loan practices and procedures are similar with very few exceptions. Until recently, these institutions confined loan funds to conventional type lending, but many of them have entered the field of government sponsored loans.

Prior to 1970, savings and loan associations were generally limited to granting new loans in amounts not to exceed 80 percent of appraised value or sales price, whichever was lower, due to government regulations and lending practices established by individual associations. In instances where a loan transaction involved prime properties and buyers, a 10 percent down payment, with the seller carrying 10 percent on a second mortgage, was and still may be possible.

In 1970, the Federal Home Loan Bank Board revised certain regulations, one of which permitted 90 percent financing under conditions that such loans were guaranteed or insured by private "mortgage insurance" companies approved by the F.H.L.B.B. However, many savings and loan associations retained their general lending policies of 80 percent of appraisal or sales price in granting mortgage loans.

In 1972, the Federal Home Loan Bank Board relaxed lending regulations still further in permitting member associations to grant 95 percent loans on single family dwellings. These loans must also be guaranteed or insured by private mortgage insurance companies approved by the F.H.L.B.B.

Savings and loan associations are not required to participate in these new percentage of appraisal or sales price ratios. They may do so provided the general economic conditions of their financial circumstances and their own individual lending policies will allow it. It is, therefore, advisable to predetermine the availability of such funds prior to commiting a sale on the basis of these high percentage loans.

The percentage ratio of loan to appraisal or sales price may decline also according to location, condition and age of the property along with the capabilities to repay the loan. Interest rates and term of the loan may also be adjusted in accordance with the above factors.

Interest rates charged on loans are a general reflection of the interest rates paid to depositors. Loans on prime properties to prime buyers may carry an interest rate of approximately two percent over the rate paid to depositors. Where loans are on other than prime properties and/or buyers, interest rates may be adjusted upward according to the increased risk.

Loan fees normally paid by the purchaser are often referred to as "points," which means that the loan fees are to be one percent of the loan amount times the number of "points" quoted. Since reference is actually made to loan origination fees, the term "points" on a conventional loan should not be confused with the "discount points" charged on government-sponsored loans, which must be paid by the seller.

When a new loan is originated, the loan fees may vary from one percent to three percent depending on the property, the buyer, the terms of the transaction and current economic conditions.

Prepayment penalties may range from two percent of the loan balance to an amount equal to six months' interest on the unpaid balance. Penalties for full payment of a loan prior to maturity are generally influenced by the money market and general economy at the time a loan is granted.

Savings and loan associations' conventional loan mortgage instruments usually contain an acceleration and alienation clause in addition to provisions for prepayment of loans. However, such mortgage instruments may be revised in connection with restrictive and penalty clauses when there is a good chance that the mortgage may be placed on the "secondary market" through the Federal National Mortgage Association (F.N.M.A.) procedures.

Commercial Banks

Commercial banks, both state and nationally chartered, are an extremely important source of conventional and government backed F.H.A. and V.A. loan funds.

From the standpoint of "prime" properties and borrowers, commercial banks pattern lending requirements generally along the same lines used by insurance companies concerning conventional loans.

Being more tightly controlled under state and federal banking laws and the Federal Reserve Bank Board, banks are usually more conservative than savings and loan associations. However, there is no uniformity in lending policies on conventional loans on a nationwide basis because of the varied state banking laws throughout the country. These laws are being continually revised in order to keep pace with the local and national economy. For that reason, bank lending policies may be in effect on a temporary basis depending upon the money market, ratio of outstanding loans to deposits, interest rates and a number of other economic factors.

189

All national banks are federally chartered and are required by law to be members of the Federal Reserve System. They are under the jurisdiction of the Comptroller of Currency, Washington, D.C. and carry the designation "national" in their title. Depositors' accounts are insured by the Federal Deposit Insurance Corporation.

State banks are chartered by the state in which they operate and are controlled by the State Superintendent of Banks or some other supervising public agency formed for that purpose. Membership of state banks in the Federal Reserve System is optional in most states. All depositors' accounts are insured by the Federal Deposit Insurance Corporation.

As members of the Federal Reserve System, lending funds and interest rates are directly and indirectly controlled by the Federal Reserve Bank Board through discounts in purchasing or lending on portfolios of commercial loans. The Board may also adjust other requirements such as loan ratios to deposits, or some other regulations concerning lending practices. For example, the whole structure of the money market is affected upward when the Federal Reserve Board increases interest rates charged to members. Mortgage loan discounts increase and loan interest rates to borrowers are higher. The situation is reversed when interest rates to member banks are lowered.

Bank mortgage loans are generally placed into two categories. Class A loans are granted on prime properties and prime mortgagors. Class B loans are those placed on average properties and borrowers. These classifications are in relation to property condition and location and to the borrower's credit history and financial circumstances.

Recent regulation changes provided for Class A loans to be granted on the basis of 80 percent ratio to appraisal for 30 years. Class B loans may now be granted at 70 percent of appraisal for a term of 25 years. Secondary financing may be allowed on Class B mortgage loans, but is not generally allowed on Class A mortgage loans.

Banks usually maintain a staff of real property appraisers and base their loans according to the bank appraiser's estimate of value in connection with conventional loans. This arrangement more or less provides a certain amount of control as to mortgage loans granted in accordance with the individual bank's financial situation and current lending practices. A high appraisal during one period may be lowered the next month depending on the general economy at the time.

Some banks confine their mortgage loans to residential properties and others enter the commercial property lending field. This may be particularly true in short-term construction loans, which are ultimately converted to long-term conventional loans or the government-sponsored loan programs.

Interest rates fluctuate according to current money markets throughout the country, but the amount of risk involved with properties and borrowers has a more definite bearing on conventional mortgage loans and the rates of interest charged. Interest rates paid to depositors are also an important factor in the amount generally charged on mortgage loans. F.H.A. and V.A. interest rates are the same in all localities due to government controls.

Loan origination fees may vary from $100, including appraisal fees, to 1 or 2 percent of the loan amount plus appraisal fees. New construction loans generally involve higher loan fees, the degree of which will depend largely on the amount of paper work, inspections and "take-out" money during construction which must be processed.

Prepayment penalties may vary with different banks and localities from 1 percent to 3 percent of the original loan amount when paid in full within the first two years and diminish by ½ percent each succeeding year until there is no penalty. As a general rule, twenty percent of the original loan amount may be paid each year without penalty. Banks are normally more liberal in connection with prepayment penalties than any of the other institutional lenders on conventional loans.

The lending policies of all banks change from time to time according to the money markets, general outlook of the present and future economy, adjustments of portfolios in investment programs, Federal Reserve Bank Board policy revisions and new state and national legislation. Therefore, a constant surveillance should be maintained by anyone considering the possibilities of utilizing mortgage loans from commercial bank sources.

Mutual Savings Banks

Mutual savings banks are mutual thrift banks, similar to savings and loan associations, in which the depositors are shareholders. The depositors participate in the banks's earnings after expenses, reserves and other contributions are considered.

Interest rates on deposit accounts are not established in advance, but are determined by a Board of Trustees at the end of each quarter of the year at which time each depositor's account is credited with earned interest according to the amount on deposit he may have.

Depositors' accounts are insured by the Federal Deposit Insurance Corporation, but very few banks belong to the Federal Reserve Bank system, as to do so is not usually a particular advantage to a mutual savings bank's operations. In some states, the law prohibits membership of mutual savings banks in the Federal Reserve Bank system.

Mutual savings banks are chartered by the state in which they were

191

organized and operate. They are controlled by and operate under the laws of the state in which they were chartered. Although these banks are located mainly in the northeastern states, they exist in two of the central states and in two of the northwestern states.

Conventional type mortgage loans are normally restricted to reasonable servicing areas within the bank's location, but in some instances may extend operations to any locality within their chartered state. The laws of a few states permit their operation in contiguous states where compatible laws prevail. In some states, mutual savings banks may participate in mortgage loans on an equal basis with commercial banks or other mutual savings banks, but may not be permitted to participate in mortgage loans with savings and loan associations.

Most state laws permit these banks to invest in F.H.A. and V.A. mortgage loans in any state. Therefore, they are an extremely important source of funds in the western states for government-sponsored loan programs.

NONINSTITUTIONAL LENDERS

Loan funds from sources of noninstitutional lenders account for approximately twenty-five percent of the total funds available for real estate mortgage lending in the present market.

Noninstitutional lenders are individuals, groups and companies who engage in mortgage loan investments, but are not required to conform to the rigid controls of state and federal banking laws in their operations.

Colleges and universities often invest endowment funds to strengthen resources for operation and expansion through the investment media of real estate mortgage loans. Trade and professional unions often invest pension funds and other revenues into mortgage loans for added financial strength. Funds held in trust for investment purposes by banks, title companies, estate executors and others normally include mortgage loans into their portfolios. In many instances, individuals with available investment funds prefer to invest in real estate mortgage loans.

Investment funds belonging to noninstitutional lenders are normally made available through real estate and mortgage brokers for placement of mortgage loans in various forms. In some instances, real estate and mortgage brokers may deal primarily with individuals and small groups who are mostly interested in short-term first and second mortgages bearing high interest rates and discounts.

Some loan brokers invest their own funds in the purchase and resale or in trading trust deeds or mortgages at a profit. Others work closely with their clientele in the selection of loan transactions of a preferred nature. These brokers and investors frequently make investments which may not be considered by institutional lenders who are restricted by state and federal laws.

A large number of mortgage companies operate on a diversified scale. These companies normally act as correspondents for institutional lenders such as insurance companies, mutual savings and commercial banks and other groups with huge "blocks" of investment funds to place into real estate mortgages. Mortgage companies often invest their own funds in the "primary" mortgage loan market, but they largely deal in the "secondary" market whereby they sell their processed, packaged and insured loans to other investors.

During periods of prevailing high rates of "discount points" on government-sponsored loans, mortgage companies may originate loans with funds supplied through a "line of credit" established with commercial banks and then borrow money by assignment of the mortgages as collateral until the portfolios are salable under a more favorable discount structure. The mortgages are then reassigned to an ultimate investor-purchaser.

As correspondents for institutional lenders or other investment sources, mortgage companies normally originate and package loans for funding by the lender. Servicing of the loan is most generally delegated to the correspondent who collects a small percentage fee based on monthly interest payments on the loan. Loan servicing consists of collecting the monthly payments, paying tax and insurance bills out of the mortgagor's impound account and, when necessary, attending to foreclosure proceedings.

16

Loan Assumptions

When a buyer assumes the obligation of a loan balance and the payments thereon and pays the seller the difference between sales price and the existing loan balance, it is a loan assumption type of real estate transaction. Ownership of the property is transferred to the purchaser and the mortgagee (lender) is notified to change his records accordingly. The purchaser is then responsible to meet the terms and conditions contained in the original mortgage instruments.

In states where mortgages are predominate over trust deeds it is often a practice for the purchase to be "subject to the loan." This means that although the purchaser may pay the seller for the difference between sales price and the existing loan balance, he is not assuming any responsibility for the mortgage debt. His only responsibility is to meet the prescribed monthly payments in behalf of the seller for as long as the buyer is in possession of the property.

Thus, in the event of foreclosure, the seller remains liable to the lender for any deficiencies. Deficiencies may arise unless the proceeds from the foreclosure sale are sufficient to retire the debt in full plus certain expenses involved in the foreclosure. Therefore, in a "subject to the loan" transaction the buyer's loss would be confined to his equity. Although the mortgagee may look to him first for a deficiency, he may pass the loss on to the seller.

In other parts of the country, it may be customary for the buyer to assume responsibility for an existing loan debt and in effect become a co-guarantor along with the seller. In the event of foreclosure, the lender will look to the owner of record first and then to preceding owners until any deficiencies are satisfied.

When it is written in the sales agreement that the buyer is to "assume the loan" it is presumed that he is also assuming liability for the payment of that loan debt.

In some states, where trust deeds are predominantly used over mortgages such as in California, Montana and North Carolina, there can be no deficiency judgment obtained on a "purchase money" trust deed or mortgage foreclosure. The exception to this may apply when a third party lender forecloses on a dwelling designed for more than four families and the foreclosure action is through the courts on the basis of a mortgage foreclosure rather than through a Trustee's sale.

The Veterans Administration, in guaranteeing payment of a G.I. loan, will hold the original borrower liable to the V.A. for any deficiencies. However, if the new purchaser applies to the V.A. and agrees to accept full responsibility of an existing loan and is an acceptable risk to the V.A., the original vetern-mortgagor may be released from responsibility of the debt by the V.A. This situation exists regardless of the locality in which the G.I. loan originated. (Further details in this connection may be found in the G.I. loan chapters of this book.)

There are several advantages to sellers and buyers connected with a loan assumption in the purchase of real estate.

ADVANTAGES TO SELLER

Some of the advantages to the seller in a loan assumption transaction are as follows:

1. The expense of paying discount points for a purchaser obtaining a new government-sponsored loan is eliminated.
2. The elimination of prepayment and unearned interest penalties if the loan is assumed rather than paid off prior to maturity.
3. Less transfer tax and the elimination of costs involved with removing a mortgage loan debt from the public records.
4. Escrows may close sooner when there is no delay in the processing of the property and buyer for new financing.

ADVANTAGES TO BUYER

Some of the advantages to a buyer in a loan assumption transaction are as follows:

1. The elimination of new loan origination fees and other closing costs involved with establishing a new mortgage loan.
2. Normally lower interest rates on loans which originated in an era of low interest rates as compared to present money markets.
3. Long term loans on which several years' payments have been applied will greatly reduce the overall cost of the property. For example, a loan that originated for a term of thirty years, but now has only

twenty years left for full amortization may reduce interest costs by approximately 40 percent.

4. When assuming a government-sponsored loan and some conventional type loans, the purchaser does not have to qualify from the standpoint of monthly income, past credit history and other factors which are considered when establishing a new loan. Investigation as to possible ramifications that may be involved with the assumption of conventional loans is advisable. Some conventional loans may not be assumable without some sort of penalty and others may not be assumable at all.

IMPOUND ESCROW ACCOUNT REPLACEMENT

In addition to normal closing costs charged by lenders, escrow agents, attorneys, etc., consideration should be given to the buyer's replacement of the seller's impound account, if any, held by the lender. It can involve various sums of money depending on the time of year in which escrow is scheduled to close. The impound account belongs to the seller, but is held by the lender and maintained at a certain level through monthly payments for the purpose of paying tax bills and insurance premiums as they become due and payable.

These funds are normally paid to the seller by the buyer in a loan assumption transaction, because lenders do not refund to owners as long as the loan is on their books.

CONVENTIONAL LOAN ASSUMPTION

Most conventional loans may be assumed, but trust deeds and mortgage instruments contain certain provisions and considerations under which there may be some limitations. It is advisable to review existing trust deed and mortgage documents to find out what protective clauses may be contained.

Acceleration Clause

An acceleration clause is ordinarily provided in conventional loan trust deeds and mortgages. It gives the lender the right to the immediate collection of all sums owing to him on the debt upon the happening of certain events. These events normally pertain to the proper maintenance of the property, retirement of the debt, sufficient insurance coverage and transfer of ownership to another party. A violation or an occurrence of one or more of these conditions may motivate the lender to require a remedy to the situation or full retirement of the debt.

Alienation Clause

An alienation clause contained in a trust deed or mortgage is intended to prevent the mortgagor from transferring the subject property to another party's ownership without written permission from the mortgagee. Failure to comply may give the mortgagee the right to demand full payment of the obligation.

The mortgagee will usually grant permission in consideration of some sort of a cash penalty from either the seller or the buyer, provided the buyer is financially capable of meeting the loan payments and has a good credit history.

This condition is based on the theory that the money was loaned to a qualified original borrower only. Subsequent mortgagors may be more of a risk.

In addition to requiring a cash penalty or fee, the lender may also increase the existing loan interest rate if it is substantially lower than prevailing interest rates on the current mortgage market.

Escalator Clause

This provision in a contract of sale, trust deed or mortgage instrument may permit an adjustment on the lender's behalf in interest rates, loan payments or other conditions of the obligation upon the happening of certain events. In most instances, one of the events included is upon the transfer of ownership as when the property is sold on the basis of a loan assumption there may be an increase of interest rates to the new owner.

The escalator clause may also provide for an adjustment in the interest rate according to current prevailing interest rates even though there is no change in ownership of the mortgage property. It may additionally provide for increased property taxes and insurance premiums.

Prior Approval of Buyer

When any of the above conventional loan protective clauses appear in a contract of sale, trust deed or mortgage instrument, it is possible the lender will require a financial statement, credit report and employment verification from the buyer prior to waiving any rights the lender may posess in allowing the existing loan to be assumed or the property to change ownership unless the entire loan is paid off.

Prior to, or immediately upon, placing the property for sale on the market, the conventional lender should be contacted as to the condition of the loan as well as to any conditions that may affect the assumption of that loan and what penalties may be charged if the loan should be paid off prior to maturity.

Under certain circumstances, the lender may be happy to learn there is the possibility of a new owner becoming responsible for future loan payments. Lenders seldom, if ever, desire to be placed in the position of being forced to foreclose on trust deeds or mortgages in order to protect their investments.

G.I. LOAN ASSUMPTION

There are a number of benefits connected with the assumption of G.I. loans guaranteed by the Veterans Administration and for that reason these loans are normally sought out more frequently than other types of existing financing.

Lower Interest Rates

Although there are relatively few four percent loans still in existence, there are some with low balances that were originated in the late 1940s and early 1950s. In 1953, G.I. loan interest rates increased to 4½ percent and from that time have ranged to 9 percent in accordance with changing money markets through the years. Since the early part of the 1960s, interest rates on G.I. loans have been commensurate with those of F.H.A. loans with the only difference being the mutual mortgage insurance of ½ percent charged on F.H.A. loans.

No Mutual Mortgage Insurance

F.H.A. and Veterans Administration G.I. loans carry the same rates of interest. However, F.H.A. loans have an additional ½ percent charge for mutual mortgage insurance to insure the lender against loss in the event of foreclosure losses.

G.I. loans do not have this ½ percent annual charge on loan balances since the Veteran Administration guarantees only 60 percent of the original loan amount to the lender and limits the guarantee to $12,500. In the event of foreclosure losses, the V.A. will collect the loss from the original veteran or another party accepted by the V.A. as a substitute mortgagor. Since G.I. loans do not entail the ½ percent additional charge, monthly loan payments are lower. *(Note:* The guarantee of $12,500 is expected to increase after this writing.)

199

No Prepayment Penalty

G.I. loans may be paid in full at any time prior to maturity without any prepayment penalty. Virtually all other types of loans provide for some degree of prepayment penalty in the mortgage instruments, if the loan is paid off prior to the specified term.

Remaining Term of Existing Loan

As it normally is the case when any existing loan is assumed, when a G.I. loan is assumed, fewer years are required to amortize full payment of the loan. A thirty-year term loan, which has existed for ten years, has only twenty remaining years to be fully amortized. Thus, the overall cost of a home is greatly reduced.

Secondary Financing Allowed

G.I. loans bearing low interest rates normally require a substantial amount of cash difference between sales price and the existing loan balance. This is true primarily because of equity buildup and increased property values through the years.

Under such circumstances, when the prospective purchaser does not have sufficient cash for all the seller's equity at one time, but is in a financial position to make a higher monthly payment, he may condition his offer on the basis of the seller carrying a second trust deed or mortgage for a portion of the equity. The seller is ordinarily entitled to a higher interest rate and a shorter amortization for full payment of the secondary financing, but when the debt is retired, leaving only the payments on the first trust deed or mortgage, the purchaser will be further ahead in the end results.

However, since the original veteran-mortgagor remains liable to the Veterans Administration for any deficiencies involved with a foreclosure, unless released from liability by the V.A., there is a definite advantage for the seller to carry some secondary financing on a G.I. loan.

In taking a note and second trust deed or mortgage, the seller could record a "Request for a Notice of Default" concerning the first loan. If the borrower should default on the first loan, the seller could instigate his own foreclosure and recover the property and escape liability to the V.A. for any deficiencies that might otherwise result.

Anyone May Assume G.I. Loans

There are no restrictive clauses contained in the mortgage instruments on G.I. loans from the standpoint of the lender's option as to the loan's being assumed by a new mortgagor. An existing G.I. loan may be assumed by anyone, if the seller is willing, with no changes made in the terms of the original mortgage security instruments.

However, as mentioned in the preceding paragraphs, the original veteran-mortgagor may be held responsible for any deficiencies resulting from a subsequent foreclosure on the property. This liability remains in all states regardless of any antideficiency judgment laws concerning trust deeds and mortgages prevailing in some of the states. It is a matter of reimbursing the Veterans Administration for any loan guarantee losses that agency may suffer as a result of foreclosure.

If upon a foreclosure sale, the property does not bring a sufficient price to offset the outstanding debt plus all other expenses of the sale, the Veterans Administration will look to the original veteran-mortgagor for the amount of deficiency. The obligation may appear in the public records against the liable party regardless of where he may reside until it is paid.

Buyer May Assume Responsibility

When the original veteran-mortgagor plans to sell his property on the basis of a loan assumption and wants to be released from liability to the Veterans Administration, provisions for it should be contained in the listing agreement. At the same time, the Veterans Administration should be contacted for the necessary application forms for his release of liability and the transfer of responsibility of the loan to a new mortgagor.

If the buyer is willing to assume full responsibility for payment of the G.I. loan balance, it should be written into the sales agreement. The new purchaser will fill out the application for responsibility of the loan and mail it into the Veterans Administration along with his financial statement, credit statement and the required fees. If the purchaser's credit history and financial situation is acceptable to the V.A., he will be approved and from that time forward will be held responsible for the mortgage debt and the original veteran-mortgagor will be released from the obligation.

Processing of the application may require from thirty to sixty days' time, depending on the V.A.'s current work load and delays involved with obtaining a credit report and clearance on the applicant.

The transfer of ownership may be accomplished while the application is being processed, but there is always the possibility of the purchaser's being turned down by the V.A. for some reason. If escrow is closed and ownership of the property is transferred to the purchaser prior to his approval by the V.A., and he is turned down, there is usually nothing that can be done about it except to re-apply at a later time.

201

Release Does Not Reinstate Entitlement

The release from liability and acceptance of a new mortgagor does not reinstate the veteran's entitlement to another G.I. loan. Full entitlement may be restored only when the Veterans Administration is no longer liable to the lender for the loan and then only under the following conditions:

1. If the veteran is forced to sell his residence and thereby lose benefit of his G.I. loan because of his health, employment, or otherwise through no fault of his own, or;
2. If his property is lost through the process of eminent domain;
3. If, while in military service, he must dispose of his home due to a military transfer, or;
4. If his property is destroyed by fire or some other natural hazard.

More Than One Entitlement

A veteran who did not use his World War II housing entitlement prior to the effective date of Public Law 550 on July 16, 1952 and was then engaged in the Korean conflict, lost his W.W. II entitlement in favor of the Korean War entitlement. If he used his W.W. II entitlement prior to July 16, 1952, he may have a new entitlement resulting from subsequent active military service provided he no longer owns the first home and the V.A. guaranteed mortgage is not in default.

(*Restoration of Entitlements and Additional Entitlements* are discussed in the chapter concerning new G.I. loans.)

F.H.A. LOAN ASSUMPTION

F.H.A. loans rate second in desirability to the assumption of a G.I. loan. Because the Federal Housing Administration insures the full loan amount against the lender's losses through mutual mortgage funds, there are some differences in the mortgage security instruments of F.H.A. as compared to the mortgage documents implemented by the Veterans Administration G.I. loans.

Lower Interest Rates

Since the early 1960s, interest rates on F.H.A. loans have been on par with G.I. loans. F.H.A. loans originated prior to that time may be of a higher interest rate in comparison to G.I. loans originated in the same period. In either case interest rates are somewhat lower than conventional loan interest rates in any given period for F.H.A. and G.I. loans.

Mutual Mortgage Insurance

F.H.A. mutual mortgage insurance premiums are computed annually on the basis of ½ percent of the loan balance on each anniversary date of when the loan was originated. Funds collected on all F.H.A. loans, for M.M.I., provide the means of reimbursing lenders for any losses sustained in the event of foreclosure on properties on which an insured F.H.A. loan exists. This ½ percent is collected monthly along with regular principal and interest payments and held in the mortgagor's trust account by the lender. The preceding year's premium is due on the date of loan anniversary, at which time the funds are forwarded to the Federal Housing Administration.

This item of expense is in addition to the interest rate specified and should be set forth as such in a listing agreement. For example, if the interest rate on an existing loan is 5¼ percent, the listing should specify—"Interest 5¼ percent plus ½ percent MMI." When stated in this manner on the listing form, all interested parties will know the exact interest rate if the loan is to be assumed. Otherwise, if the ½ percent M.M.I. is not mentioned separately, it may be presumed to be included in with the only percentage figure stated on the information portion of a listing agreement.

Prepayment Penalty

F.H.A. loans formerly carried a prepayment penalty of one percent of the original loan balance, when paid in full prior to ten years or 120 regular monthly payments. Such penalties were collected by the Federal Housing Administration.

Effective May 1, 1972, this prepayment penalty was eliminated and is no longer collected by F.H.A. even though prior mortgage instruments may provide for it.

Term of Existing Loan

It is normally a distinct advantage to assume an F.H.A. loan from the standpoint of a lower interest rate. However, the fewer remaining years for amortizing the loan balance may be more of an advantage in the assumption of any loan. Most F.H.A. loans are for a term of thirty years, but when only twenty or twenty-five years remain in which to amortize the entire balance, the overall cost of the property is greatly reduced.

Secondary Financing Allowed

When there is a substantial amount of equity, which is the difference between sales price and loan balance, it is often more difficult to find a buyer with sufficient funds to pay all cash to the existing loan. After an F.H.A. loan has been established and the mortgagor desires to sell the property to another party who is not in position to pay all cash for the equity, it may be profitable to both principals if the seller takes part cash and the balance of his equity on a note and second trust deed or mortgage. (See also *Loan Assumption—Secondary Financing.*)

Anyone May Assume F.H.A. Loans

F.H.A. mortgage security instruments do not contain any clauses prohibiting assumption of the loan based on a subsequent purchaser's credit or financial situation. Lenders seldom, if ever, know any of the subsequent buyer's qualifications until after the property ownership has been transferred and escrow is closed. The lender's security lies in the fact that the loan is insured by F.H.A. and in the event of foreclosure losses mutual mortgage insurance funds are used to reimburse him.

In the event of a foreclosure, responsibility for deficiencies rests with each mortgagor on the loan from the last to the first in the order of ownership.

When a loan is to be assumed, the escrow agent will request an offset statement or mortgagee's statement that provides all the vital information concerning the loan balance, impound account, principal and interest payments due, hazard insurance and the general condition of the loan account. The lender or loan servicing agent may enclose forms for the purchaser to fill out along with the condition of loan statement. A statement fee is normally requested by the lender for providing this service and an assumption is also collected to off-set the costs involved with changing over their records of ownership.

Limitations to Seller

There is no limitation as to the number of loans one person or a group may assume. However, there are certain limits imposed on the number of new loans an individual may obtain and the conditions under which he may allow a loan to be assumed and be eligible for a new loan, particularly when applying for another F.H.A. loan within two years from the time of allowing an F.H.A. loan to be assumed.

When an applicant for a new F.H.A. loan is obligated on an outstanding F.H.A. insured mortgage property that has been or is to be sold or traded within two years prior to the date of application, the F.H.A. insurance contract must be terminated or a substitute mortgagor must be approved to assume the mortgage obligation. However, if the new loan applicant has sufficient income to qualify for the prior mortgage obligation and the new loan too, these conditions would not apply.

The owner who plans to sell his property on which an F.H.A. insured loan exists and purchase another home in the same general locality by obtaining a new F.H.A. insured loan, should be aware that unless the purchaser is approved through the required process, the owner may not be approved by F.H.A. for a new loan. When listing his property for sale, provisions should be entered on the listing form to the effect that the buyer is to be so approved as a substitute mortgagor.

Processing for a substitute mortgagor begins with F.H.A. Form 2210, "Request for Credit Approval of Substitute Mortgagor." The form is submitted to the lender and if the purchaser is approved Form 2210-1, "Approval of Purchaser and Release of Seller," is to be submitted to F.H.A. by the lender and a nominal fee is charged by the lender for processing the substitution. The charge may vary with different lenders. Therefore, it may be advisable to obtain full information in this connection from the lender and agreement noted in the sales agreement as to which party is to pay the expense.

There are certain exceptions to the necessity of obtaining a Form 2210-1, "Approval of Purchaser and Release of Seller." These exceptions are when:

1. The unpaid balance of the outstanding insured mortgage does not exceed 85 percent of the original principal amount, or
2. The outstanding mortgage on which the mortgagor is obligated is insured under the escrow commitment procedure, or
3. The date of transfer of the property securing the insured mortgage was approximately two years prior to the purchase of the property to be financed, or
4. The insured mortgage is on a property located in a distant community, the property has been sold and transferred and it is apparent that the sale is in no manner related to the purchase transaction.

The seller is assured, through the 2210 procedure, that he will not be held responsible for any deficiency occurring as a result of foreclosure after transferring the property to the acceptable purchaser. He may use the statement of release to support a subsequent application for an insured mortgage.

When the Form 2210 procedure is used, the F.H.A. credit analysis and approval of the new mortgagor will be based upon the actual terms of the

205

sales transaction as agreed by the buyer and seller. A minimum cash investment is not required for the approval of a purchaser when the sale is from one owner-occupant to another owner-occupant and long-term occupancy is anticipated. There is a minimum cash investment required in connection with sales to nonoccupant owners, sales under the escrow commitment procedure and sales to fill short-term housing needs of purchasers.

The seller may use the statement of release to support a subsequent application for an insured F.H.A. mortgage. However, in the event this has not been accomplished, the following may be required by F.H.A. if the insured property has been sold within the past six months of application:

1. Evidence that the F.H.A. insurance on that property has been terminated, or
2. A current credit report on the substitute borrower is obtained.
3. A statement from the mortgagee as to current status of the assumed loan is obtained.
4. The payment record of the substitute borrower is to be obtained from the mortgagee of the assumed loan.

For F.H.A. insured property sold prior to the last six months but within the last two years the following will be required:

1. Evidence that the F.H.A. insurance on the property has been terminated, or
2. A statement from the mortgagee as to the current status of the assumed loan is obtained.
3. The payment record of the substitute borrower is to be obtained from the mortgagee of the assumed loan.

Whether a formal release agreement is to be executed and recorded is a decision to be made by the mortgagee (lender). F.H.A. does not require, prescribe or pass on the form or method by which the original mortgagor is released and the liability of the new mortgagor is substituted.

LOAN ASSUMPTION—SECONDARY FINANCING

Loan assumptions normally require a considerable amount of cash difference between the purchase price and existing loan balance. In many instances, the buyer may not have sufficient funds on hand to pay the required amount of cash, although he would otherwise purchase the property. During an era of high interest rates on new mortgage loans, the purchaser may find it beneficial to condition his offer to purchase on the basis of the seller accepting a portion of his equity in cash and the balance on a note and second trust deed or mortgage.

It may be particularly advantageous to the purchaser when the loan to be assumed is of a low interest-bearing nature. For example, use an assumable six percent interest bearing mortgage in the amount of $25,000, with principal and interest payments of $119.92, which would fully amortize in thirty years. At the end of five years, the balance would be $23,250 with twenty-five years left for payments to be made.

To purchase the property at a fair market value of $30,000, the buyer would need a $6,750 cash down payment plus closing costs of $350 to assume the loan.

On the other hand, the buyer could refinance and obtain a new loan of $27,500, bearing an interest rate of 8 percent per annum with principal and interest payments of $201.79 to amortize the loan fully in thirty years. Thus, his down payment would amount to only $2,500 plus closing costs estimated to be $600 for a total amount of cash outlay of $3,100.

For the sake of this example, say the buyer could afford to invest as much as $4,100 total cash. Under those circumstances, it would be beneficial to the buyer to offer the seller $3,750 cash down payment, which would leave enough cash to pay the closing costs of $350, if the seller would carry the balance of $3,000 equity on a note and second trust deed or mortgage, payable at $63.75 per month, including 10 percent interest, to amortize fully at the end of five years.

If the sellers were willing to accept this offer, the buyer's payments would total $183.47 per month rather than $201.79 on the basis of a new loan. At the end of the five-year period, the buyer would be obligated only on the existing mortgage payments of $119.92 and would fully amortize the debt within twenty additional years. Otherwise, if the buyer elected to obtain the new loan, he would still be paying $201.79 per month and at the end of the first five-year period would still have twenty-five years of such payments to meet.

In the event the sellers refused the offer and insisted on all the cash for their equity, it would pay the buyer to borrow the money from another source on a similar basis with which to pay the sellers all their cash and assume the existing loan.

Whether or not the seller would be willing to accept the buyer's offer would naturally depend on the seller's financial situation and plans for the future.

If the sellers plan to place a portion of their net proceeds into some sort of savings account or a low-return investment, they would be far ahead to draw 10 percent interest on a note and second trust deed or mortgage. This is particularly true since they are familiar with the property and when the buyer has a relatively large cash investment in the property.

The primary objective may be reflected in the actual number of net dollars the seller may receive. For example, if the buyer should be forced to condition his offer on the basis of obtaining a new F.H.A. or G.I. loan, the seller would be faced with several additional expenses that would reduce his net proceeds.

Under F.H.A. and V.A. regulations, the purchaser is not permitted to pay "discount points" involved in new loans to be insured or guaranteed by these two government agencies.

If the current money market demanded two "discount points" in this particular instance, the new lender would withhold approximately $600 from the seller at the time of funding the loan. The seller would be faced with other expenses such as prepayment penalties, unearned interest penalties, reconveyance fees and other expenses that could amount to approximately $400, which would bring the total extra expense to $1,000 in a new F.H.A. or G.I. loan transaction. On that basis, the sellers would have only $2,000 more spendable cash than they would have by accepting the buyer's offer of $3,750 cash down payment along with a $3,000 second trust deed or mortgage.

It follows then, that the seller would have only $2,000 invested in a $3,000 second mortgage instrument on which he would be drawing 10 percent interest. Almost any private investor would be willing to buy the second from the seller under those conditions at any time. If the sellers should decide to sell the mortgage later at a discount, the mortgagor (buyer) should have first opportunity equal to an outsider's bid for it.

Terms and Conditions of Note and Mortgage Instrument

There is a natural tendency to keep the terms and conditions more or less relaxed and comfortable for the purchaser at the time of submitting an offer involving secondary financing. In many instances, there is no choice for the buyer but to have low monthly payments on a second note and trust deed or mortgage if he is to be in financial position to meet the obligation. However, the terms and conditions of a mortgage instrument should be considered on the premise that the seller may be forced to sell the investment to another investor prior to maturity of the debt.

Investors who deal in negotiable secondary security instruments ordinarily consider the term (number of years), conditions (protection clauses), risk, interest rate and yield in arriving at a percentage of discount on the principal balance. When all the factors are favorable, the percentage of discount may be lower. For example, a second trust deed with all favorable factors may be discounted at 30 percent of the principal balance while another trust deed with some of the factors missing may be discounted by as much as 40 to 50 percent. A 30 percent discount on a $3,000 note and trust deed or mortgage would amount to $900; thus the seller would receive $2,100 for it. The discount of 40 percent on the same amount would be $1,200 and the seller would receive only $1,800 cash for it. If the situation is too unfavorable, the average investor would not be interested at any price.

From the standpoint of term, the most desirable from the investor's view is from three to five years and no more than seven years. The conditions usually are expected to include an acceleration and alienation clause, prepayment penalty, late charges and provisions for the mortgagor to pay any attorney fees and foreclosure costs involved in collection of the debt.

As for the risk involved, the mortgagor's financial capabilities and his cash investment in the transaction is an important assurance of the debt retirement without any problems. The investor will also consider the salability of the property in the event he is forced to foreclose on the security instrument.

Yield is the primary objective of investors. Therefore, a substantial rate of interest is essential to a reduced percentage of discount.

All terms and conditions pertaining to the mortgage instruments must be provided in the original offer by the buyer, or stated in a counter-offer by the seller prior to acceptance, as there can be nothing added afterwards without the mutual consent of both parties.

Provisions for a penalty in the event mortgage payments are not paid on or before the specified due date is often effective in motivating the mortgagor to be prompt in his monthly payments. This is called a "late charge" and may vary from two to three percent of the payment due.

It is advisable for the seller, who is taking part payment for his equity in the form of a note and trust deed or mortgage, to record a "Request for Notice of Default" in the public records. In the event the mortgagor fails to make current monthly payments on the first loan, or for some reason forces the holder of the first mortgage to file a "Notice of Default" with intent to foreclose, a copy of the notice will be mailed to the holder of the second mortgage.

Upon receipt of the notice, the holder of the junior mortgage may protect his interests by instigating his own foreclosure action and removing the default on the senior lien. He may then collect any advances from the mortgagor or complete his own foreclosure proceedings. Foreclosure on a senior lien will eliminate most junior liens unless they are tax liens or mechanic's liens.

LOAN ASSUMPTION—CASH FOR EQUITY ONLY

Prospective purchasers frequently have only a certain sum of money to invest in the purchase of property. Their financial position may be such that there is no latitude for a lower existing loan balance or an excessive impound account balance.

In order to eliminate the possibility of a purchase requiring more cash than the buyer has available, it may be advisable for the offer to be made on the basis of a specified amount of cash for the seller's equity with no prorations and the impound account to be transferred free to the buyer. Monthly payments should be paid currently by the seller and the seller should pay any earned interest on the loan prior to the subsequent payment becoming due.

When the seller has maintained his impound account at the proper level to pay for property taxes and insurance bills when they become due, he should not be required to pay any prorations of these two items of expense. On the other hand, the buyer presumably does not have sufficient cash to replace the seller's impound account or enough money to pay any prorations to the seller. Thus, the reason for stating "no prorations," in the sales agreement.

The sales agreement would be written on the basis of the sales price being "approximately, but not to exceed $_____" because the exact balance of the existing loan may be unknown until the lender issues an "offset" statement disclosing the exact balance as of a certain date. The "not to exceed" provision protects the buyer in the event the exact loan balance proves to be materially higher than was anticipated.

Since the exact sales price is unknown until receipt of the lender's offset statement, the sales commission should be based on the total of the loan balance and amount of cash the buyer is paying. Therefore, the sales agreement should specify the normal percentage of commission is to be paid on the final determined sales price.

It is not always advisable to use this method of purchasing, as it is more equitable for the trust fund or impound account to be replaced by the purchaser and to allow prorations to fall where they may. However, the buyer is assured of paying only an exact amount of cash and the seller may be fairly sure of what his net proceeds are to be.

Loan balances and impound account balances can usually be computed from the lender's most recent year end loan statement by applying any principal payments made subsequent to the balance shown on the statement and adding any payments into the impound account less any potential impound funds distributed after the statement was received. A great amount of care should be exercised in these computations, because an error of material consequence could be fatal to the transaction.

INSTALLMENT SALES CONTRACT

An installment sales contract, as it applies to real property sales, is an instrument in which the seller agrees to convey title to real property to the buyer after certain specified conditions in the contract have been accomplished provided conveyance of title is not required within one year.

This type of sales agreement is used to varied degrees in many parts of the country and may be variously referred to as "Real Property Sales Contract," "Land Contract of Sale," "Agreement for Purchase and Sale," "Land Sale Contract" and "Agreement to Convey."

The general concept in usage is when the seller prefers to retain title to the property until the buyer has paid a specified sum of money towards the principal balance due the seller. When the agreed payment has been performed, the seller will transfer title of ownership to the buyer. Buyers are attracted to this type of contract because in many instances very little cash down payment is required.

Sellers often prefer this type of contract over a trust deed or mortgage from the standpoint of enforcement in the event of a default in payment and/or some other condition upon which the contract agreement was based, which relieves the necessity for otherwise appropriate foreclosure proceedings.

However, it does not always work out to an avoidance of some sort of litigation in court from the standpoint of possession immediately on default. In some cases, where the contract has not been drawn by a competent attorney, the court may rule that the seller had an unfair advantage and on that basis may order both parties to be restored to their original positions. It is extremely important to have legal counsel in drawing up this type of sales agreement.

In some states, title insurance or other protective devices are available in this type of transaction, which is commendable, but when the seller retains title there may be nothing to prevent him from later encumbering the property or actually deeding the property to another party. In the event of some sort of civil suit, judgment or lien against the seller, it may be impossible for him to deliver good title to the buyer as originally agreed.

As a general rule, the buyer's payments are made directly to the seller who in turn is to pay the necessary payments on any existing loans or liens against the property. Principal and interest payments plus impounds are

211

normally based on the total obligation to the seller while he pays principal and interest plus impounds on existing loans.

It is customary in most areas for the seller to deliver a policy of title insurance or some other title protective device to the buyer after the terms and conditions have been met and title of ownership is transferred to the buyer. At that time, the buyer assumes the existing loan balances and the installment contract is converted to a secondary trust deed or mortgage if there is any balance still due the seller. Otherwise, the contract is completed and eliminated.

In instances where existing loans are to be assumed, it is advisable first to determine if the loans are assumable or if the mortgage instruments contain some restrictive clauses in that connection.

In most instances, the buyer's equitable interests in an installment contract are not assignable in the event he should desire to sell prior to full performance nor are his equitable interests normally acceptable collateral in the event he desires to borrow money.

There may be many potential imperfections connected with this type of real property financing. Therefore, all hazards should be considered and provided for in the contract by an attorney who specializes in real estate transactions of this nature.

ALL-INCLUSIVE TRUST DEED OR MORTGAGE

The all-inclusive trust deed or mortgage type of financing is often referred to as the "Hold Harmless," "Overriding" or "Wrap Around" trust deed or mortgage. It is similar to the installment sales contract in the general concept of purpose. The primary difference being that title of ownership is transferred and the purchaser receives a policy of title insurance, or other protective device, at the time the mortgage instrument becomes effective at close of escrow.

It is more often used from an investment and tax-shelter approach in the sale of income property, but may also be applied to residential properties to an advantage. Sellers often prefer this type of transaction over the usual loan assumption with secondary mortgage being the only amount due them, while with this type of financing they are entitled to collect interest on the balance of sales price less the cash down payment.

It is a "subject to the loan" type of transaction whereby the mortgagor pays specified monthly payments to the seller at a higher rate of interest on the balance of purchase price after making a down payment. The seller, in turn, pays the senior mortgage payments on the basis of usually lower interest rates.

212

The all-inclusive trust deed or mortgage is a junior lien held by the mortgagee. In the event of a foreclosure, the proper proceedings are taken according to the laws affecting trust deeds or mortgages in the locality in which the property lies.

When the seller has received full payment for his equitable interest, he will issue the necessary reconveyance or mortgage release and the buyer will continue on with the payments involved with any remaining loan balances.

Prior to the execution of the agreement, the purchaser should make certain to have any existing mortgage instruments examined by a competent attorney to verify whether or not the existing obligations are assumable.

Where it is not physically possible to examine the mortgage instruments, a written statement and verification should be obtained from the mortgagee to whom existing obligations are payable.

If an existing mortgage instrument contains an alienation clause or an escalation provision, the lender may waive his rights and grant permission for the loan to be assumed. Without a waiver, the lender may call for the entire loan balance upon transfer of the seller's interests.

There are a great many terms and conditions to be considered in an all-inclusive trust deed or mortgage instrument. Consideration must be given to the application of payments to existing loans, impounds, sufficient principal payments on the all-inclusive instrument, at what point in time or event the buyer assumes responsibility of any existing loans, restrictive conditions on the transfer of equitable interests, leasing, refinancing and prepayment penalties. Therefore, all details of the transaction and precautionary measures and clauses should be developed through the aid of legal counsel who is experienced in drawing the necessary and proper agreements for this type of transaction.

Exhibit 16-1 illustrates the utilization and net results of an all-inclusive trust deed or mortgage.

LOAN ASSUMPTION

Apartment house—10 Units—Sales Price—	$100,000
Buyer's Down Payment	10,000
Balance on All-inclusive Trust Deed—	$ 90,000

Above balance payable at $900 per month—including 8½% interest—plus impounds.

Principal and Interest payment first month	$ 900
Interest first month— (8½% X $90,000)	$ 637.50
Applied to Principal first month—	$ 262.50

By mutual agreement, buyer makes payments to a third party—XYZ Bank.

XYZ Bank makes payments to holders of existing mortgages as follows:

1st Trust Deed—$40,000—Payable at $250 per month—5% interest.
2nd Trust Deed—$20,000—   " $175 "   " —6% "

Seller receives	(8½% X $90,000) interest		$ 637.50
			(first month)
Seller pays	(5½% X $40,000) "	$166.67	
" "	(6% X $40,000) "	100.00	
Total Interest paid by seller			$ 266.67
Net effective interest seller receives first month—			$ 370.83
Amount applied to principal by buyer first month—			263.50
Total cash received first month			$ 633.33

EXHIBIT 16-1
THE EFFECT OF AN ALL-INCLUSIVE
TRUST DEED OR MORTGAGE

17

Financing–Veterans Loans– Guaranteed

In 1944 Congress passed the Servicemen's Readjustment Act (Public Law 346), which was signed by the President on June 22, 1944. This act was designed to provide assistance to veterans of World War II in making the necessary readjustments from military service to civilian life.

In general, the act provided for the following established benefits:

1. Title I—Hospitalization, Claims and Procedures.
2. Title II—Education of qualified veterans.
3. Title III—Section 501—Purchase or construction of homes.
   Section 502—Purchase of farms and farm equipment.
   Section 503—Purchase of Business property.
   Section 505—Secondary Financing.

Through the years following enactment of the law, there have been numerous changes, decisions, rulings, interpretations and opinions rendered by the Administrator of Veterans Affairs and the Veterans Administration Counsel regarding procedures, policies and practices of the Veterans Administration and lenders who participate in the G.I. loan program.

Congress has also provided a number of amendments to the act and there will, no doubt, be additional amendments. Therefore, it may be advisable to watch for current publications in this connection.

The Veterans Administration does not provide funds for loans except in isolated areas where funds from private lenders are not available. The primary function of the V.A. is to guarantee repayment of loans made to qualified veterans by accredited lenders. Thus, with this degree of protection, lenders are in better position to grant lower interest-bearing loans for a longer term.

At the inception of the Servicemen's Readjustment Act of 1944, a guarantee of up to 50 percent of the loan amount, not to exceed $2,000, was provided to accredited lending institutions and builder-lenders. However, on December 28, 1945, Congress amended the act through Public Law 268, which increased the guarantee to 50 percent of the total loan with a maximum guarantee of $4,000.

Effective September 1, 1951, the maximum guaranty was increased to 60 percent of the loan amount not to exceed $7,500 and on May 7, 1968 the guaranty was increased to 60 percent of the loan amount, not to exceed $12,500, whichever is smaller.

ENTITLEMENTS

The Veterans Housing Act of 1970, under Public Law 91-506 effective October 23, 1970, restored all expired home loan guaranty entitlements to veterans until such entitlements have been used. Prior to that date, veterans of World War II and Korean Conflict veterans were entitled to G.I. home loans according to their individual tenure of service.

World War II Veterans

World War II veterans, with other than a dishonorable discharge, are eligible for a G.I. home loan provided they served on active military duty for 90 days or more and when at least one day of service occurred during the period between September 16, 1940 and July 25, 1947. Service after July 25, 1947, and prior to June 27, 1950, may not qualify a veteran for a home loan entitlement. Therefore, it may be advisable to establish such eligibility prior to a purchase commitment.

Korean Conflict Veterans

Korean Conflict veterans with other than a dishonorable discharge are eligible for a G.I. home loan provided they served on active military duty during the period between June 27, 1950, and January 31, 1955.

Cold War Veterans

The Veterans Administration's program for Cold War veterans, also known as the Post Korean Conflict veterans, was made effective in 1966 by congressional action. Veterans with other than a dishonorable discharge who served on active military duty for more than 180 days after January 31, 1955, are eligible for a home loan entitlement. Service in the National Guards or reserves does not create eligibility. However, such service may place the veteran in position to obtain an F.H.A.—Veterans home loan.

Vietnam Veterans

Vietnam veterans normally qualify for a home loan entitlement under the Post Korean Conflict (Cold War) veterans program.

DUAL ENTITLEMENTS

In the event a veteran has served in two or more periods and received other than a dishonorable discharge both times, he may be eligible for a second G.I. loan even though the first loan is still open. However, the prior loan must not be in his name as owner of the property and all payments must be current with no delinquencies on the existing loan.

Women who served in qualifying periods are also eligible for the same benefits as men. Where both man and wife have entitlements, the use of either entitlement does not affect the other.

ADDITIONAL ENTITLEMENTS

Effective October 23, 1970, cut-off dates for G.I. loan entitlements were eliminated and a more liberal program for unused portions of expired and unexpired entitlements was initiated through the Veterans Housing Act of 1970. All entitlements are now effective indefinitely until used.

The veteran who used his entitlement when the loan guaranty was only $2,000 now has an additional entitlement of $10,500.

If the veteran used his entitlement when the loan guaranty was only $4,000, he may be eligible for an additional entitlement of $8,500.

Those veterans who used their entitlements when the loan guaranty was only $7,500 may now be eligible for an additional $5,000 entitlement.

These additional entitlements are based on the present maximum loan guaranty of $12,500 less the prior amount used. The remaining entitlement balance is multiplied by four to find the maximum loan guaranty now available for qualification under the F.N.M.A. secondary purchase program.

F.N.M.A. has established limitations of $50,000 on 100 percent loans based on the full $12,500 entitlement (4 x $12,500 = $50,000). Entitlements for 100 percent loans based on the unused portion of prior used entitlements multiplied by four are as follows:

1. $10,500 remaining—times four—equals $42,000 allowable maximum loan. No down payment.
2. $8,500 remaining—times four—equals $34,000 allowable maximum loan. No down payment.
3. $5,000 remaining—times four—equals $20,000 allowable maximum loan. No down payment.

The above maximum loans are limitations if the lender expects the loan to qualify for F.N.M.A. to purchase the mortgage instrument. However, there are some lending institutions which do not intend to enter the F.N.M.A. secondary mortgage purchase program with all their loans and may offer higher limits of 100 percent loans.

In any event, the additional entitlements may be used even though the original loan still exists, provided the prior property is no longer in the veteran's name and the loan is not delinquent.

REINSTATEMENT OF VETERANS LOAN ENTITLEMENTS

Full entitlement for a second or subsequent G.I. loan may be restored to veterans under certain circumstances and conditions. However, reinstatement of an entitlement can not be obtained unless the Veterans Administration has been relieved from liability to the lender on the previous loan. This normally implies that the previous loan must have been paid off. In addition, reinstatement of an entitlement may be accomplished only if:

1. The veteran was forced to sell his previous home, which was financed under the veteran's loan guaranty entitlement being restored, as a result of an employment or military transfer.
2. The veteran was forced to sell due to personal or family health reasons.
3. The veteran's home was taken for public use through eminent domain processes.
4. The veteran's home was destroyed by fire or other natural causes.

Documentary proof will be required in connection with applicable circumstances and it may also be necessary to substantiate the fact that the previous loan was paid off.

ENTITLEMENT FOR UNREMARRIED WIDOWS OF VETERANS

The unremarried widow of any person who met the service requirements for benefits under the Serviceman's Readjustment Act of 1944 and who died either in service or after separation from service as a result of injury or disease incurred or aggravated by such service in the line of duty, shall be eligible for the benefits under Title III of the act, provided the veteran's discharge was not dishonorable.

ENTITLEMENT FOR CONDOMINIUMS

When purchasing an individual residence unit, a veteran may use his G.I.

218

entitlement for a condominium unit. However, this applies only under the condition that at least one loan to a purchaser of an individual unit in such project has been insured by the F.H.A. under Section 234 of the National Housing Act.

ENTITLEMENT FOR MOBILE HOMES

Any veteran who has eligibility for a $12,500 loan guaranty, may receive a 30 percent mobile home loan guaranty entitlement. Use of the mobile home loan guaranty entitlement does not reduce the $12,500 home loan entitlement. However, any veteran obtaining a guaranteed mobile home loan cannot use his $12,500 guaranty entitlement to purchase a conventionally constructed home until his mobile home loan is paid in full.

Maximum loans in connection with mobile homes are as follows:

1. $10,000 for 12 years and 32 days in the case of a loan covering the purchase of a mobile home only and such additional amount as is determined by the Administrator of Veterans Affairs to be appropriate to cover the cost of necessary site preparation where the veteran owns the lot, or,
2. $15,000 (but not to exceed $10,000 for the mobile home) for 15 years and 32 days in the case of a loan covering the purchase of a mobile home and an undeveloped lot on which to place such home and such additional amount as is determined by the administrator to be appropriate to cover the cost of necessary site preparation, or,
3. $17,500 (but not to exceed $10,000 for the mobile home) for 15 years and 32 days in the case of a loan covering the purchase of a mobile home and a suitably developed lot on which to place such home.

The V.A. administrator is authorized to establish a loan maximum for each loan. The maximum loan amount may be based on the mobile home manufacturer's invoice cost to the dealer and other cost factors considered to be proper. The down payment will be approximately 10 percent. Interest rates may vary according to the money market, but there may be a different fixed rate between interest charged on the mobile home purchased and the lot or land purchased for its location.

ELIGIBLE PROPERTIES

The primary purpose of the Veterans Administration's home loan guaranty program is to provide the veteran an opportunity to purchase a residence within his financial capabilities of repayment of the loan. It is not

219

intended to provide funds solely for speculative investment purposes. However, it is possible for the veteran to purchase a single family residence, a duplex, triplex or a quadruplex structure provided one unit is to be used as the veteran's residence. If the dwelling is to be owned by two or more veterans, it may be possible to purchase a residential structure consisting of four units plus one additional unit for each qualified veteran participating in the loan.

Farm loans may be obtained for the purchase of land containing buildings, or construction of buildings, livestock, equipment, etc. to be used in farming operations; for working capital necessary for farming operations; and for purchasing stock in a cooperative association where purchase of such stock is required by federal statute incident to obtaining the loan.

A business loan may be obtained for engaging in business or pursuing a gainful occupation; for purchasing lands, buildings, supplies, equipment, machinery, tools, inventory and stock in trade for the purposes of engaging in business or pursuing a gainful occupation.

It would be advisable to contact the nearest V.A. district office for full details involving farm and business loans. In any event, G.I. loans may be available to qualified veterans even though they may be receiving benefits under Title II for education at the time of application.

LOAN PROCEDURES

Although there is no maximum loan limit imposed by the V.A., lenders most generally will not grant loan funds in excess of the present $50,000, based on the $12,500 times four entitlement acceptable to F.N.M.A. in the secondary mortgage market. However, there may be some lenders in various localities who do not always grant G.I. loans with the intentions of entering the F.N.M.A. secondary market and will exceed the established F.N.M.A. limitation. It is the lender's option.

A Certificate of Eligibility for the veteran must be obtained from the V.A. in order for the lender to receive the loan guaranty from that agency. The veteran may apply for the certificate directly through the V.A. or, upon application for a G.I. loan, the lender may submit the necessary forms to the V.A. for a Certificate of Eligibility.

Proof of service in the form of original discharge or separation papers must be provided in either case. In the event such proof of service has been lost, the veteran may sign a statement of fact to that effect and receive the Certificate of Eligibility. It is sometimes only a matter of a few days for the lender to obtain a certificate from a centralized facility where complete records on individual veterans are maintained.

There are times when a large volume of veterans home loan applications are being processed by the V.A., which may create a long period of time in waiting for loan approval. Under such circumstances and where it is of great importance for a loan or loans to be funded without prior approval by the V.A., some lenders may process home loan applications on the basis of "automatic guaranty."

Lenders do not ordinarily utilize this privilege unless they are confident of the veteran's eligibility for entitlement and have every reason to believe the veteran will otherwise qualify for the loan. If loan funds are provided and for some reason the veteran is not subsequently approved by the V.A., the loan guaranty is not issued. Such circumstances would leave the lender strictly without protection in the loan investment.

At the time of application for a G.I. loan, the veteran should be prepared to pay for the appraisal fee and CRV (Certificate of Reasonable Value). The CRV determines the loan amount on which the V.A. will issue a guaranty to the lender.

The CRV is ordered through the V.A. who in turn will assign an independent fee appraiser to the case. V.A. appraisal fees in California are presently $40 for a single family residence, $55 for two units, $75 for three units and $95 for four units under the same structure. However, CRV appraisal fees may vary in different localities and states.

A CRV is effective for 129 days. Owners and builders will sometimes obtain a CRV prior to finding a veteran purchaser. In such cases, the CRV appraisal fee can not be collected from a veteran purchaser. A veteran can pay the CRV fee only when his name appears as purchaser of the subject property involving the Certificate of Reasonable Value.

At the time of loan application, the lender will require a credit statement and a financial statement from the veteran. The lender may also ask the veteran to sign an authorization form whereby his employer may verify employment history and income. Another authorization form may be required for verification of bank accounts from the veteran's banking institution.

Ordinarily, the lender will submit a "Request for Determination of Reasonable Value" immediately upon the veteran's application for the loan and payment of the CRV fee. While waiting for the CRV to be processed, the lender normally processes the credit information, financial statement and verification of employment and banking forms.

When the CRV is received and when all other necessary documents are in the lender's hands the "package" is submitted to the Veterans Administration for "prior approval." If and when the veteran and the property are approved for the loan, the loan papers are drawn and forwarded along with lender's instructions to the escrow holder.

When all loan papers and other documents are signed by the buyer and seller, the escrow holder is in position to order loan funds from the lender. After the necessary documents have been recorded, the appropriate funds are distributed and escrow is complete.

LIABILITY RELEASE FROM G.I. LOANS

After a G.I. loan has been established, it may be assumed at any time by another purchaser. There are no restrictive conditions in the mortgage instruments pertaining to such loans from the standpoint of a loan assumption. Anyone may assume a G.I. loan without having to qualify for it from the standpoint of military service, credit history, employment or financial capabilities for repayment of the loan obligation.

However, if the veteran were to sell the property securing his own G.I. loan entitlement, he would still be legally liable on that loan, even though ownership of the property is transferred to another party. The situation will exist unless the loan is paid in full in connection with the sale or the Veterans Administration issues a written release to the veteran from all future liability on the loan.

If the loan is not paid in full, and the veteran is not released from liability by the V.A. in writing, and any subsequent owner defaults on the loan, any amount which the V.A. is required to pay to the holder of the mortgage instrument under the loan guaranty contract will represent the amount the veteran will owe to the United States Government. This is so even though subsequent purchasers may assume personal liability for repayment of the loan obligation.

Immediately upon deciding to sell property secured by his own G.I. loan entitlement, the veteran should write to the V.A. office that guaranteed the loan and request the necessary forms and instructions for release from personal liability to the V.A. due to a default on the loan by a future owner of the property.

The Veterans Administration will promptly mail a form for the new purchaser to sign in agreement to accept responsibility and liability to the V.A. for the veteran's loan and the veteran will sign the form in agreement to those conditions.

It will also be necessary for the new purchaser to fill out and sign a credit and financial statement supplied by the V.A. A money order or cashiers check in an amount subscribed by the V.A. must also be attached to the credit statement as payment for a credit report to be obtained by the Veterans Administration.

Buyers with a past credit problem are not usually acceptable to the V.A. even though they may have a good credit rating and sufficient income at the time of applying for responsibility of the loan debt.

If the new purchaser is approved and accepted in substitution of the veteran for liability of the loan, the V.A. will notify all parties concerned. However, if the new purchaser is not acceptable to the V.A., only the veteran-seller is notified and it is his option, if provided in the sales agreement, as to whether to allow the loan to be assumed and remain liable or to look for another buyer who may be acceptable to the Veterans Administration in substitution for the veteran from the standpoint of future liability. It is often a matter of from thirty to sixty days before the Veterans Administration completes processing of the request.

The release from liability to the V.A. does not restore the same loan entitlement to the veteran for another G.I. loan except when using the unused portion of the entitlement, as discussed in previous pages herein, which is possible with or without having been released from liability.

CASH REQUIREMENTS FOR NEW G.I. LOANS

When property is purchased at a price within the maximum amount of value indicated on the Certificate of Reasonable Value or less, there is no down payment required of the veteran by the Veterans Administration. However, certain lenders may require some down payment due to varying circumstances and conditions pertaining to the buyer, the property or the existing money market and will not grant a 100 percent G.I. loan.

In the event a price exceeding the CRV value amount is paid for the property, the veteran may pay the difference in cash from his own assets and obtain his G.I. loan up to the indicated value. The veteran will be required to sign a statement to the effect that the difference between the purchase price and the CRV amount was paid from his own personal cash assets.

The veteran will ordinarily pay his own closing costs to obtain the new loan plus establishing the impound account, consisting of prepaid taxes and insurance, but the Veterans Administration, unlike F.H.A., will permit the seller or anyone else to pay all or any portion of the closing costs and impounds. The V.A. will not permit the veteran-purchaser to pay for lender's discount points, a termite inspection fee, a Truth in Lending statement fee and, unless the veteran's name appears as purchaser of the subject property on the CRV, he can not pay the CRV fee. There may be other local charges imposed in some states that the V.A. will not permit a veteran to pay when obtaining a new G.I. loan, in which case consideration to these should be given.

REFINANCING PRESENT HOME

Eligible veterans may refinance existing mortgage loans, or other liens of record, on an owned and occupied home used as his residence. Under these circumstances the veteran is permitted to pay discount points to the new lender when discount points are required for refinancing. The veteran is not allowed to pay a lender's discount points in the event of purchasing a residence on his G.I. entitlement.

PREPAYMENT OF G.I. LOANS

Since April 20, 1950, the maximum maturity on a V.A. home loan has been 30 years. Regardless of the terms of maturity of mortgage instruments, the debtor has the right to prepay at any time the entire indebtedness or any part thereof without premium or fee. If desired, the lender is permitted to withhold application of the credit for the prepayment until the next following installment date or 30 days after the prepayment, whichever is earlier. This entitles the lender to some unearned interest.

REVISIONS IN GOVERNMENT-SPONSORED LOANS

Each year, Congress enacts new laws affecting V.A. and F.H.A. regulations. Therefore, it may be advisable to keep abreast of these revisions by subscribing to some of the various publications that keep their readers informed in connection with major changes. In some instances, when the changes are newsworthy, local newspapers will print the details.

Lenders are naturally kept informed on such matters and are an excellent source of information concerning government-sponsored lending practices, rules, and regulations.

18

Financing–F.H.A.-Insured Loan Programs

The National Housing Act of 1934 (Public Law 479–73rd Congress) was passed by Congress in June of that year and was signed by the President on June 27, 1934. This act created the Federal Housing Administration and the F.H.A. mutual mortgage insurance plan. The preamble to the act reads as follows: "To encourage improvement in housing standards and conditions, to provide a system of mutual mortgage insurance, and for other purposes."

When the F.H.A. plan went into effect, the lending industry more or less resented the government's entrance into such an enterprise. In particular, there was a great resentment from the standpoint of controlled interest rates and regulations concerning participating lenders, borrowers, appraisals and properties. However, as time passed, the basic concept of the Federal Housing Administration and the protection it provided to lender and borrower alike, was accepted and is now generally recognized as one of the most essential government agencies in operation.

There have been many changes and revisions through subsequent legislation from the standpoint of regulations concerning F.H.A. programs, qualifications of borrowers and properties for each of the programs and financial arrangements including maximum loan percentages and interest rates. In each case of new legislation, revisions were instigated in order to keep pace with national economic and housing conditions. As time goes on, there will be additional regulatory revisions and new programs may emanate from those in effect.

Regardless of past, present and future revisions, F.H.A.-insured loans are intended to benefit borrowers in the following manner:

1. Enable borrowers to obtain long-term mortgage loans based on a high ratio of loan amount to property value.
2. Reduce financing costs and cash outlay upon loan origination.

225

3. Monthly payments of taxes and insurance included with fixed principal and interest payments in order to insure having sufficient funds to meet tax and insurance obligations when they become due and payable. Fixed monthly principal and interest payments will amortize the loan to a full repayment of the obligation.

4. The borrower's financial capabilities are analyzed in order to determine whether or not there is the possibility of overextension of debt and subsequent financial loss through foreclosure on the property being purchased.

5. Regulatory measures concerning minimum structural standards required on F.H.A. insured loans.

6. Standardized appraisal techniques in determining the market value of properties prior to issuing a commitment for F.H.A. loan insurance to the lender.

F.H.A. MORTGAGE INSURANCE

The Federal Housing Administration does not advance loan funds to borrowers, but through the establishment of the Mutual Mortgage Insurance Fund, lenders are protected or insured against loss in the event of default in repayment of the loan and resulting foreclosure.

Only those lenders approved by F.H.A. may participate and receive a commitment for loan insurance through the F.H.A. Mutual Mortgage Insurance Fund. All approved mortgagees (lenders) are required to service insured loans in accordance with the mortgage practices of prudent lending institutions. Other requirements for a mortgage to be eligible for insurance are as follows:

1. The mortgage must be executed on F.H.A. forms prescribed by the F.H.A. for use in the jurisdiction in which the property covered by the mortgage is situated.

2. The borrower's credit standing must be satisfactory to the F.H.A. Both the lender as well as the F.H.A. must analyze each application in order to make as certain as possible that the proposed monthly payments bear a proper relationship to the borrower's anticipated income and expenses.

It must also be established that after the mortgage is recorded, the mortgaged property is free and clear of all liens other than the insured mortgage and in the case of a home purchase there will not be outstanding any other unpaid obligation involving the acquisition of the subject property except obligations that are secured by

226

property or other collateral owned by the mortgagor independently of the mortgaged property.

The mortgagor need not be an occupant of the property covered by the mortgage; however, the owner-occupant mortgagor will receive a higher ratio of loan amount to property value.

3. The mortgage must be a first lien on property that conforms with the property standards prescribed by the F.H.A. and must cover the type property designed principally for residential use for not more than four families.

4. The mortgage must involve a principal obligation not in excess of the prescribed maximum loans as they apply to the various F.H.A. insured loan programs.

5. The mortgagor is obliged to establish to the satisfaction of F.H.A. that he has invested in cash or its equivalent not less than the amount of the required down payment and costs prescribed by the F.H.A. as set forth on the commitment for insurance.

6. Interest rates may not exceed those established by Congress or by the President when Congress has vested him with such authority.

7. In addition to the interest charge each mortgage provides for payment by the borrower of a sum equal to ½ of 1 percent of the average outstanding principal obligation to provide for payment to the F.H.A. of the annual mortgage insurance premium.

8. The mortgage must also provide for such equal monthly payments in advance that will amortize ground rents, taxes, special assessments, if any, and fire and other hazard insurance premiums within a period ending one month prior to the dates on which such payments become due.

9. The mortgage must contain provisions for complete amortization of the loan by its maturity. The sum of the principal and interest payments in each month shall be substantially the same. The mortgage must also become due on the first day of a month.

10. The mortgage must be executed with respect to a project that in the opinion of the Federal Housing Commissioner, is economically sound.

Application for Mortgage Insurance

It is necessary that an application for mortgage insurance be made on standard forms furnished by F.H.A. and submitted through an approved F.H.A. lender. In areas where F.H.A. financing prevails in residential sales, it is common practice for sellers to obtain an F.H.A. "conditional" commitment prior to obtaining a home buyer. These commitments cost $40 for existing structures and $50 for proposed structures. Such fees may differ in the case of some "special assistance" and multifamily projects. (This chapter primarily applies·to one to four family housing units.)

Upon receipt of the application and appropriate fee, the servicing F.H.A. office will send an appraiser to the property for inspection and an appraisal of value. If the structure meets with the established minimum structural requirements, a "conditional" commitment is issued on the basis of a regular loan program. In case the property does not meet the established standards, F.H.A. will write a letter of explanation to the lender who submitted the application.

The property value is indicated on the commitment and the buyer's estimated loan costs are added to that amount as a vehicle to increase the loan amount for the buyer. The maximum loan amount is computed on the basis of the total value and buyer's estimated nonrecurring or one time costs in obtaining the new loan. Commitments are mailed to the lenders who apply for them.

When a buyer is found who desires a new F.H.A.-insured loan, the lender will process his loan application. If from the buyer's credit report financial statement and verification of employment and bank account, the lender and F.H.A. determine the buyer is qualified for the loan requested, the existing "conditional" commitment is converted to a "firm" commitment of mortgage insurance to the lender on the. basis of the loan amount.

If no "conditional" commitment exists at the time the buyer applies for the loan, his application and fee, credit report, financial statement and verifications are submitted to F.H.A. at the same time. Inspection and appraisal of the property is then made and a "firm" commitment is issued by F.H.A. along with approval of the purchaser. In the event the purchaser is not approved, only a "conditional" commitment is issued and the lender is notified of the purchaser's rejection by F.H.A. and for what reason.

When, as a result of a preliminary examination, a lender rejects the loan application, the application fee is returned by the lender. If the case is submitted to F.H.A. and rejected, the application fee is not returned.

"Conditional" and "firm" commitments are the property of the submitting lender. After a commitment has been issued to one lender and another lender is chosen to process the loan, the commitment may be reassigned to the new lender at the original lender's option. In most instances, the assignment from one lender to another is done as a matter of courtesy, but where considerable work has been completed beforehand, there may be a charge levied for the transfer of a commitment.

Commitment for F.H.A. Mutual Mortgage Insurance

Upon completion of the processing of an application for mutual mortgage insurance, the F.H.A. will either issue a Commitment of Insurance or forward a letter rejecting the application. Each commitment outlines the terms and conditions under which the loan will be insured. Full compliance with the terms and conditions must be accomplished in order that the lender may obtain the insurance endorsement. If repairs to existing structures are required, a compliance report must be ordered from the F.H.A. and final approval obtained thereof prior to the disbursement of loan funds.

In the case of new construction, it is essential that compliance inspections be ordered at specified intervals designated and that any corrections called for in resulting reports be remedied if the lender is to secure final approval for insurance of the loan.

Funding an F.H.A.-Insured Loan

The note and mortgage forms signed by the borrower must be the F.H.A. forms as prescribed for the state or area in which the mortgaged property is located. When all conditions indicated on the Commitment for Insurance have been fulfilled, the mortgage instruments may be recorded and loan funds disbursed.

At the time of closing an F.H.A. loan, the lender is required to collect accrued taxes and hazard insurance premiums in order that subsequent monthly payments collected will provide sufficient funds to pay the obligations as they become due and payable. It is also necessary to collect one month mutual mortgage insurance premium in advance when the first regular monthly payment does not become due until the first day of the second month following date of recording. The lender is to maintain these monthly mutual mortgage insurance payments in a "reserve" account, which is a part of the loan "trust fund" or "impound account."

Upon closing an F.H.A.-insured mortgage, the lender is permitted to collect an initial service charge (loan origination fee) not to exceed one percent of the loan amount. The usual recording and title fees, tax service fees and other one time loan costs customarily charged to the buyer in various localities are also collected at that time. (These costs are discussed more in detail in the chapter *Buyer's Closing Costs—New Loans.*)

Monthly Payments

Payments on F.H.A. loans are on a monthly basis and are required to be applied in the following order:

1. Mortgage Insurance premium.
2. Ground rents, taxes, special assessments and fire and other hazard insurance premiums.
3. Interest on the mortgage.
4. Amortization of the principal amount.

F.H.A. and V.A. loan payments are always due on the first day of a month and delinquent after the fifteenth day of that month if not paid. Payments not received by the fifteenth of the month in which they become due are subject to a two percent penalty based on the total monthly payment. Lenders are authorized to collect this penalty to offset the expenses involved in collecting delinquent accounts.

Partial payments are not acceptable and, as a general rule when the loan is in delinquency for more than two payments, the lender cannot accept less then the total amount of payments and penalties due. This is in connection with default reports required to be submitted to F.H.A. covering delinquent loans in order for the lender to be eligible to collect the mutual mortgage insurance in the event of foreclosures.

Lender's Recovery Through M.M.I. Funds

Approved lenders are obligated to "service" insured loans in accordance with prudent lending practices. In the event of default, the lender or the servicing agent handling the account is required to use due diligence in collecting the amounts due. The F.H.A. holds the mortgage holder responsible for proper servicing even though the actual servicing may be performed by an agent of the mortgagee (lender). However, either party may report to F.H.A. on a "Notice of Default Status" form completely executed periodically as required by the F.H.A.

At any time within one year of the default, the lender must acquire title to the property by means other than foreclosure or must institute foreclosure proceedings to foreclose the mortgage. When foreclosure proceedings have been instituted, the lender must notify F.H.A. on the appropriate forms.

Upon foreclosure, the lender obtains title to the property and has the option of conveying title to the property to the Federal Housing Commissioner within a period of thirty days, at which time application is made for debentures of the Mutual Mortgage Insurance Fund. Otherwise, the lender may hold the property for speculative purposes and not apply for debentures of the M.M.I. fund, in which case the M.M.I. contract is terminated. Most lenders convey the property to the Commissioner and apply for debentures.

It is mandatory that the foreclosed property must have a good merchantable title and be undamaged by fire, other hazards or waste.

Debentures

Debentures, as applied against Mutual Mortgage Insurance Funds, are a government voucher of indebtedness issued to the lender as a repayment of the loan balance, advanced taxes and interest at the debenture rate of interest from start of foreclosure, which were lost through the process of default foreclosure of the property to satisfy the obligation. These debentures are guaranteed as to both principal and interest by the United States government and are highly marketable. Interest rates and maturity dates vary.

In addition to the debentures, the lender will receive a Certificate of Claim that becomes payable after the property is resold by the F.H.A., provided sufficient funds are obtained through the F.H.A. resale.

The Certificate of Claim is to cover the lender's "out-of-pocket" foreclosure expenses, interest from default to the start of foreclosure, interest due over the debenture rate to the face of the note, and reasonable amounts to cover the costs of foreclosure and maintenance of the property prior to the conveyance of the property to the F.H.A. Commissioner.

This certificate specifies the amount to which the holder is entitled, contingent and dependent upon the net amount realized from the property and payable only upon the full liquidation of that property. The Commissioner deducts from the net realized for the property all expenses incurred by him in handling, dealing with and disposing of the property. If there be an excess then realized over the debentures and cash advanced for interest on them such excess is paid over to the certificate holder.

BUYER'S FINANCIAL QUALIFICATIONS

The primary objective of the Federal Housing Administration is to assist the general public into becoming homeowners. The various low-interest, long-term loan programs requiring a small percentage of the purchase price as a cash investment, are not intended as a trap whereby the purchaser becomes financially overextended and cannot meet the monthly payments on a current basis. Therefore, F.H.A. has developed certain guidelines for qualifying applicants desiring a new F.H.A.-insured loan in order to minimize the possibility of hardship and/or subsequent foreclosure on insured loans.

Financial Capabilities

The fact that an applicant for a new F.H.A.-insured loan earns a high monthly salary is commendable. However, grave consideration is given to "net effective" income, which is the amount left over after all fixed living expenses and monthly installment payments are paid. As a general rule, installment contract payments such as those paid on a car, T.V., furniture, etc., that have less than nine months to run, are often not counted. This would depend largely on the purchaser's stability and buying habits.

In any case, it may be advisable to multiply the total monthly payments of a prospective new F.H.A. loan by four. If the amount exceeds the "net effective income," the purchaser is liable to be rejected for that amount of loan. In such case, the purchaser-applicant would be forced to reduce the loan amount to a point within his limitations or buy a less-expensive home.

F.H.A. may consider the applicant's base salary plus 50 percent of the usual overtime and bonuses that are verified by an employer. A Veterans Administration school allotment or any other income that may be verified may also be included in the total income. Net income from rental properties may be considered when substantiated by a schedule.

Up to 100 percent of the wife's income, at the time of this writing, may be included if she is over 32 years of age with at least four years employment history, because at that age she is not considered to be so vulnerable to having to leave her employment to raise a family. By submitting a certificate issued by a qualified physician that states that pregnancy is impossible, a wife of a lesser age may be counted in on the basis of 100 percent of her income.

When the wife is over 25 years of age and is employed as a professional practitioner such as a nurse, teacher, etc. 100 percent of her income may be included with the husband's income for qualifying. Only 50 percent of her income may be considered if she is under 25 years of age.

If the wife is under 25 years of age and is employed other than on a professional status, but has been on the same job for over two years, 50 percent of her income may be included. However, if she is under 25 years of age with less than two years employment history, her income will receive little or no consideration.

The maximum amount of income a co-signer or co-mortgagor may contribute toward the qualifying monthly income is an amount equal to the monthly payment or the difference between the buyer's montly earnings and expenses, whichever is smaller.

In some instances, child support or alimony is considered when it is

232

verified in writing by the attorney who handled the divorce case or a copy of the interlocutory decree must be submitted.

All income must be verified or documented by the applicant when applying for a new F.H.A. loan. It is considered perjury to falsify an applicant's financial statment concerning income, obligations, or employment.

Employment History

The applicant's history of employment is an extremely important factor in obtaining a new F.H.A.-insured loan. One who changes employment frequently is normally not considered a good risk from the standpoint of stability. Under ordinary circumstances, the applicant must have been on his present job for at least one year, or in the same type of work for that length of time. If an applicant has been on his present job for less than six months, his previous employment must be verified.

In any case, his credit report must verify a two-year history of employment. A small amount of credit may be allowed for part-time employment provided the applicant has been so employed on the same job for at least one year and it does not conflict with his full-time employment.

Anyone employed in the trades such as a construction worker may be required to provide W-2 tax forms at least for the previous two years. His standing in the trade union also may have to be verified.

Self-employed applicants will be required to prove their capacity to pay monthly house payments by providing a current profit and loss statement showing the condition of the business. If his business is new, he may be required to substantiate at least two years' experience related to his new business.

Graduating college students who have received a job offer in the near future and have accepted it may possibly qualify by providing proof of the proposed employment.

Salesmen who work only on a commission basis must prove actual earnings on the job by providing W-2 tax forms or an income tax return for the previous two years.

A convicted felon on parole must be released from parole prior to obtaining an F.H.A.-insured loan.

Qualified single or unmarried persons may purchase a home, but if they have been married and the divorce is not yet final, it may be necessary to obtain a quit claim deed signed by the ex-spouse. This may be particularly true in the states where community property laws are a factor in property ownership between husband and wife.

233

When an applicant has a serious problem in the matter of qualifying for a new F.H.A. loan, it may be beneficial to contact someone in authority at the nearest F.H.A. office serving the area in which the property lies.

Credit History

At the time of applying for a new F.H.A. loan, the applicant will be required to complete a credit information form. Some of the information required will pertain to the applicant's full name and marital status; if married, his wife's full name and how long the marriage has existed.

There will be questions concerning present address and previous addresses, where employed, how long on the job, and the employment history for husband and wife for the past five years or more. Information concerning banking habits, credit references, character references, and past credit difficulties will also be required.

There will be questions concerning various cash, real property, and personal property assets including a description of existing insurance policies and the cash surrender value on them, if any.

A credit report fee is normally collected by the lender at the time of applying for the new loan. The fee may vary from one locality to another and will depend to a great extent on whether or not investigation of the applicant's credit history necessitates out-of-town inquiries.

Applicants who have always paid cash for previous purchases and have never established a credit history are normally at a great disadvantage in obtaining a new F.H.A.-insured loan since it is necessary for a credit report to accompany the loan application being submitted to F.H.A.

The lender, as a member of a local credit-reporting agency, will submit the credit information form to the proper reporting agency. The agency will verify the applicant's information and refer to their own files for any additional information they may have. The reporting agency will then issue a complete written credit report to the lender to submit to F.H.A. If the credit report is satisfactory to the lender, it is submitted.

The lender and F.H.A. will evaluate the written credit report from the standpoint of character, dependability, any domestic difficulties, the applicant's buying habits, income management, general attitude concerning obligations, bankruptcies, foreclosures, suits, and if it has been necessary for previous creditors to turn the applicant's account over to a collection agency.

When the credit report is of a satisfactory nature and all other factors concerning the buyer and the property qualifications are in order, the buyer will be approved by F.H.A. for the loan. A derogatory credit report may motivate the lender or F.H.A. to reject the applicant as a mortgagor. However, in some instances the applicant may be able to disprove the derogatory claims or otherwise provide a sound and plausible explanation. In that case, the application may be resubmitted for consideration.

The primary objective in the requirement for a satisfactory credit rating is to minimize the possibilities of the lender's having collection problems or a subsequent foreclosure suit on his hands.

Cash Investment Requirements

F.H.A. regulations do require the new loan applicant to have some sort of financial interest or cash investment in property on which a loan is to be insured. Cash investment requirements vary with each of the current programs, depending on the buyer's qualifications for one of the "special assistance" programs and the price of the property.

In some instances, the purchaser-applicant may be required to invest a cash down payment and establish an impound account. Other programs may require only an impound account to be paid in cash and established by the applicant.

Impound accounts are prepaid items consisting of taxes, special assessments, insurance, and mutual mortgage insurance reserves. These accounts are often referred to as "trust funds" or "trust accounts." Once established, impound accounts are maintained by being paid to the lender along with the monthly principal and interest payments. The lender holds the funds in spearate accounts and disburses payments for taxes, special assessments, hazard insurance, and mutual mortgage insurance when these items of expense become due and payable.

Sellers are not permitted to pay any portion of the buyer's impound account, but they are permitted to pay any of the buyer's loan expenses or costs that have no bearing on impound account funds.

Buyers are not allowed to pay any part of the loan "discount points" involved in obtaining a new F.H.A. loan. However, lenders may collect one percent of the loan amount from the buyer, which is called a loan origination fee or a service fee, for processing and "packaging" the loan for submission to F.H.A. (More details in this connection will be found in the chapter *Buyer's Costs—New Loans.*)

New loan "discount points" are based on one percent of the loan amount for each "point" charged by the lender for funding the loan and are withheld from the seller's funds at the time of "funding the loan." (This item of cost is discussed in the chapter *Seller's Costs—New Loans.*)

Secondary financing on the property on which a new F.H.A. loan is

235

being obtained is not permitted. However, secondary financing involving another property may be utilized in lieu of down payment and closing costs in cash provided the buyer has sufficient equity in the other property or an existing mortgage document and the seller is willing to take such in lieu of cash.

Any asset owned by the buyer that may be converted to cash by the seller is allowed by the F.H.A. to be used as down payment and/or closing costs if the seller is willing to accept it instead of cash. Such assets must equal or exceed in value the amount being allowed for it by the seller. Boats, automobiles, or any personal or real property assets of material value may be used as a down payment and/or closing costs in a new F.H.A. loan transaction.

Cash received from blood relatives for the required cash investment is acceptable in the transaction by the F.H.A. provided it is a gift. The relatives lending the money to the borrower must sign and submit a "gift letter" stating that the funds are a gift and repayment is not expected.

F.H.A. loan applicants may borrow money on life insurance policies, savings accounts, stocks and bonds, or other assets to obtain the necessary funds provided the facts are made known on the financial statement portion of the loan application. The F.H.A. is concerned only to the extent that repayment of such borrowed funds will not cause the applicant's total obligations to become out of balance in ratio to net effective income.

The purchaser must certify on the F.H.A. loan application that he is to be an owner-occupant of the subject property if he is to be approved for the maximum available loan under the program for which he is qualified to purchase.

There is no limitation concerning the price an applicant may pay for a home. However, any difference between the purchase price of the property and the value indicated on an F.H.A.-insured loan commitment must be paid by cash or with other assets owned by the buyer.

In order for the home to qualify for the maximum F.H.A. loan, the structure must have been built under F.H.A. specifications or it must have been constructed for at least one year if not built under F.H.A. specifications. Otherwise, the maximum loan will be reduced by an amount equal to approximately 15 percent.

All home-purchase maximum F.H.A. loans are based on sales price of the property or on F.H.A. appraised value, whichever is less. "Conditional" commitments for F.H.A. loan insurance are issued on the basic percentage ratio of maximum loan to F.H.A. value. When the sales price is less than appraised value indicated on the commitment, the maximum loan will be reduced accordingly upon final approval.

F.H.A. commitments indicate appraised value plus the estimated amount of the buyer's nonrecurring closing costs, which are one-time expenses customarily paid by the buyer in the locality in which the property lies. The total of the appraised value and closing costs is the amount on which maximum loans are computed. The purpose of adding the buyer's estimated costs to the appraised value is to provide a higher loan for the buyer, thereby reducing his overall cash outlay.

In effect, the buyer is financing the greater portion of his nonrecurring costs because the maximum loan percentage is applied to them as well as to the appraised value of the property. This is done only when the buyer is paying his own nonrecurring costs in cash. If the seller pays the buyer's nonrecurring closing costs, they are not added to the appraised value amount; therefore, the maximum loan will be lower. However, if the buyer pays the total amount of the value and closing costs for the property, the seller should pay the buyer's nonrecurring closing costs or otherwise the buyer will be paying them twice. He would be paying them once in the form of an increased loan and again in cash.

When a transaction is made in areas where property normally sells at F.H.A. value and if the sale is to be financed by a new F.H.A. loan, a fair and equitable arrangement is for the buyer to pay the appraised value price for the property plus his own recurring and nonrecurring closing costs and the seller pays his own normal closing costs. If the purchase and sales agreemnt specifies the buyer is to pay his own nonrecurring closing costs, the loan will be proportionally higher percentagewise to offset the major portion of cash the buyer will have to lay out for those costs when final settlement for the purchase is made to close escrow.

Borrower's Loan Costs

Loan costs of the borrower are outlined briefly below, but are explained in detail in the chapter *Buyer's Costs—New Loans.* Closing costs may vary in amount and structure in different sections of the nation. Therefore, consideration must be given as to the customary costs and fees charged buyers and sellers in the locality in which the property lies.

Interest and Rate

F.H.A. mortgages may bear interest at any rate agreed upon between the mortgagee and mortgagor. However, it cannot exceed the rate specified in a loan commitment or published in the Federal Register. Interest must be paid in monthly installments on the outstanding principal balance of a loan.

237

Mutual Mortgage Insurance Charge

The mortgage may provide for monthly payments by the mortgagor to the mortgagee of an amount equal to one-twelfth of the annual mortgage insurance premium. Mortgage insurance premiums are based on one-half of one percent of the loan balance at the inception of the loan and on each anniversary of the recording date thereafter.

Taxes, Special Assessments, and Hazard Insurance

A mortgage must provide for such equal monthly payments by the mortgagor to the mortgagee as will amortize the ground rents, if any, and the estimated amount of all taxes, special assessments, if any, and fire and other hazard insurance premiums.

Other Charges or Costs

In addition to the foregoing charges, which are referred to as "recurring costs" or "prepaids," the mortgagor may be required to pay the following "nonrecurring costs": F.H.A. application fee, an initial service charge in an amount equal to one percent of the mortgage amount (loan origination fee), recording fees, credit report, survey, title search, and title insurance.

Mortgage Discounts

The lender is permitted to charge "discount points" to the borrower on an F.H.A.-insured loan only under the following conditions:
1. When the borrower is building a home for his own occupancy.
2. If the borrower is a builder constructing homes for sale and taxes the mortgage in his own name.
3. If the borrower is refinancing a mortgage on property that he owns.
4. If the borrower is purchasing the property from a governmental agency or municipal corporation that is precluded by statute from paying a mortgage discount.

Property Qualifications for F.H.A.-Insured Loan

In localities where FHA financing is extensively utilized, a commitment for an F.H.A. loan should be ordered immediately upon placing a home on the market for sale.

Since all F.H.A.-insured loan commitments and loan applications must be submitted through an F.H.A.-approved lender, it would be necessary to contact an F.H.A.-approved mortgage broker, a bank, savings and loan association, or a real estate agency, which may assist in applying for a commitment. It will be necessary to supply information concerning the structures, property description, taxes and special assessments, utilities, and so on, to the institution who will process the application and submit a request form along with the $40 application fee to F.H.A.

An F.H.A. representative will appraise the property and, provided the property meets the necessary requirements, a commitment for F.H.A. loan insurance will be issued. It is a "conditional" commitment when issued prior to the sale of a home. If the request for appraisal and the $40 fee is submitted along with a buyer's loan application, a "firm" commitment is issued.

The commitment will indicate the F.H.A. estimate of property value, estimated closing costs for the buyer, and a total of the two for loan insurance purposes. It will also disclose the maximum loan amount and maximum term of the loan on that particular property.

It is possible that certain conditions concerning structural defects will be noted on the commitment that must be corrected prior to the final issuance of loan insurance. Under those circumstances, the seller will know what must be done and may take the costs into consideration before accepting an offer lower than the listed price for sale of the property.

F.H.A. commitments are effective for six months and may be extended for an additional period of time for a $25 fee.

Sweat Equities

When painting, repairs, and reconditioning are specified as conditions to an F.H.A. commitment, it is commonly referred to as Panel D requirements and the work must be completed before mortgage insurance will be issued. A termite and dry rot inspection and clearance also comes under Panel D requirements, but can be cleared only through a licensed pest control operator when he issues a certification of clearance that the structure is free from damage or infestation by termites, fungus, or other wood-destroying organisms.

The F.H.A. will allow the buyer to supply labor and materials for correctional work appearing on the commitment and to receive credit from the seller for a fair and reasonable amount toward the down payment and closing costs. For obvious reasons, this is called a "sweat equity."

The valuation section of the F.H.A. will estimate the cost of sweat equity labor and materials as a guide in preventing an excessive allowance to the buyer. A credit of $500 will not be allowed if the estimate is $400.

However, when there is a difference of opinion and the estimate is proven to be in error, a reasonable adjustment in allowable credit will be made.

The buyer is required to have sufficient cash to provide the material or the credit will not be allowed. Any work must be completed, inspected, and approved prior to close of escrow. Inspection may be made by an F.H.A. field appraiser or, in some instances, by a representative of the lender.

This plan was primarily initiated in order to help the buyer who has a small amount of cash to work his way into owning his home. In effect, if the work must be done the seller hires the buyer to do it instead of hiring outside labor.

Sweat equity work should not be commenced by the buyer until his loan is approved and escrow is certain to close. Otherwise, if escrow failed to close and the buyer never received the property in his name, he would lose his invested time and materials.

19

Property Exchanges

In essence, the exchange of real estate is a method of selling and purchasing properties by two or more principals accomplished under the terms and conditions of one agreement.

Under certain circumstances, the one agreement may be dependent upon the consummation and finalization of other agreements. That is, it is sometimes necessary to create a multiple type of transaction with more than two principals and with more than two properties being involved. For example, A may be interested in trading for property owned by B, but B may prefer to trade for property owned by C who would be interested in A's property. In such case, A and C could exchange under an agreement that stipulated that, as a condition, B is to in turn exchange his property with A for the property A received from C. Thus, each party would eventually wind up with the property he wanted.

Other circumstances may necessitate an outright sale of a property in order to facilitate an exchange. This may be where A wants to sell his property and is not willing to exchange it. B is in a tax situation where he can only exchange and cannot sell his property, but is interested in A's property. The solution would be to find a buyer for A's property who would then exchange with B. This arrangement should be accomplished in two separate transactions under separate closings as to use the term "sale," or "purchase" in a tax-free exchange agreement could possibly negate a full tax savings for one or more of the principals to the exchange.

On the face of it, the entire procedure could be simplified through outright sales and purchases. However, under ordinary circumstances, most investors are primarily interested in tax savings, tax shelters, and minimum taxable gains as to income tax consequences.

INCOME TAX FACTORS

The Internal Revenue Service is regulated by laws that provide for a

241

deferment of tax payment on gains resulting in a property exchange type of transaction, provided certain conditions prevail in the exchange. In some transactions, an exchange may be considered "tax-free" where there is no cash or property other than real estate, except a personal residence, received by the taxpayer.

The receipt of cash, stocks, bonds, etc., is called "boot." Boot also includes real estate used solely for a residence and the assumption of a mortgage. The taxpayer who receives boot is not going to receive a full tax deferment in an exchange, as taxable gain is recognized to the extent of boot received.

There are also other qualifications required in connection with tax savings as to the taxpayer's operational classification—whether or not the properties being exchanged are of a "like-kind" nature and if any properties received are to be held for resale.

Real estate exchanges, for the most part, are complex transactions that can either work to an advantage or a disadvantage for the average client. Therefore, prudent exchange brokers and agents are continually aware of the many pitfalls into which their clients may fall, but at the same time, they must be aware of the potential advantages for clients in order to properly guide them. Brokers and their agents must obtain all the facts concerning the client's present property, tax situation, and reasons for a contemplated sale or exchange in order to be an effective service to the client in the selection of new properties and the disposal of the client's present property.

In many instances, after analyzing and evaluating the client's tax situation, the broker may find it advisable to consult a tax accountant or an attorney trained in tax matters and knowledgable as to current Internal Revenue Service regulations. Local and state regulations must also be considered in income and investment properties.

An explanation of the more commonly used technical words and phrases that have a bearing on property exchanges as to income tax consequences pertaining to investment and income properties, is given briefly in the following paragraphs. This information is merely to provide a general idea of the factors into which further counseling, study, and understanding should be applied.

CAPITAL ASSETS

As a general rule, most property owned by a taxpayer may be considered as being a capital asset. Interpretation by the Internal Revenue Service as to whether or not a capital asset may receive capital gains treatment on income tax returns may depend on the taxpayer's occupation and the intended purpose or usage for which the property is being held.

Under the Internal Revenue Code, the following properties, and the circumstances for which they are being held, are eliminated as to qualifying as capital assets whereby capital gain or loss treatment may be applied for income tax purposes.

1. The taxpayer's stock in trade, which may be included in inventory.
2. Real or personal property held primarily for sale to customers in the ordinary course of the taxpayer's trade or business.
3. Depreciable property used in the taxpayer's trade or business.
4. Real property used in the taxpayer's trade or business. (Such property may qualify for special treatment under Section 1231, which is discussed later.)
5. A copyright, a literary, musical, or artistic composition, or similar property, whether created or acquired by the taxpayer.
6. Accounts or notes receivable acquired in the ordinary course of trade or business for services rendered or from the sale of stock in trade or property primarily held for sale to customers in the ordinary course of trade or business.
7. Certain government obligations purchased on a short-term investment basis.
8. Although the taxpayer's personal residence is considered to be a capital asset, a loss resulting from the sale or exchange of it is not deductible for income tax savings purposes.

There are exceptions to the properties listed which, although not being considered as capital assets, may receive the same preferential treatment on sale or trade at a gain as capital assets subject to the depreciation recapture rules. This means that all or a portion of gains may be treated as ordinary income. However, the full deduction of losses are allowed. These exceptions are contained in provisions under the Internal Revenue Code Section 1231.

Section 1231 Property

Various types of property such as livestock, crops, timber, certain mining products and real estate under specified conditions are included in this section. The primary condition of qualifying the above for special capital asset income tax treatment is that such property must be held for more than six months.

Where real property used in a trade or business is held for more than six months, a gain or loss from the sale or exchange of it is treated as though it were a capital gain or loss as the case may be. The same may apply to any depreciable property used in a trade or business held for more than six months and not considered a capital asset.

Real Property as a Capital Asset

When real estate is held by the taxpayer for the sole purpose of investment or income production and is not used in his trade or business and is not held primarily for sale to customers, the property may be considered as a capital asset. Upon sale or exchange of such property, capital gains tax treatment may be applied. Capital losses may offset capital gains and taxes are paid on the net results.

Even though a noncapital asset may receive the capital gains treatment under Section 1231, there could be a difference in the tax consequences, when offsetting gains with losses if one property is a capital asset and the other is a Section 1231 property.

Classification of the Taxpayer

The capital gains treatment is available only to investors. Where the taxpayer is considered by the Internal Revenue Service to be a "dealer," the capital gain benefits do not apply and any gains are taxed on an ordinary income basis. The question often arises with the IRS as to whether the taxpayer is to be classified as an investor or a dealer when the taxpayer's principal occupation and source of income is as a real estate broker, subdivider, developer, or builder. However, any taxpayer, regardless of occupation, may be classified as a dealer when an unusual number of sales, purchases, and exchanges occur within a short span of time.

CAPITAL GAINS

Capital gains are classified as "long-term" or "short-term." Long-term capital gains treatment is allowed on capital assets or Section 1231 assets that have been held for more than six months at the time of sale or exchange. Short-term capital gains treatment is given when qualified capital assets or Section 1231 assets have been held for six months, or less, at the time of sale or exchange.

Holding Period

In order to determine whether applicable assets are short-term or long-term capital or losses, the day of purchase is excluded and the day of sale is included. The six-month period is in reference to full calendar months regardless of the number of days involved. The dates of purchase and sale of real estate are normally established according to dates on which title is passed.

Property not acquired by purchase such as by gift or inheritance is governed by special rules. Gift property is usually based on the date on which the donor acquired it. On property acquired by inheritance, the holding period begins on the date of the decedent's death.

Separate Computations

In the event of capital gains or losses, it is necessary to compute short-term gains or losses and then long-term gains or losses in order to determine the net results of each. The two net results are then added together or one deducted from the other as the case may be.

When a long-term gain results, the taxpayer will pay taxes on only 50 percent of it. In the case of a net short-term gain, it is included in with the taxpayer's other income. However, short-term losses and long-term losses may be deducted for long-term gains, thereby reducing the net amount of gain, 50 percent of which is taxable.

As to net long-term capital loss deductions, the rules were modified in 1970 to provide that deduction for such losses are allowed only to the extent of gains plus the smallest of:

1. Taxable income for the year, or
2. $1,000 ($500 if married and filing a separate return), or
3. The sum of:
   (a) excess of the short-term capital loss over net long-term capital gain, and
   (b) one-half of the excess of net long-term capital loss over net long-term capital gain.

Internal Revenue Service regulations and rulings are revised periodically. If for no other reason, it would be advisable to subscribe to informational sources on the subject.

TAX BRACKET

Income tax rates graduate in an ascending scale of percentages in accordance with increased taxable ordinary income.

It is not uncommon for individual and corporate investors to seek properties on which, through depreciation and other factors, a "paper loss" may result. The effect may be to reduce their net taxable income through an investment loss and thus fall into a lower percentage bracket for tax computations. Such losses may be advantageous in an exchange type of transaction.

245

Investment "paper losses" are particularly beneficial to individuals who, in their prime periods of earning ordinary income, need to reduce their income tax percentage bracket. In their later years, when their earning power has subsided through tax-free exchanges and other tax-deferment vehicles, they could remain in the lower tax percentage brackets even with taxable gains.

COST BASIS

When a property is purchased outright, the purchase price plus acquisition expenses would be the cost basis. There are also many additional and different ways of acquiring property such as by gift, inheritance, exchange, foreclosure, replacement of seized or destroyed property, and property converted to business or rental use.

The establishment of a cost basis is extremely important since that is the amount attributable to the taxpayer's property that thereafter may be partially recovered in depreciation, except in the case of a personal residence. A portion of the acquisition cost is allocated to the improvements, which may be depreciated, and the balance to the land, which cannot be depreciated.

ADJUSTED COST BASIS

The original established cost basis may increase or decrease in time, resulting in an adjusted cost basis.

An increase in the original cost basis may occur when improvements that have an estimated life in excess of one year are added to the property. Escrow expenses, purchase commissions, legal fees and certain other capital expenditures at the time of purchase plus the purchase price are included in the establishment of the original cost basis.

A decrease in the established cost basis occurs when depreciation has been taken and deductable losses have been allowed. Also, in the event a portion of the property is sold, the amount of consideration must be deducted from the original cost basis. The amount allowed on an exchange that is in excess of basis of property traded also decreases the original established cost basis.

The following simplified example will illustrate the importance of the original cost basis and the adjusted cost basis for the purpose of computing the capital gain or loss upon disposal of the property.

246

Original Cost Basis	$80,000	Sales Price	$120,000
Capital Improvements	5,000	Less Selling Expenses	10,000
Total	$85,000	Net Proceeds	$110,000
Depreciation Deducted	6,000	Less Adjusted Cost Basis	79,000
Adjusted Cost Basis	$79,000	Capital Gain	$ 31,000

The capital gain in the above example is $31,000. To apply the capital gain treatment, deduct 50 percent, or $15,500, from the above capital gain and the difference of $15,500 is the amount on which taxes would be paid.

TAX-FREE EXCHANGE

In a tax-free exchange, the cost basis of the property traded in is to be transferred to the property received. When cash is given and/or a mortgage is assumed, the amounts involved are added to the transferred cost basis less any mortgage balance assumed on the property traded away, if such was the case.

The term "tax-free" simply means that no taxable gain is recognized by the Internal Revenue Service at the time of exchange of qualified properties. In the true sense, it is only a "tax deferment" until recognized taxable gains are evident upon the sale or exchange of the property at a later time. Certain distinctive advantages normally exist in tax deferments, although much would depend on the client's income tax situation and purpose in trading.

Provisions under Section 1031 of the Internal Revenue Code state that no gain or loss is recognized in an exchange transaction when applied under the following conditions:

1. Properties exchanged are to be solely of a "like-kind" nature.
2. Properties exchanged are to be held for investment or for use in a trade or business.
3. The basis of property exchanged is to be transferred and to become the basis of the property received.

Like-Kind Properties

If real estate is exchanged, the property received may be considered as "like-kind" provided it is real estate and both the property given up and the property received are held for use in a trade or business or for investment purposes and not held for resale or as a personal residence.

The Internal Revenue Service is not normally sympathetic from the

247

standpoint of "mistake" and "intent" in tax-free exchanges. Therefore, in the event of properties involved in a contemplated tax-free exchange being "borderline cases," it would be advisable to make certain of the qualifications prior to finalizing the exchange agreement.

Basis and Holding Period

Where it is a tax-free exchange, the basis of the property given up is transferred to the property received. The holding period of the property given up is also transferred to the property received.

Boot

It may not be an entirely tax-free exchange for all parties to the exchange where "boot" is given or received.

Boot is cash or any other nonqualified property or assets given or received in an exchange. It is considered to be a recognized gain to the extent of the boot and is, therefore, subject to tax at the time of exchange. Nonqualified property other than cash would consist of stocks, bonds, notes, personal residence, etc., and if a mortgage is assumed on the property given, it is treated as cash and considered to be boot.

When both the property given and the property received are subject to mortgages, each exchanging party receives boot in the amount of the mortgage on the property he trades away. However, each is entitled to deduct from this type of boot the amount of mortgage on the new property received for purposes of determining the recognized gain subject to tax. The difference between two mortgages could mean an increased basis for the party assuming the higher mortgage. If one party transfers cash, his basis is increased in a tax free exchange.

DEPRECIATION

The primary factor in relation to tax shelters and tax consequences for investors is the depreciation allowances available on investment- and income-producing properties. Only the improvements are depreciable; land is not.

Depreciation does eventually run out, leaving the owner of such property with very little to deduct from the income produced on which taxes are paid. In such case, the owner would be wise to exchange his property for one of a higher value and subject to a larger mortgage. Thus, a new basis and a substantial depreciation schedule could be established as an offset to income and reduction of income tax obligations.

An owner with a small remaining basis and a low mortgage balance on his income-producing property can substantially improve his tax situation by entering into a tax-free exchange transaction. In this type of exchange, the basis for the new property is the basis for the old property plus the low mortgage on the property given and the higher mortgage assumed on the property received. The following example will illustrate the point.

Jones owns a property worth $75,000 with a remaining cost basis on the building of $5,000 and a mortgage balance of $10,000. He trades for Brown's property the building on which is worth $190,000 and is subject to a mortgage of $125,000.

The basis on Jones's new property is his old basis of $5,000 plus the difference of $115,000 between the two mortgages. His new basis is $120,000 on the property received, which places Jones in a much improved tax position. He can now increase annual depreciation and at the same time increase mortgage interest and property tax deductions. In addition, he paid no capital gain taxes as such taxes are deferred until the time when he sells or exchanges the property resulting in a recognized taxable gain on which taxes must be paid.

Determining Depreciation

In order to determine properly the basis of depreciation, an allocation of real property costs must be considered. First the land and other nondepreciable property values must be established. The balance of the property cost may then be allocated to improvements such as buildings and other depreciable property.

In ordinary exchanges and sales, capital gains taxes are paid at the time taxes are paid for the year in which disposal of the property occurred. Upon receiving new property in an exchange or purchasing it, the purchaser may start out fresh in establishing a new original cost basis for acquired depreciable property. In tax-free exchanges, such is not the case since the adjusted basis of the old property is transferred to the new property. The depreciation of improvements is based on the cost value plus any additional improvements that are depreciable in other than tax-free exchange transactions.

Salvage Value

The salvage value of property that qualifies for an annual depreciation may be required to be determined and deducted from the cost basis of the asset when either the straight line or the sum of the digits methods of depreciation is used. Salvage value is the remaining value of an asset at the end of its useful life.

Determination of salvage value, as applied to real property, should be worked out and decided between the taxpayer and his accountant. Since real property tends to increase in value, accountants most often use only the allocated portion of the property to the purchase price when establishing a depreciation schedule.

Depreciation schedules, which refer to the accepted useful life term of assets by the Internal Revenue Service, may be obtained from the U.S. Treasury Department under Publication 62-21 of Revenue Procedures. Depreciation guidelines for all types of assets, including the various forms of real properties, may be found in the publication.

METHODS OF DEPRECIATION

It is the taxpayer's responsibility to establish a method of depreciation upon acquiring depreciable property and use it as an income deduction. Any reasonable method may be acceptable to the Internal Revenue Service, but the three methods most generally used are the straight-line, declining-balance, and sum-of-the-digits methods. The latter two are accelerated methods that may be used under more limited conditions and circumstances.

Straight-Line Method

The straight-line method is more commonly used for most assets that qualify for depreciation. However, if a real property qualifies for one of the accelerated methods, the taxpayer may not be receiving full tax benefits with the straight-line method.

In brief, the total cost of the asset is allocated over a prescribed number of years of useful life and depreciated in equal amounts each year. For example, a building with a cost basis of $20,000, scheduled for forty years would depreciate at $500, or 2½ percent per year, beginning with the first year.

Declining-Balance Method

This system was designed to accelerate the depreciation allowance in the first few years of the property's useful life. The allowed limitations, under certain circumstances, may vary from 125 percent, 150 percent, or 200 percent of the amount that would be allowed by using the straight-line method of depreciation.

The Tax Reform Act of 1969 created a great many revisions of rules and regulations pertaining to properties and conditions under which each of the above percentages may be utilized.

In general, properties acquired after July 25, 1969, by second and subsequent owners of residential construction may apply only the 125 percent rate, provided there is a remaining useful life of more than twenty years to the building. For structures with a remaining useful life of less than twenty years, it may be necessary to use the straight-line method.

First owners of nonresidential properties, such as commercial and industrial buildings, may be limited to the 150 percent declining-balance allowance. This would mean 1½ times the amount allowed under the straight-line computations.

Under certain circumstances, first owners of residential structures such as apartment houses, may be entitled to the 200 percent declining-balance rate, which would mean double the amount allowed under the straight-line method.

To illustrate how the declining-balance methods accelerate depreciation for the first three years, use the example given under the straight-line method and apply it to the 150 percent rate of declining balance.

The building worth $20,000, scheduled for a forty-year depreciation allows $500, or 2½ percent per year under the straight-line method, would be accelerated to one and one-half times 2½ percent to equal 3¾ percent per year. The 3¾ percent times $20,000 the first year would equal $750 depreciation allowance. Deduct the $750 from $20,000 and the remaining balance is $19,250 at the beginning of the second year.

At the end of the second year, the 3¾ percent is applied to the remaining $19,250 and works out to $721 depreciation for the second year and is deducted from the $19,250, leaving a remaining balance of $18,529 at the beginning of the third year.

At the end of the third year, the 3¾ percent applied to the $18,529 balance would amount to $694 depreciation allowance. The total depreciation allowance for the three-year period under the 150 percent declining balance would amount to $2,165, which is $665 more than would have been allowed for three years at $500 per year, or $1,500 allowance under the straight-line method.

Sum-of-the-Digits Method

When a property qualifies for the 200 percent declining-balance method, it may also qualify for the alternate sum-of-the-digits method of depreciation, which provides an even more rapid return of invested capital. Under this method, the useful life of the asset is first determined and the years are totaled to establish a fraction denominator.

Again, using the example illustrated under the straight-line method, the building with a cost basis of $20,000, after deducting salvage value, is scheduled for 40 years' depreciation.

The digits from 1 through 40, which would be 1, 2, 3, 4, through 40, totaled up would be 820. Therefore, the numerator would be 40 and the denominator would be 820. Thus, 40 divided by 820 X $20,000 for the first year would equal $975 in depreciation. The numerator decreases by 1 each succeeding year, so for the second year it would be 39 divided by 820 X $20,000 to equal $951 depreciation. The third year would be 38 divided by 820 X $20,000 to equal $925 depreciation.

Over a three-year period, the total allowable depreciation would amount to $2,851 compared to $1,500 allowed for the same period under the straight-line method. The difference of $1,351 is accelerated depreciation, the nature of which is referred to in following paragraphs under *Recapture of Depreciation.*

There is a point in time after three to five years, depending upon which method is elected, when the accelerated methods will no longer exceed the amount of annual depreciation established under the straight-line method. Under certain circumstances and conditions, it may be possible to obtain the approval of the Internal Revenue Service to switch methods of depreciation from an accelerated method to the straight-line basis. Otherwise, the owner may improve his tax situation by exchanging the property.

RECAPTURE OF DEPRECIATION

The term "recapture" is used in reference to depreciation allowances that are recovered in the sale price of the property at the time of sale. For example, if the original established cost of a building was $50,000 and the cost basis was reduced to $40,000 through depreciation and if the building sold at that time for $60,000, there would be a gain of $20,000, but $10,000 of the gain would be recaptured depreciation.

An investor's primary concern is whether the accelerated portion of the recaptured depreciation would be subject to capital gains or ordinary income treatment.

Prior to initiating the Tax Reform Act of 1969, real estate depreciation recapture rules applied to all types of real estate in a uniform manner from the standpoint of depreciation deductions taken on an accelerated basis in excess of the amount that would have been allowed under the straight-line method. Much depended on the holding period of the property. If a sale occurred within the first twelve months of ownership, ordinary income tax was paid on all recaptured depreciation deductions. If the property sold within the first eight months of the second year of holding, only 100 percent of the accelerated depreciation recaptured in excess of the straight-line method would be taxed at ordinary income rates.

After the 21st month of ownership, the 100 percent applied to the excess or accelerated depreciation recaptured, declined at the rate of 1 percent per month. Therefore, after ownership for 120 months, none of the depreciation was taxed on the basis of ordinary income and all recaptured depreciation received the capital gains treatment.

The Tax Reform Act of 1969 virtually eliminated the above allowances for all types of depreciable property except residential rental properties.

Only residential rental properties are presently qualified to receive capital gains treatment at a 1 percent per month decline of the 100 percent recapture of accelerated depreciation allowances taken in excess of straight line. However, the 1 percent per month decline does not now begin until after ownership of 100 months. After 200 months' ownership, the entire gain may conceivably receive capital gains treatment.

The 1969 law has no effect on initial owner-investors of housing projects insured under F.H.A. 221(d)(3) rent supplement or 236 rental housing projects acquired prior to January 1, 1975. Additionally, such initial owner-investors may defer tax on capital gains that may otherwise be payable, provided the subject property is sold to a nonprofit organization or cooperative and the owner reinvests the proceeds in a comparable project within one year. In such case, the nonrecognized gain would have to be used toward reducing the basis of the newly acquired rental housing project.

As to owners of nonresidential depreciable properties, under the 1969 law any accelerated depreciation taken in excess of allowable straight-line depreciation is subject to recapture as ordinary income to the extent of gain resulting from the sale regardless of how long the property is held. This rule applies to depreciation taken subsequent to December 31, 1969, on prior acquired properties as well as to later acquired properties.

There may be numerous points to be reviewed by a tax accountant or a tax attorney regarding depreciation recapture prior to entering into an exchange agreement.

EXCHANGE OF PERSONAL RESIDENCE

Upon the sale or exchange of personal residence, if held for more than six months, a capital gains treatment is allowable, but losses are not deductible. Where the structure is used solely as a personal residence, the cost basis will ordinarily consist of the original cost plus improvements, acquisition costs, and expenses. Disposition costs are a factor of deduction in determining the adjusted sale price if and when the property is sold.

In general, the sale of a residence has the same tax effect as though it were exchanged, provided any gains are invested in another residence of a value exceeding the adjusted sale price of the old residence within twelve months; or eighteen months if the new home is being constructed. Persons in active military service may also be allowed additional time under certain circumstances. The main advantage of an exchange of residences is that each party may have a place to live when the exchange is completed without the necessity of having to select another home afterwards.

Owners often exchange their residences for residential income properties in order to establish a foundation for a future estate through investment and income properties. For example, an owner may exchange his home for a duplex or a small apartment complex and have a place to live while building an equity in an income-producing property. By starting out in a small way and trading up every few years, a sizeable estate can be accumulated and at the same time establish a valuable tax shelter as a hedge against ordinary income.

Taxable gains are transferred to the residence acquired to replace it, resulting in a lower basis to be used upon the eventual sale or exchange of it. Where the adjusted sale price, which is sale price less selling expenses, exceeds the purchase price of the replacement residence, the gain taxed in the year of sale is limited to: (a) gain realized on sale of old residence, or (b) the excess of the adjusted sale price of the old residence over cost of the new. A loss on the sale or exchange of the old residence is not deductible, nor does it have any effect on the basis of the new residence.

Age 65 or Older

Once in a lifetime, persons of age 65 or older who sell or exchange their principal residences during the year may exclude a part of all their gain from gross income provided:

1. The sale or exchange is made after attaining age 65.
2. They owned and used the property as their principal residence for an aggregate total of five years or more within the eight years immediately preceding the date of sale or exchange.
3. The adjusted sale price is $20,000 or less for full exclusion of gain from gross income.

In case the adjusted sale price exceeds $20,000, only a part of such exclusion may be allowed. The part that may be excluded is the portion bearing the same ratio of percentage to the entire amount of gain as $20,000 is to the adjusted sale price. For example, if $20,000 is 90 percent of the adjusted sale price, then 90 percent of the gain may be excluded.

Widows and widowers who meet the above requirements are allowed the exclusion and if only one of a man and wife ownership is 65, they may elect the special exclusion. However, both may be eliminated from such election at a later time.

PERSONAL RESIDENCE DEPRECIATION

When a personal residence is used solely for that purpose, depreciation is not allowed. However, when a structure accommodates both a personal residence and income, or use in a trade or business, that portion of the structure so used may be allowed depreciation plus capital gain and loss treatment.

For example, a duplex where the owner lives in one side and rents the other side out to a tenant would qualify for depreciation on the rented side. In addition, an owner may depreciate any portion of his personal residence that has been allocated for use in a trade, business, or income that may contribute to his gross income. This could be a room set aside for an office, storage, display of merchandise, and numerous other uses that contribute to the owner's income on which he pays taxes.

EXCHANGE LISTINGS

In theory, any property listed for sale is potentially an exchange listing, provided an exchange is agreeable to the owner and is compatible with his future plans. A notation on listing of property for sale as to the type of property for which the owner may be willing to acquire may be sufficient.

On the other hand, there is often the situation where the owner cannot afford to sell and for tax reasons must exchange in order to receive full benefit in tax consequences. In such cases, it may be possible to modify an "authorization to sell" listing to an "authorization to exchange" listing.

Most exchange brokers, however, use printed forms devised specifically for exchanges only. Such listing forms may be of a nature to fit the individual broker's operation or the forms may be provided through local or national property exchange organizations for the purpose of conformity in the exchange of listing information.

The exclusive listing for exchange is preferable from the standpoints of

255

protection and an inventory of listings, but along with that goes the responsibility of certain promotional and advertising expenses. Since some properties for exchange are in the category of "hard to sell," which is necessary to accomplish in disposing of the property, some brokers may prefer only an "open-listing arrangement. Thus, they have the necessary information for use with prospective clients, but no particular obligation as to advertising and promotional expenses, unless of course, it is a condition contained in the open listing contract.

In many instances, exchanges are created without benefit of any type of listing and the broker's protection lies in the terms and conditions of a signed exchange agreement.

Most exchange transactions are accomplished through cooperative efforts between two or more brokerage firms or between salespeople who are members of the same brokerage firm. Exchange transactions are strictly a matter of matching up two or more clients with two or more properties, as the case may be.

THE EXCHANGE AGREEMENT

Exchange agreements should be drawn only under the supervision of experts in the field of property exchanges, which would include knowledgeable exchange brokers and/or attorneys. This would be particularly true in complex transactions where all angles of tax consequences are to be considered prior to the signing of an exchange agreement.

The format of exchange agreements is more or less uniform throughout the nation, although there may be some deviation in the phrasing of legal terminology indigenous to various states and localities.

In most instances for income tax purposes, it is necessary that offer, acceptance, and details of the terms and conditions as to the exchanged properties are contained in the same document. Payment of commission to the broker by each principal is also normally included in the exchange agreement.

The steps generally taken in the drawing of an exchange agreement are outlined in the following paragraphs.

1. The full names, addresses, and legal ownership status of the offerors, who are making the first move. Reference may be made to them as "party of the first part" or reference may pertain to the "first property," depending upon local laws and customs.
2. A complete description and address of the property owned by the first party, including details of any existing mortgage liens, tax liens,

covenants, restrictions, and any other existing conditions to be considered by the second party.

3. A complete description of the second property for which the first party proposes to exchange and the full names and addresses of the second party who owns it. The status of mortgage liens, convenants, restrictions, and any other conditions known, or believed to exist, as to the second property is also set forth at this point.

4. Specific details of terms and conditions to the exchange, beginning with the proposed value of each property, less existing mortgage liens, in order to establish equities in each of the properties. When the equities are of different amounts, it is specified as to which party is to equalize them and the manner in which it is to be accomplished. If it is to be assets other than cash, to equalize the equities such as a note, stocks, etc., the other assets are described in detail. Expenses, costs and prorations of taxes, insurance and rents, connected with the exchange properties, as well as possession dates, are set forth at this point.

5. The broker's authorization to act as agent for the first party and a statement of expected performance on the part of both parties to the exchange as to the manner in which marketable title is to be given and received may be specified at this point. The type and cost of title guarantee or insurance, according to local custom, where each property lies, is also provided for at this point in the agreement.

6. Next in order is a statement providing for the amount of and payment of commission to the authorized broker previously nominated as agent. The signatures of the first party are dated and placed under this statement of authorization for payment of commission.

7. The final statement provides for the second party's acceptance of the proposal offered by the first party, provisions for marketable title and authorization for amount and payment of commission to the designated broker acting as agent for the second party.

When a proposal, and the acceptance of it, has been signed by all parties to an exchange transaction, a legal and binding contract is in effect. As previously mentioned, there may be variations in the format of exchange agreements in relation to local laws and customs. In some states and localities, it may be legally customary for any type of real estate agreement to be drawn only by an attorney at law, while in other states, printed forms providing blank spaces to be filled in are permitted in real estate transactions. Exhibit 19-1 is a representative example of such printed forms whereby blank spaces may be filled in.

257

In any case, exchange agreements should be drawn, or blank spaces filled in, only under the supervision of persons knowledgeable in the field of property exchanges.

AGREEMENT FOR EXCHANGE

THIS AGREEMENT WITNESSETH: *That*..

...., *owner of the following described:*

FIRST PIECE *of property situate, lying and being in* ....,

County of ...., *State of* ....,
particularly described as follows, to wit:

.... *which* .... *agree to exchange for the following*

SECOND PIECE *of property owned by*...
situate in

TERMS:

is hereby authorized
to act as .... *agent......* *in negotiating an exchange,* .... *agree.... that if*
.... *shall secure an acceptance of the proposition to exchange the above described*
property on the above terms, that .... *will, within* .... *days, furnish a*
.... *from a reputable and*
reliable .... *and to furnish a good and*
sufficient Deed conveying title to the property first above described. It is also presumed and
understood that all principals to this agreement have investigated the respective properties,
and the agent or broker is hereby released from all responsibility regarding valuation of same.
The agent of any of the parties to this exchange agreement may act for and receive a com-
mission from any of the other parties hereto.

AND IT IS FURTHER AGREED *with said*...

that when .... *ha......* *secured an acceptance of the proposition to exchange the*

above described property on the above terms, ... *then pay the sum*

of .... *Dollars*
as commission for services rendered. And will allow a reasonable time for the furnishing

of a .... *and good and sufficient*
Deed conveying the second of the above described properties.

DATED AT .... *this* .... *day of* ...., *19.......*

....

EXHIBIT 19-1 AGREEMENT FOR EXCHANGE (FRONT SIDE) *
*Illustrated form courtesy of Wolcotts, 214 So. Spring St., Los Angeles, C A.

259

THIS AGREEMENT WITNESSETH: *That* ....

of ...., *owner.... of the second piece of property*

described within, hereby accept.... the proposition of exchange made therein, and upon the

terms therein stated, and agree.... to furnish a...

.... *within* .... *days, showing the*

title to said property vested in...

....*and then to furnish a good and sufficient Deed*

conveying title to said property to...

....*or assigns or* .... *representatives.*

And .... *further agree.... to pay* ....

.... *Dollars*

commission for services rendered.

DATED AT ....*this*.............*day of* ...., *19*.......

....

_____

DO NOT RECORD

This standard form covers most usual problems in the field
indicated. Before you sign, read it, fill in all blanks, and make
changes proper to your transaction. Consult a lawyer if you
doubt the form's fitness for your purpose.

EXHIBIT 19-1 AGREEMENT FOR EXCHANGE (REVERSE SIDE) *

*Illustrated form courtesy of Wolcotts, 214 So. Spring St., Los Angeles, C A.

20

Real Estate Leases

There are numerous considerations to be given as to real estate rental agreements and lease contracts. First the federal, state, and local laws must be considered in order that none of the conditions contained in the agreement are unlawful and thereby not enforceable. Next, consideration as to the suitability of the property in relation to the tenant's needs, desires, and intents must be given. Finally, consideration must be given as to the reliability and capability of both parties to deliver under the covenants, terms, and conditions designated in the agreement. The timeworn adage that, "Any agreement is only as good as the parties who make it," is particularly true in rental agreements regardless of the contract's being oral or written.

In most states, a lease for one year or less may be of a verbal nature and for a term of more than one year it must be a written contract. It is not true in all states, however; in Pennsylvania, Maryland, Indiana, and Ohio a lease for more than three years must be in writing. The maximum term for which a lease may be written may vary from state to state, but it is generally limited to ninety-nine years with exceptions pertaining to farm, grazing, and mineral lands. The recording requirements pertaining to leases also differ in various states as to the protection of third parties.

MONTH-TO-MONTH TENANCY

A month-to-month tenancy may be created at the outset through either an oral or written agreement or a written lease may ultimately become a month-to-month tenancy.

Where rents are paid on a month-to-month basis with no expressed termination period in the agreement such as would be contained in a lease, it is usually considered to be a tenancy from month to month. Thus, the tenant is a "tenant at will."

When a written or oral lease does not specify an annual rent and does not fully comply with federal, state, or local laws, it may become a

261

month-to-month tenancy. In many instances near the end of a leasing period, the landlord and tenant may mutually agree that the tenant is to remain in possession on a month-to-month basis.

A month-to-month tenancy cannot be terminated by either the landlord or tenant without one giving notice to the other under ordinary circumstances. In most states, the required termination notice must be given at least thirty days in advance, although in some states it may be shorter such as in Arizona and Alabama where the required notice may be only ten days and in North Carolina and Florida it is fifteen days.

A tenancy from month to month is considered to be a continuous agreement until terminated according to local laws. The landlord is liable to the tenant from the standpoint of possession and quiet enjoyment and the tenant is liable for rents and normal care until the proper notice has been served by one or the other.

Although a month-to-month tenancy may be only an oral agreement wherein protection for both parties is in the reliance of local and state laws, it is usually advisable to specify certain terms and conditions of the tenancy in the form of a written agreement. Thus, each party is on notice as to what is expected of him in the way of performance.

The month-to-month "tenancy at will" agreement is used primarily in the rental of residential properties rather than for business and professional types of properties. As a general rule, the business and professional tenant prefers a written lease as assurance that a move to another location will not be necessary for at least the specified term of lease.

Residential rentals are generally on a more personal level and, depending on the landlord's future plans and purpose in renting, the tenant may often remain in that capacity for as long as he likes, provided he pays his rent and meets all other contractual obligations either written or oral.

When a "tenant at will" defaults, it is simply a matter of the landlord serving the proper termination notice as prescribed by local laws. The tenant has the same rights of termination and may vacate the premises upon serving proper notice.

The required termination notice, the number of days in advance it must be served, and the conditions under which it may be given will vary from state to state. Termination is discussed more fully later in this chapter in connection with leases.

Since there is no specified expiration of a month-to-month tenancy regardless of how long the tenant remains in possession, the agreement need not be in writing as it is with leases for terms of one year or more in most states and up to three years or more in other states. In the absence of a written condition in an agreement, local laws become operable and apply to a tenancy at will or a tenancy at sufferance. A written lease in effect under certain conditions for which a termination may occur usually reverts to a tenancy at will or to a tenancy at sufferance and the operation of it will then become subject to local laws pertaining to such classified tenancies.

Most residential printed general lease forms may be modified to become a month-to-month tenancy agreement simply by so stating the fact in the form and eliminating the ending, or expiration, date of the agreement. Otherwise, in the absence of such agreement being drawn by legal counsel, printed forms for month-to-month tenancies may ordinarily be found in any stationery store in most localities.

The effect of such written agreements is more or less to provide a memorandum of the transaction as to terms and conditions and the performance expected of the landlord and the tenant. For example, a month-to-month tenancy agreement for the rental of a residence may be outlined as follows:

MONTH-TO-MONTH TENANCY AGREEMENT

This agreement, executed in duplicate at _____, on this day of _____, by and between _____ Landlord and _____ Tenant.

Witnesseth: That for and in consideration of the payments of rents and the performance, by Tenant, of the herein contained covenants, the Landlord does hereby demise and let unto the Tenant, and Tenant hires from Landlord, for use as a residence, those certain premises with appurtenances located at_____

_____.

This month-to-month tenancy shall commence the _____ day of _____ and at a monthly rental of $_____ per month payable in advance on the _____ day of each and every month.

It is further mutually agreed between Landlord and Tenant as follows:

The covenants and conditions of the agreement are then itemized by number and stated. A few of the more common points to consider are:

1. The number of occupants, adults and children to be allowed.
2. That the tenant is not to violate any local ordinances or state laws on the premises.
3. Whether or not the Tenant may sublet all or part of the premises.
4. The termination of the agreement in the event of default.
5. The required tenant's care and maintenance of the premises, including grounds.
6. Which party is to pay water bills and other utilities.
7. Which party will be responsible for repairs to plumbing and heating.

8. That the consent of the Landlord is necessary prior to Tenant making any alterations or improvements to the premises.
9. The landlord's right to enter the premises at reasonable hours for purposes of inspection of premises; this normally extends rights to agent for landlord.
10. The number of days required by either party for termination of the agreement.
11. That the tenant is to pay expenses of any legal action necessary as to termination, eviction and other.
12. The required security and cleanup and damage deposits and disposition of them.

A receipt for any monies tenant pays at the time of signing the agreement is also often included, for example: "$_____ hereby received as deposit to be applied to first month rent. $_____ hereby received as cleanup and damage deposit," and so on.

YEAR-TO-YEAR TENANCY

In some instances, where the tenant needs the assurance of at least one year in possession of the property such as some types of farm operations, a year-to-year tenancy may be created. Like a month-to-month tenancy, a year-to-year tenancy is a continuous agreement until the proper notice of termination is given. Rents may be paid on an annual basis, but there is no lease for a definite period of time.

If the tenant remains in possession for one day in excess of a given year, he may be considered to be "holding over" and may be liable for another year of rent in some states. In other states the laws in this connection have been either abolished or restricted as to the additional term of liability.

The periods of termination notice as to a year-to-year tenancy may vary under the laws of different states from thirty days to six months. Either party is bound by the required advance notice of termination prescribed by local laws.

LEASE AGREEMENTS

A lease agreement may be of an oral nature when it is for a term of one year or less, but in most states it must be a written agreement for a term in excess of one year. An agent may be required under the laws of some states to have a written authorization from the landlord to execute a lease for a period in excess of one year.

The laws of some states provide that a written lease of an extended term must comply with the requirements applicable to deeds. In other states, a written lease may be considered only as a contract without such requirements. In effect, a lease is a contract and also a conveyance by the lessor (landlord) to the lessee (tenant) of the right of occupancy as to the property for a definite term specified in the lease agreement.

The requirements mentioned above may be that the lessor and spouse must sign the instrument under acknowledgment of signatures for the purpose of recording in the public records. Also, as a contract in any state, the lessor and lessee must be of age, of sound mind, and be capable of delivery. If either the lessor or lessee is a corporation, the signatures must be of those persons authorized by the directors or stockholders to act in behalf of the corporation.

The lessor's signature to a lease and delivery to the lessee is necessary for it to be valid and effective. However, it may not always be necessary for the lessee to sign it if he accepts the lease and takes possession of the premises. As a general rule, where there is no intent or requirement that the lease is to be recorded, the lessor may sign one copy of the lease for the lessee and the lessee will sign a copy of the lease for the lessor. An agent will often retain a copy of the lease containing the signatures of both parties.

For purposes of later recording the instrument in public records, the signatures of lessor and lessee should be acknowledged by a notary public or an official who may function in that capacity for recording purposes.

TERM OF THE LEASE

Leases are often classified as "short-term" or "long-term." The laws of most states have the same effect on one as to the other with the possible exception being in some states where certain properties are limited as to the number of years a lease may be in effect.

For example, a short-term lease is generally considered to be for a period of ten years or less, while a long-term lease may extend to ninety-nine years with the right of renewal. But, the laws of Nevada may restrict the lease term of agricultural and grazing land to ten years and land to be used primarily for mining may be limited to a lease term not to exceed thirty-five years. Land for horticultural or agricultural purposes may be limited to fifteen years in California.

Other states' laws may prohibit long lease terms on various types of properties, which would make it advisable to become familiar with local laws in this connection in order to avoid entering into an unlawful lease contract.

Exact specification of the lease term is essential for complete under-standing. Under certain circumstances, the phrasing, "one year from date" or "from one date to another date" may be technically questionable. To specify the term "commences on a certain date and ends at a certain time on a certain date" may eliminate future disagreement.

LEASE FORM

Since there are so many different types of income properties, it is often necessary to revise, modify, or add to printed lease forms even though there may be a distinct similarity of purpose as to two different properties. For example, a lease form devised to apply to store space in a shopping center would necessarily contain terms, conditions, and considerations that would be different than those contained in application to the identical type of business leasing an independent store building located elsewhere. As another example, the lease forms used in large apartment complexes may differ from those used in a small apartment house.

LEASING METHODS

There are many different methods on which the payment of rents on a lease may be based. Those most commonly used are as follows:

Fixed Rent Lease

Rents are specified for an agreed amount for the full term of the lease, usually paid on a monthly basis in equal amounts. Tenant normally pays his own utilities in addition to rents. Most leases contain an Escalation Clause, which provides for increased rents in direct proportion to future property tax increases.

Net Lease

Rents are specified in a fixed amount for the lease term. In addition, the tenant pays all leasehold expenses such as utilities, insurance, property taxes, maintenance of improvements, and repairs to the improvements except structural.

Participating Expense Lease

Rents are specified in a fixed amount for term of lease. This method is often used in multi-office buildings where the proportionate share of expenses such as utilities, building maintenance, increased property taxes, and increased hazard insurance are proportionately shared by the tenants and paid in addition to rents.

Escalator Lease

This method is also called a Step-Up Lease. The rents are established on a lower basis at first and are then increased periodically to a larger amount. It is often used in the instance of a new business where increased sales volume and profits are anticipated in the future. It may also be used as a hedge against future inflationary increases in expenses.

Percentage Lease

Minimum rents may be established in this type of lease and are then increased in direct proportion to gross sales or income volume. This method is often used for tenants who conduct retail and services types of operations located in shopping centers, although it is not limited to such locations.

Sale and Lease Back

This type of leasing arrangement is normally accomplished by the larger corporate tenants such as chain store operations or industries with specific needs in design and utilization of the premises. Smaller operations may often use this device also to fit their requirements. In addition to having the desired premises design for operational function, the sale-lease-back arrangement provides many other advantages.

For example, a company may buy the land and erect the desired improvements then sell the entire package to an investor. The investor is then the lessor and the company becomes the lessee on a long-term lease basis. Thus, their invested capital in real estate is regained for use in the stock in trade of the business or for other purposes.

In another instance, a company may need some investment capital for their business operation. Rather than to mortgage the premises on which the business is located, where the property is owned by the company, it will sell the property and lease it back from the investor.

In a sale-and-lease-back transaction, the lease term is usually from twenty to thirty years with a renewal clause for an extended period of time. The lease term will normally amortize the lessor-investor's purchase price. In some cases, the lease may provide the company with an option to repurchase the property at a predetermined figure. Extreme caution is advisable in this connection since such arrangements have, on occasion, been ruled by the courts as nothing more than a long-term loan.

Ground Lease

In effect, as to the lessor, this method of leasing could be compared to a net lease, with the primary difference being that the lessee will construct the improvements and pay for it. In addition, the lessee will pay property taxes, insurance, maintenance costs and repairs to the improvements.

At end of the lease term, ownership of the improvements will revert to the lessor. There are a great many advantages for both the lessor and lessee in this type of lease and also some potential disadvantages, which could result in the lessee's failure in the enterprise and a building of a design for which there may be a limited demand in the future.

LEASE FORM ESSENTIALS

There are certain specific essentials to be included in the format of a written lease in order that it may become a valid instrument.

Although there is no such thing as a lease form adaptable for use in all situations for all properties, the general lease form illustrated as Exhibit 20-1 contains most of the covenants, terms, conditions, and provisions fundamentally incorporated into most lease contracts. The information generally required in the formation of a valid contract is as follows:

Date

The date on which the instrument was drawn may be vital for a future reference.

Names and Addresses

The full names, addresses and ownership status of the lessors as well as the lessees is important for proper identification.

Intended Usage of Premises

It is advisable to establish within the contract, the exact nature of the lessee's business and his intended usage of the premises. The tenant must be in a compatible situation with other tenants and must also be capable of utilizing the property in a lawful capacity under existing zoning and other local laws.

Complete Description of Leased Premises

The full address of the property and a complete description of the area included in the contract, including extra storage space, parking spaces allocated, etc., will eliminate future disagreements.

268

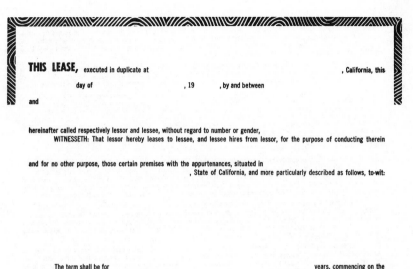

THIS LEASE, executed in duplicate at   , California, this

day of   , 19   , by and between

and

hereinafter called respectively lessor and lessee, without regard to number or gender,

WITNESSETH: That lessor hereby leases to lessee, and lessee hires from lessor, for the purpose of conducting therein

and for no other purpose, those certain premises with the appurtenances, situated in
, State of California, and more particularly described as follows, to-wit:

The term shall be for   years, commencing on the
day of   , 19   , and ending on the
day of   , 19   , at the total rent or sum of
($) Dollars,

lawful money of the United States of America, which lessee agrees to pay to lessor, without deduction or offset, prior notice or demand, at such place or places as may be designated from time to time by lessor, in installments as follows:

It is further mutually agreed between the parties as follows:

1. If lessor, for any reason, cannot deliver possession of said premises to lessee at the commencement of said term, this lease shall not be void or voidable, nor shall lessor be liable to lessee for any loss or damage resulting therefrom; but there shall be a proportionate deduction of rent covering the period between the commencement of said term and the time when lessor can deliver possession.

2. Lessee shall not use, or permit said premises, or any part thereof, to be used, for any purpose or purposes other than the purpose or purposes for which said premises are hereby leased; and no use shall be made or permitted to be made of said premises, nor acts done, which will increase the existing rate of insurance upon the building in which said premises may be located, or cause a cancellation of any insurance policy covering said building, or any part thereof, nor shall lessee sell, or permit to be kept, used, or sold, in or about said premises, any article which may be prohibited by standard form of fire insurance policies. Lessee shall, at his sole cost, comply with any and all requirements, pertaining to the use of said premises, of any insurance organization or company, necessary for maintenance of reasonable fire and public liability insurance, covering said building and appurtenances.

LEASE—GENERAL—WOLCOTTS FORM 973. REV. 2-73   8 pt. type or larger

EXHIBIT 20-1 GENERAL LEASE FORM*

*Illustrated forms in this chapter courtesy of Wolcotts, 214 So. Spring St., Los Angeles C A.

3. Lessee shall not commit, or suffer to be committed, any waste upon said premises, or any nuisance, or other act or thing which may disturb the quiet enjoyment of any other tenant in the building in which the demised premises may be located. Lessee shall not make, or suffer to be made, any alterations of the said premises, or any part thereof, without the written consent of lessor first had and obtained, and any additions to, or alterations of, said premises, except movable furniture and trade fixtures, shall become at once a part of the realty and belong to lessor.

4. Lessee shall not vacate or abandon the premises at any time during the term; and if lessee shall abandon, vacate or surrender said premises or be dispossessed by process of law, or otherwise, any personal property belonging to lessee and left on the premises shall be deemed abandoned, at the option of lessor, except such property as may be mortgaged to lessor.

5. As part of the consideration for rental, lessee shall, at his sole cost, keep and maintain said premises and appurtenances and every part thereof (excepting exterior walls and roof which Lessor agrees to repair), including sidewalks adjacent to said premises, any store front and interior of the premises, in good and sanitary order, condition and repair, and replace broken glazing, and except as to any condition which renders the premises untenantable, hereby waiving all right to make repairs at the expense of lessor as provided in Section 1942 of said Civil Code of the State of California, and all rights provided for by Section 1941 of said Civil Code. By entry hereunder, lessee accepts the premises as being in good and sanitary order, condition and repair and agrees on the last day of said term, or sooner termination of this lease, to surrender unto lessor all and singular said premises with said appurtenances in the same condition as when received, reasonable use and wear thereof and damage by fire, act of God, or by the elements excepted, and to remove all of the lessee's signs, from said premises.

6. Lessee shall, at his sole cost, comply with all of the requirements of all Municipal, State and Federal authorities now in force, or which may hereafter be in force, pertaining to the use of said premises, and shall faithfully observe in said use all Municipal ordinances and State and Federal statutes now in force or which may hereafter be in force. The judgment of any court of competent jurisdiction, or the admission of lessee in any action or proceeding against lessee, whether lessor be a party thereto or not, that lessee has violated any such ordinance or statute in said use, shall be conclusive of that fact as between lessor and lessee.

7. Lessee as a material part of the consideration to be rendered to lessor, hereby waives all claims against lessor for damages to goods, wares and merchandise, in, upon, or about said premises and for injuries to persons, in, upon, or about said premises, from any cause whatsoever arising at any time, and lessee will hold lessor exempt and harmless from any liability, loss, cost and obligation on account of any damage or injury to any person, or to the goods, wares and merchandise of any person, arising in any manner from the use or occupancy of the premises by the lessee.

8. Lessee shall not conduct or permit to be conducted any sale by auction on said premises. Lessee shall not place or permit to be placed any sign, marquee or awning on the front of said premises without the written consent of lessor; lessee upon request of lessor, shall immediately remove any sign or decoration which lessee has placed or permitted to be placed in, on, or about the front of the premises which, in the opinion of lessor, is objectionable or offensive, and if lessee fails so to do, lessor may enter said premises and remove the same. Lessor has reserved the exclusive right to the exterior sidewalls, rear wall and roof of said premises, and lessee shall not place or permit to be placed upon said sidewalls, rear wall or roof, any sign, advertisement or notice without the written consent of lessor.

9. Lessee shall pay for all water, gas, heat, light, power, telephone service and all other services and utilities supplied to said premises.

10. Lessee shall permit lessor and his agents to enter into and upon said premises at all reasonable times for the purpose of inspecting the same or for the purpose of maintaining the building in which said premises are situated, or for the purpose of making repairs, alterations or additions to any other portion of said building, including the erection and maintenance of such scaffolding, canopies, fences and props as may be required, or for the purpose of posting notices of non-liability for alterations, additions, or repairs or for the purpose of placing upon the property in which the said premises are located any usual or ordinary "for sale" signs, without any rebate of rent and without any liability to lessee for any loss of occupation or quiet enjoyment of the premises thereby occasioned; and shall permit lessor, at any time within thirty days prior to the expiration of this lease, to place upon said premises any usual or ordinary "to let" or "to lease" signs.

11. In the event of (a) a partial destruction of said premises or the building containing same during said term which requires repairs to either said premises or said building, or (b) said premises or said building being declared unsafe or unfit for occupancy by any authorized public authority for any reason other than lessee's act, use or occupation which declaration requires repairs to either said premises or said building, lessor shall forthwith make such repairs, provided such repairs can be made within sixty (60) days under the laws and regulations of authorized public authorities, but such partial destruction (including any destruction necessary in order to make repairs required by any such declaration) shall in no wise annul or void this lease, except that lessee shall be entitled to a proportionate deduction of rent while such repairs are being made, such proportionate deduction to be based upon the extent to which the making of such repairs shall interfere with the business carried on by lessee in said premises. If such repairs cannot be made within sixty (60) days, lessor may, at his option, make same within a reasonable time, this lease continuing in full force and effect and the rent to be proportionately rebated, as in this paragraph provided. In the event that lessor does not so elect to make such repairs which cannot be made within sixty (60) days, or such repairs cannot be made under such laws and regulations, this lease may be terminated at the option of either party. In respect to any partial destruction (including any destruction necessary in order to make repairs required by any such declaration) which lessor is obligated to repair or may elect to repair under the terms of this paragraph, the provisions of Section 1932, Subdivision (2), and Section 1933, Subdivision (4), of the Civil Code of the State of California are waived by lessee. A total destruction (including any destruction required by any authorized public authority) of either said premises or said building shall terminate this lease. In the event of any dispute between lessor and lessee relative to the provisions of this paragraph, they shall each select an arbitrator, the two arbitrators so selected shall select a third arbitrator and the three arbitrators so selected shall hear and determine the controversy and their decision thereof shall be final and binding on both lessor and lessee who shall bear the cost of such arbitration equally between them.

12. Lessee shall not assign this lease, or any interest therein, and shall not sublet said premises or any part thereof, or any right or privilege appurtenant thereto, or suffer any other person (the agents and servants of lessee excepted) to occupy or use said premises, or any portion thereof, without the written consent of lessor first had and obtained. Furthermore, this lease shall not, nor shall any interest therein, be assignable, as to the interest of lessee, by operation of law, without the written consent of lessor first had and obtained. A consent by lessor to one assignment, subletting, occupation or use by any other person, shall not be deemed to be a consent to any subsequent assignment, subletting, occupation or use by any other person. Any such assignment or subletting, whether by operation of law or otherwise, without such written consent first had and obtained shall be void, and shall, at the option of lessor, terminate this lease.

13. Either (a) the appointment of a receiver to take possession of all or substantially all of the assets of lessee, or (b) a general assignment by lessee for the benefit of creditors, or (c) any action taken or suffered by lessee under any insolvency or bankruptcy act shall constitute a breach of this lease by lessee, and shall, at the option of lessor, terminate this lease.

EXHIBIT 20-1 SECOND PAGE

14.A In the event lessee breaches the lease and abandons the property before the end of the term or, if his right to possession is terminated by the lessor because of a breach of the lease, this lease shall thereupon terminate. Upon such termination, lessor may recover from lessee: (a) the worth at the time of award of judgment of the unpaid rent which had been earned at the time of termination, together with interest thereon at the rate of nine (9%) percent per annum; and (b) the worth at the time of award of judgment by which the unpaid rent which would have been earned after termination until the time of judgment exceeds the amount of such rental loss that the lessee proves could have been reasonably avoided, together with interest thereon at the rate of nine (9%) percent per annum, and (c) the worth at the time of award of judgment of the amount by which the unpaid rent for the balance of the term after the time of award exceeds the amount of such rental loss that the lessee proves could be reasonably avoided discounted by the discount rate of Federal Reserve Bank of San Francisco at the time of award of judgment plus one (1%) percent; and (d) any other amount necessary to compensate the lessor for all the detriment proximately caused by the lessee's failure to perform his obligations under the lease or which in the ordinary course of things would be likely to result therefrom, together with costs of suit and reasonable attorney's fees.

14.B If default be made by lessee in payment of rent or in the observance, payment or performance of any of the other provisions, terms or conditions of this lease, or if any conduct of the lessee, his family, servants, employees, agents, invitees or licensees shall obstruct or interfere with the rights of other occupants, or annoy them by unreasonable noises or otherwise, or should they commit or perform any nuisance on the premises or commit or suffer any illegal or immoral act to be committed thereon, the lessor may, at its option, terminate **this lease and, any holding over thereafter by lessee shall be construed to be a tenancy from month to month only, for the same rental rate and payable in the same manner as herein specified.**

15. The voluntary or other surrender of this lease by lessee, or a mutual cancellation thereof, shall not work a merger, and shall, at the option of lessor, terminate all or any existing subleases or subtenancies or may, at the option of lessor, operate as an assignment to him of any or all of such subleases or subtenancies.

16. If lessor is made a party defendant to any litigation concerning this lease or the leased premises or the occupancy thereof by lessee, then lessee shall hold harmless lessor from all liability by reason of said litigation, including reasonable attorneys fees and expenses incurred by lessor in any such litigation, whether or not any such litigation is prosecuted to judgment. If lessor commences an action against lessee to enforce any of the terms hereof or because of the breach by lessee of any of the terms hereof, or for the recovery of any rent due hereunder, or for any unlawful detainer of said premises, lessee shall pay to lessor reasonable attorneys fees and expenses, and the right to such attorneys fees and expenses shall be deemed to have accrued on the commencement of such action, and shall be enforceable whether or not such action is prosecuted to judgment. If lessee breaches any term of this lease, lessor may employ an attorney or attorneys to protect lessor's rights hereunder, and in the event of such employment following any breach by lessee, lessee shall pay lessor reasonable attorneys fees and expenses incurred by lessor, whether or not an action is actually commenced against lessee by reason of said breach.

17. All notices to be given to lessee shall be given in writing personally or by depositing the same in the United States mail, postage prepaid, and addressed to lessee at said premises, whether or not lessee has departed from, abandoned or vacated the premises. All notices to be given to lessor shall be given in writing personally or by depositing the same in the United States mail, postage prepaid, and addressed to the lessor at the place designated by lessor for the payment of rent, or at such other place or places as may be designated from time to time by lessor.

18. If any security be given by lessee to secure the faithful performance of all or any of the covenants of this lease on the part of lessee, lessor may transfer and/or deliver the security, as such, to the purchaser of the reversion, in the event that the reversion be sold, and thereupon lessor shall be discharged from any further liability in reference thereto. Lessee hereby waives notice in the event of lessor's transfer of its interest in the leased premises.

19. The waiver by lessor of any breach of any term, covenant or condition herein contained shall not be deemed to be a waiver of such term, covenant or condition or any subsequent breach of the same or any other term, covenant or condition herein contained.

20. Any holding over after the expiration of the said term, with the consent of lessor, shall be construed to be a tenancy from month to month, at a rental of
($) Dollars a month, and shall otherwise be on the terms and conditions herein specified, so far as applicable.

21. ESCALATION CLAUSE: The lessee agrees that should the leased premises be taxed at a higher rate than the rate for the "present" tax year, then said increase shall be paid by the lessee monthly and shall be prorated over the twelve month period to which said tax is attributable and shall be due and payable as rent.

The "present" tax year heretofore referred to is the fiscal year 19___-___. The tax bill for the leased premises for the "present" tax year is $

22. SUBORDINATION CLAUSE: This lease is subject and subordinate to all existing leases and to all mortgages and deeds of trust which may now or hereafter affect the real property of which the leased premises form a part, and to all renewals, modifications, replacements and extensions thereof. The lessee hereby agrees to execute any instruments for the benefit of the lessor as may be necessary to effectuate this provision of the lease.

23. TAKING BY EMINENT DOMAIN: In case the whole of the leased premises are taken by right of eminent domain or other authority of law during the period of this lease, or any extension thereof, this lease shall terminate. In case a part of the leased premises are taken by right of eminent domain or other authority of law, this lease may, at the election of the lessor, be terminated.

If a part of the premises are taken by the right of eminent domain and the lessor does not elect to terminate the lease the rent herein stipulated shall be decreased proportionally according to the value of that part of the premises taken. If the entire premises are taken or if a part of the leased premises are taken and the lessor elects to terminate the lease, then all compensation paid for the taking shall belong to the lessor.

24. The covenants and conditions herein contained shall, subject to the provisions as to assignment, apply to and bind the heirs, successors, executors, administrators and assigns of all the parties hereto; and all of the parties hereto shall be jointly and severally liable hereunder.

25. Time is of the essence of this lease.

IN WITNESS WHEREOF, lessor and lessee have executed these presents, the day and year first above written.

--(Seal)   --(Seal)

--(Seal)   --(Seal)

--(Seal)   --(Seal)

            LESSOR   LESSEE

EXHIBIT 20-1 THIRD PAGE

271

Term of Lease

The number of years and/or months for which the premises are being leased and the dates when the lease is to commence and end.

Total Rent for Lease Term

The total amount for the full lease term. For example, if the lease is for a term of thirty-six months at a monthly rental of $200 per month, the full amount would be $7,200.

How the Total Rent Is to Be Paid

This may be varied, but if the rent is to be paid in equal monthly installments, which is usual, the number of installments would equal the number of months in the lease term.

Security Deposits

Provision is made for the number of designated months for which advance payments are being paid. In some agreements, the security deposit may be only the first month and last month of the lease term in advance; however, it is not unusual for the lessor to insist on the lessee paying from two to six months in advance to be applied to the last months of the lease term. Thus, in the event the lessee defaults in the lease contract, the lessor's loss is reduced. Under ordinary circumstances, the lessor may have a cause of action for a suit in a court of law for any rents due, but it may be a case of "suing a beggar and getting a louse."

Cleanup and Damage Deposit

In addition to security deposits in the form of advanced rents, it is common practice for the lessor to collect a cleanup and damage deposit as the tenant's guarantee that the premises will be left in a clean, orderly and tenantable condition upon vacating at which time the deposit monies will be refunded. If those conditions are not met, the lessor will have the right to retain the deposit to apply toward the expenses of hiring the necessary cleaning and repairing to be done.

This is often an area for disagreement when it is time for a decision to be made as to whether or not the cleanup and damage deposit is to be refunded to the tenant. The lessor may feel the premises are in a deplorable condition and wants to retain the deposit. On the other hand, the tenant may feel he has conformed to the obligation and demands the deposit to be refunded to him. In many instances, both parties are correct in their thinking if the premises were in poor condition and repair at the time of the lessee taking possession.

One way to prevent the situation from arising is for both parties and/or their agents to inspect the premises thoroughly together and make note of any defects or general condition existing prior to signing the lease and an agreement as to what must be done, if anything, stated in writing. This agreement could be placed in the lease instrument or in an addendum to it.

Upon vacating the property at the end of the lease term, an inspection is made and consideration given to prior conditions that were not remedied. Reasonable wear and tear is also a factor to be taken into account.

In some apartment houses, a lease or month-to-month tenancy agreements provide that such deposits automatically become the property of the lessor and are not refundable regardless of condition upon vacating the premises. The main line of reasoning is that a certain amount of cleaning, painting, repairing and fixing will be necessary anyway in preparation for new tenants. The deposit helps to defray such preparation expenses.

Option to Renew Lease

It is a common practice for the lessor to give the lessee an option to renew the lease for a specified term. This may be under the same terms and conditions as are in the original agreement or there may be some form of adjustment in the amount of rent or some other condition. Any changes should be included in the clause and also some minimum term of prior notice as to whether the tenant intends to remain in tenancy should be stated.

OPTION TO PURCHASE

A lease transaction, whereby the lessee may have an option to purchase the premises, is a common practice. The details of such option may be written into the lease or the option may be a separate instrument with reference made to it in the lease agreement.

There are several different reasons for a lease with option to purchase. It is sometimes used as a means for the lessee to accumulate a sufficient down payment by paying additional monies each month along with the specified amount of rent until an agreed total has been paid in. At this point, the lessee has the right to exercise his option and complete the purchase. In other instances, the lessee may be anticipating the receipt of sufficient funds

273

some time in the future with which to make the purchase and would pay a certain lump sum at the time of leasing for the privilege of an option to purchase.

Such option contained in a lease agreement may specify a fixed purchase price or it may extend the right of refusal to purchase at a price offered for the property by a third party or it may provide both a fixed price and the right of refusal at a price offered by someone else.

The agent normally protects his commission rights in the agreement in the event the lessee exercises his option and a sale is consummated.

RIGHTS AND OBLIGATIONS

The rights and obligations of lessor and lessee, in application to the ordinary eventualities of lease agreements, are generally provided for under the laws of individual states and localities unless otherwise set forth in a written lease contract within the framework of such laws.

As to the lessee, the rights, privileges and quiet enjoyment of the leased premises are either stated in writing or implied, or both, by virtue of the granting by the lessor of the leasehold estate in the first part of the lease instrument. The obligations of the lessee may be stated or implied throughout the entire contract.

In most printed forms of lease agreements, the lessor's obligations are mostly implied, unless otherwise stated in writing, and his rights are more or less merged with the conditions set forth as obligations of the lessee.

In order to make certain that neither party is giving up his legal rights or escaping any of his obligations, it is usually advisable for the lessee and the lessor to have any lease agreement to be either written or reviewed by their own legal counsels.

In reference to the general lease form in Exhibit 20-1, some of the printed clauses as conditions to the lease contract will be discussed in the following paragraphs. These conditions are more or less universal in application for the most part in a majority of the states, but may have to be modified from the standpoint of legality in some instances in a few states.

DELAY IN POSSESSION

Most leases provide for an unforeseeable delay in delivering possesssion of the premises on the date rents are to commence. It is generally provided that the lease period is to be extended by the period of delay and rents are to be adjusted accordingly. In some instances, it may not be to the lessee's best interest for the lease expiration date to be extended, in which case there should be a further stipulation to that effect in the clause.

The situation may arise as the result of a delay in completion of new construction or it may be a matter of a tenant, already in possession, not vacating at the end of his lease term which is called "holding over." In any event, the lessor will normally hold himself free of any resulting liability as to the new lessee and at the same time will keep the lease contract operable.

Another point for the lessee to consider is in a prolonged delay in possession resulting in some form of hardship. For example, if the lessee has to vacate another location due to his lease's expiring, he may suffer the consequences of "holding over," which can be severe in some states such as Mississippi where the rents may be doubled or in Missouri where the tenant may be liable for double the amount of damages awarded plus double the amount of rents and profits when found guilty of unlawful detainer.

There may be numerous factors to be weighed in connection with the delay in possession clause, which is the first condition indicated in Exhibit 20-1—general lease form.

USAGE OF PREMISES

The second condition restricts the lessee to use of the property to the type of business and operation thereof, in conformance to that as specified at the top of the lease form. The lessor is entitled to retain his existing insurance protection without the threat of cancellation of the policy or an increase in premiums.

For example, say the lessee was in the wholesale greeting card business when he took possession of the property. Within a few months, the lessee decided to print his own greeting cards on the leased premises, which meant that he would have flammable materials around that were not considered in the lessor's fire insurance policy. The insurance company would, no doubt, increase the insurance premiums or under some circumstances might cancel the policy altogether.

This clause protects the lessor to the extent that the lessee has defaulted in the agreement, which would give the lessor the right to terminate the lease.

ALTERATIONS AND FIXTURES

Condition number three is almost always contained in leases. In effect the lessee agrees not to disturb any other tenants and also agrees to obtain permission from the lessor prior to making any alterations to the premises. Most leases provide that any moveable furniture and fixtures belong to the lessee, at the end of the lease term, but any that are attached to the premises may become a part of the realty and revert in ownership to the lessor.

Frequently, the lessee must attach certain trade fixtures and equipment to the floor or the walls. In such cases, it may be advisable to provide, in addition, that those attached fixtures may be removed and any resulting damage is to be repaired at the lessee's expense. The laws of some states provide for such repairs in any case where damage is done.

ABANDONMENT

Reference is made to abandonment of the premises in paragraphs 4, 14-A, 14-B and 17 of the lease form in Exhibit 20-1.

Abandonment of leased premises by the lessee is one of the most frequent causes of lease termination; therefore, much reference is made to it in the lease agreement. If the tenant abandons the property prior to the expiration of the lease term, he may still be liable for any rents remaining due under the lease agreement without obligation on the lessor's part to relet the premises. Thus, the lessor may allow the premises to remain vacant and in such case, may sue the lessee for the full amount due plus costs of such suit under the laws of most states.

Under ordinary circumstances, however, the lessor will usually relet the property rather than to have it remain vacant. But, to do so may constitute a termination of the lease, thereby releasing the tenant from a further liability to the lessor under the laws of some states.

The laws in application to abandonment are at a great variance from state to state and should be examined carefully prior to taking action.

INSURANCE

Paragraphs 7 and 11 of the illustrated lease form are in reference to insurance.

As a general rule, the lessor will carry hazard insurance on the improvements and liability insurance on the premises. The lessee should carry hazard insurance on his own property on the premises and in addition may be required by the lessor to carry liability insurance under an owner-landlord-tenant policy as protection in the event an invitee of the lessee is injured on the premises. Required insurance should be specified in the lease agreement.

Additionally, the lessee may be wise to include a "loss of business" clause in his insurance coverage in the event of a fire partially or fully destroying the premises.

The conditions contained in most lease forms provide that in the event of partial or whole destruction of the premises, it is the lessor's option as to whether or not the lease is to remain in effect. The laws of some states provide for termination of the lease in the event improvements are destroyed unless it is otherwise written into the agreement. In other states, the statutes provide an automatic termination of the lease in such cases.

This point should be cleared up prior to the drawing of a lease as to application in the locality in which the property lies.

ASSIGNMENT AND SUBLEASE

Paragraphs 12 and 15 of Exhibit 20-1 refer to assignments and subleases.

All leases contain a clause that provides that the premises cannot be subleased, nor can the lease be assigned to another party without the lessor's consent. In the absence of such provisions, the tenant may have the right to assign or sublet the premises to someone else, provided there is no conflict of the sublessee's operation as to other terms and conditions contained in the original lease agreement.

When a lease is assigned, the assignee becomes liable to the original lessor for rents. With a sublease, the sublessee is liable only to the original lessee, who in turn is liable to the original or subsequent lessors.

In some states, the original term of the lease may have a bearing on whether or not a lease may be assigned, even with the lessor's consent. For example, in the states of Kentucky and Missouri, a lease for a term under two years may not be assignable.

HOLDING OVER

Paragraph 20 refers to "holding over."

This term is applied to the lessee who remains in possession of the property past the date of lease termination. Any resulting eventualities of holding over would depend on whether or not it is by consent of the lessor.

If it is by consent of the lessor and a new lease is not signed, the lessee may become a "tenant at will." A tenancy at will may be terminated by either party at any time proper notice as prescribed by local law is delivered.

Where a tenant has been in lawful possession of the premises, as under a lease, and without the lessor's consent remains in possession past the expiration of the lease, the tenant is called a "tenant at sufferance." A tenant at sufferance may be entitled to varied periods of advance notice of termination and eviction, which range from no period of advance notice to thirty days under the laws of different states.

For instance, in North Carolina a tenant holding over may be dispossessed by summary proceedings, while a tenancy from month-to-month may be terminated in seven days. In New York, a tenancy at will or at sufferance may be entitled to at least thirty days written notice. For further comparison, no notice may be required in a tenancy at sufferance in Indiana, but a tenant at will must receive thirty days' notice. Local laws in this connection should be examined thoroughly prior to taking action.

ESCALATION CLAUSE

Paragraph 21 in Exhibit 20-1 is an escalation clause.

Rents are normally a reflection of invested capital, fixed expenses, and other costs, including annual property taxes. In anticipation of possible increases in such taxes, most leases contain an escalation clause for the automatic increase of rents proportionately to any increased property taxes.

Without this provision in the lease, rents would be locked in and could not be increased during the term of it. The lessor could be hurt financially, in such event, without the tenant's participation in the added expense.

In a month-to-month tenancy, the landlord may increase rents by serving proper notice to that effect in accordance with the laws of the state in which the property lies.

CONVEYANCE OF LEASED PREMISES

Paragraphs 18, 22, and 23 provide for the transfer of ownership of the property in the event the lessor sells or otherwise disposes of it.

Under such circumstances, the new owner-lessor normally takes title to the property subject to all existing leases and periodic tenancies. The new owner, by virtue of the deed, has the right to collect future rents and to declare a default in rent or lease payments or other conditions upon the failure of the lessee to perform as agreed.

However, where provisions other than those relating to rent are contained in a lease agreement, the original lessor should give a subsequent lessor an assignment of all the rights under the lease contract. Thus, the technical rights to enforce provisions that may not "run with the land," have been conferred.

Unless otherwise notified, the tenant may have the right and obligation to pay rent to the original lessor. In receiving title to the property and the rights thereof, the new lessor may assume the tenant will pay the rents to him through a common knowledge of the transaction. He may then discover the tenant has paid rent to the usual place and possesses receipts as proof of such payments.

In some states, the tenant may be obligated to pay rents again to the new lessor. In other states, the rents are considered paid as to the new lessor. Upon acquiring rental property, the new owner should make it a point to notify all tenants as to where rents are to be paid and to whom payment is to be made.

TERMINATION OF LEASE

Paragraphs 14-B, 19, and 20 are to varied degrees in reference to the termination of the lease contract prior to the expiration date.

Practically all leases will contain one or more clauses providing for termination of the lease in the event the lessee fails to pay rent or is in violation of other terms and conditions of the agreement.

The "waiver" clause is also normally included and provides that the waiver of any breach of terms, covenants or conditions contained in the lease is not to be deemed a continual waiver in relation to that breach or any subsequent breach.

The waiver clause is advisable because without it the lessor, in some states, could lose his right to terminate the lease subsequently and evict the lessee under certain circumstances. An example of this could be where the lessor may accept a late payment of rents once or twice. The waiver clause may make it possible for the lessor to terminate the lease the next time rent payments are late. However, it may not be possible to terminate the lease all of a sudden because of late payment when such has been an habitual circumstance.

If, under violation of some condition by the lessee, the lessor options to terminate the lease, it may then become a month-to-month tenancy and subject to the local laws of dispossession for that type of tenancy.

NOTICE TO PAY RENT OR QUIT

The required number of days' notice prior to instigating eviction proceedings varies from state to state in connection with delinquent rent payments.

In Oklahoma, for example, a ten-day notice is required in the case of delinquent rents where it is a tenancy of three months or more, but only five days' notice is required if the tenancy is for less than three months. Rents must be tendered on or prior to the first day of the rent period in the state of Oregon and no demand for rent is necessary to render a tenant in default. A seven-day notice is required in the state of Michigan.

The required notice in several states such as Idaho, Montana, California and Ohio is three days. However, the laws of the state in which the property is located should be examined in relation to the manner necessary evictions are to be handled. In many instances, the landlord is required to post bond and conform to other legal steps in addition to serving the eviction notice.

The Notice to Pay Rent or Quit form illustrated in Exhibit 20-2 is used in California and is representative of similar forms used in many of the other states where such notice is required by law.

RECORDING

The signatures of the lessor and lessee to a lease of one year or more should be acknowledged by a notary public in order that the document could be recorded in the public records if necessary. Possession of the property, as actual notice, is considered to be sufficient notice to third parties as to the existence of a lease in a few states such as Colorado, Nevada, and Arkansas. In other states, such as Pennsylvania, possession as actual notice is sufficient as to third parties for the lease term of less than twenty-one years.

The laws of most states, however, provide that leases for terms exceeding one year must be recorded for constructive notice to third parties that such a lease exists. In some states, a lease must be recorded in order to provide protection for the tenant as well as to third parties.

Regardless of the requirements in relation to local laws, it may often be advisable to record a lease of more than one-year term, as an added measure of safety, as the recording of a lease is constructive notice to all the world that the lessee has an interest in the property for a certain period of time.

The laws of practically all states differ in one way or another with reference to leases. For that reason, it may be advisable to engage the services of local legal counsel prior to entering into a lease agreement. It is the best means of complete assurance that the document is entirely valid, operable and enforceable as to local laws in which the property lies.

NOTICE TO PAY RENT OR QUIT

(C. C. P., Sec. 1161)

TO_____

_____

_____
                                                        Tenant—in Possession

Within THREE DAYS, after the service on you of this notice, you are hereby required to PAY THE RENT of the premises hereinafter described, of which you now hold possession, amounting to the sum of_____

_____Dollars, ($_____)

at the rental rate of_____Dollars, ($_____)

per month (or week), being the_____rent due from the_____day of

_____, 19____, to the_____day of_____, 19____,

or you are hereby required to DELIVER UP POSSESSION of the hereinafter described premises, within THREE DAYS after service on you of this notice, to the undersigned, or_____agent, who is

authorized to receive the same or the undersigned will institute legal proceedings against you to recover possession of said premises with ALL RENTS DUE and DAMAGES. The undersigned, as a landlord, declares and gives notice that, if the said rent is not paid within three days after service on you of this notice, I do hereby elect to declare a forfeiture of the lease and agreement under which you occupy the hereinbelow-described property:

The premises herein referred to are situated in the_____of

_____County of_____.

STATE OF CALIFORNIA, designated by the number and street as_____

_____and more particularly

described as follows:_____

_____

_____

_____

_____

_____

_____

_____

_____

_____

Dated this_____day of_____, 19____.

_____

_____

Penal Code Section No. 594 reads: "Any person or persons who wilfully or maliciously destroys or damages any Real or Personal Property not their own will be punished by Fine or Imprisonment or both."

LEASE—NOTICE TO PAY RENT OR QUIT
WOLCOTTS FORM 1006—REV. 10-73   8 pt. type or larger

EXHIBIT 20-2 NOTICE TO PAY RENT OR QUIT

21

Payment Schedules
and Interest Charts

This chapter is devoted primarily to payment amortization schedules and interest charts plus other tables concerning remaining loan balances, income conversion, ratios of income to monthly payments and tax and insurance prorations.

A quick reference to finding information is almost as important as in having the knowledge beforehand.

The exhibits are as follows:

Interest Chart

Exhibit 21-1 is for the purpose of computing interest on a daily or monthly basis for each $100 involved.

Monthly Payment Schedule

Exhibit 21-2 may be used for a quick computation of monthly payments required to repay a $1,000 loan and interpolated commensurate with total loan amounts.

Amortization Schedule

Exhibit 21-3 schedules amortization of loans of $100 to $1,000 from 1 to 40 years at interest rates of 6% to 10%. Actual loan amounts may be computed accordingly.

Remaining Loan Balances

Exhibit 21-4 provides a means of determining the remaining balances of loans at the end of 5, 10, 15 years at interest rates most commonly used.

Income Conversions

Exhibit 21-5 is used to convert hourly, weekly, and annual incomes to a monthly basis in qualifying a borrower for monthly loan payments.

Ratio of Income to Monthly Payments

Exhibit 21-6 determines the borrower's ratio of income to monthly payments that may be required for a government-sponsored or a conventional loan.

Prorations

Exhibit 21-7 is provided for quick prorating of property taxes and hazard insurance when prorations are involved in a transaction.

AMOUNT OF INTEREST ON $100

(For Mortgage Loan and Real Estate Sales Contract

Interest Computations Only)

No. of Days	Interest Rate									
	5-1/2%	5-3/4%	6%	6-1/4%	6-1/2%	6-3/4%	7%	7-1/2%	8%	8-1/2%
1	.015278	.015972	.016667	.017361	.018056	.018750	.019444	.020833	.022222	.023611
2	.030556	.031944	.033333	.034722	.036111	.037500	.038889	.041667	.044444	.047222
3	.045833	.047917	.050000	.052083	.054167	.056250	.058333	.062500	.066667	.070833
4	.061111	.063889	.066667	.069444	.072222	.075000	.077778	.083333	.088889	.094444
5	.076389	.079861	.083333	.086806	.090278	.093750	.097222	.104167	.111111	.118056
6	.091667	.095833	.100000	.104167	.108333	.112500	.116667	.125000	.133333	.141667
7	.106944	.111806	.116667	.121528	.126389	.131250	.136111	.145833	.155556	.165278
8	.122222	.127778	.133333	.138889	.144444	.150000	.155556	.166667	.177778	.188889
9	.137500	.143750	.150000	.156250	.162500	.168750	.175000	.187500	.200000	.212500
10	.152778	.159722	.166667	.173611	.180556	.187500	.194444	.208333	.222222	.236111
11	.168056	.175694	.183333	.190972	.198611	.206250	.213889	.229167	.244444	.259722
12	.183333	.191667	.200000	.208333	.216667	.225000	.233333	.250000	.266667	.283333
13	.198611	.207639	.216667	.225694	.234722	.243750	.252778	.270833	.288889	.306944
14	.213889	.223611	.233333	.243056	.252778	.262500	.272222	.291667	.311111	.330556
15	.229167	.239583	.250000	.260417	.270833	.281250	.291667	.312500	.333333	.354167
16	.244444	.255556	.266667	.277778	.288889	.300000	.311111	.333333	.355556	.377778
17	.259722	.271528	.283333	.295139	.306944	.318750	.330556	.354167	.377778	.401389
18	.275000	.287500	.300000	.312500	.325000	.337500	.350000	.375000	.400000	.425000
19	.290278	.303472	.316667	.329861	.343056	.356250	.369444	.395833	.422222	.448611
20	.305556	.319444	.333333	.347222	.361111	.375000	.388889	.416667	.444444	.472222
21	.320833	.335417	.350000	.364583	.379167	.393750	.408333	.437500	.466667	.495833
22	.336111	.351389	.366667	.381944	.397222	.412500	.427778	.458333	.488889	.519444
23	.351389	.367361	.383333	.399306	.415278	.431250	.447222	.479167	.511111	.543056
24	.366667	.383333	.400000	.416667	.433333	.450000	.466667	.500000	.533333	.566667
25	.381944	.399306	.416667	.434028	.451389	.468750	.486111	.520833	.555556	.590278
26	.397222	.415278	.433333	.451389	.469444	.487500	.505556	.541667	.577778	.613889
27	.412500	.431250	.450000	.468750	.487500	.506250	.525000	.562500	.600000	.637500
28	.427778	.447222	.466667	.486111	.505556	.525000	.544444	.583333	.622222	.661111
29	.443056	.463194	.483333	.503472	.523611	.543750	.563889	.604167	.644444	.684722
No. of Mo.										
1	.458333	.479167	.500000	.520833	.541667	.562500	.583333	.625000	.666667	.708333
2	.916667	.958333	1.000000	1.041667	1.083333	1.125000	1.166667	1.250000	1.333333	1.416667
3	1.375000	1.437500	1.500000	1.562500	1.625000	1.687500	1.750000	1.875000	2.000000	2.125000
4	1.833333	1.916667	2.000000	2.083333	2.166667	2.250000	2.333333	2.500000	2.666667	2.833333
5	2.291667	2.395833	2.500000	2.604167	2.708333	2.812500	2.916667	3.125000	3.333333	3.541667
6	2.750000	2.875000	3.000000	3.125000	3.250000	3.375000	3.500000	3.750000	4.000000	4.250000

EXHIBIT 21-1 INTEREST CHART

MONTHLY PAYMENTS REQUIRED
TO REPAY A $1,000 LOAN

NO. YEARS	6%	6½%	6.9%	7%	7.2%	7½%	7⅝%	8%	9%	10%
5	$19.34	$19.57	$19.76	$19.81	$19.90	$20.04	$20.10	$20.28	$20.76	$21.25
6	16.58	16.81	17.01	17.05	17.15	17.30	17.36	17.54	18.03	18.53
7	14.61	14.85	15.05	15.10	15.20	15.34	15.41	15.59	16.09	16.61
8	13.15	13.39	13.59	13.64	13.74	13.89	13.95	14.14	14.65	15.18
9	12.01	12.26	12.46	12.51	12.61	12.77	12.83	13.02	13.54	14.08
10	11.11	11.36	11.56	11.62	11.72	11.88	11.94	12.14	12.67	13.22
11	10.37	10.63	10.84	10.89	10.99	11.15	11.22	11.42	11.97	12.52
12	9.76	10.02	10.24	10.29	10.40	10.56	10.62	10.83	11.39	11.95
13	9.25	9.52	9.73	9.79	9.89	10.06	10.13	10.34	10.90	11.48
14	8.82	9.09	9.30	9.36	9.47	9.64	9.71	9.92	10.49	11.09
15	8.44	8.72	8.94	8.99	9.11	9.28	9.35	9.56	10.15	10.75
16	8.12	8.40	8.62	8.68	8.79	8.96	9.04	9.25	9.85	10.46
17	7.84	8.12	8.34	8.40	8.52	8.69	8.77	8.99	9.59	10.22
18	7.59	7.87	8.10	8.16	8.28	8.45	8.53	8.75	9.37	10.00
19	7.37	7.65	7.89	7.95	8.07	8.25	8.32	8.55	9.17	9.82
20	7.17	7.46	7.70	7.76	7.88	8.06	8.14	8.37	9.00	9.66
25	6.45	6.76	7.01	7.07	7.20	7.39	7.48	7.72	8.40	9.09
30	6.00	6.33	6.59	6.66	6.79	7.00	7.08	7.34	8.05	8.78

EXHIBIT 21-2 MONTHLY PAYMENT SCHEDULE

EQUAL MONTHLY PAYMENTS NECESSARY TO AMORTIZE A LOAN

6%   **6%**

TERM AMOUNT	1 YEARS	1½ YEARS	2 YEARS	2½ YEARS	3 YEARS	3½ YEARS	4 YEARS	4½ YEARS	5 YEARS	5½ YEARS	6 YEARS	6½ YEARS	7 YEARS	7½ YEARS	8 YEARS	9 YEARS	10 YEARS	11 YEARS	12 YEARS	13 YEARS
$100	8.61	5.83	4.44	3.60	3.05	2.65	2.35	2.12	1.94	1.79	1.66	1.56	1.47	1.39	1.32	1.21	1.12	1.04	.98	.93
200	17.22	11.65	8.87	7.20	6.09	5.30	4.70	4.24	3.87	3.57	3.32	3.11	2.93	2.77	2.63	2.41	2.23	2.08	1.96	1.85
300	25.82	17.47	13.30	10.80	9.13	7.94	7.05	6.36	5.80	5.35	4.98	4.66	4.39	4.15	3.95	3.61	3.34	3.12	2.93	2.78
400	34.43	23.30	17.73	14.40	12.17	10.59	9.40	8.48	7.74	7.14	6.63	6.21	5.85	5.54	5.26	4.81	4.45	4.15	3.91	3.70
500	43.04	29.12	22.17	17.99	15.22	13.23	11.75	10.59	9.67	8.92	8.29	7.76	7.31	6.92	6.58	6.01	5.56	5.19	4.88	4.63
600	51.64	34.94	26.60	21.59	18.26	15.88	14.10	12.71	11.60	10.70	9.95	9.31	8.77	8.30	7.89	7.21	6.67	6.23	5.86	5.55
700	60.25	40.77	31.03	25.19	21.30	18.52	16.44	14.83	13.54	12.48	11.61	10.86	10.23	9.68	9.20	8.41	7.78	7.26	6.84	6.48
800	68.86	46.59	35.46	28.79	24.34	21.17	18.79	16.95	15.47	14.27	13.26	12.42	11.69	11.07	10.52	9.61	8.89	8.30	7.81	7.40
900	77.46	52.41	39.89	32.39	27.38	23.82	21.14	19.06	17.40	16.05	14.92	13.97	13.15	12.45	11.83	10.81	10.00	9.34	8.79	8.33
1000	86.07	58.24	44.33	35.98	30.43	26.46	23.49	21.18	19.34	17.83	16.58	15.52	14.61	13.83	13.15	12.01	11.11	10.37	9.76	9.25

6%   **6%**

TERM AMOUNT	14 YEARS	15 YEARS	16 YEARS	17 YEARS	18 YEARS	19 YEARS	20 YEARS	21 YEARS	22 YEARS	23 YEARS	24 YEARS	25 YEARS	26 YEARS	27 YEARS	28 YEARS	29 YEARS	30 YEARS	32 YEARS	35 YEARS	40 YEARS
$100	.89	.85	.82	.79	.76	.74	.72	.70	.69	.67	.66	.65	.64	.63	.63	.62	.60	.59	.58	.56
200	1.77	1.69	1.63	1.57	1.52	1.48	1.44	1.40	1.37	1.34	1.32	1.29	1.27	1.25	1.24	1.22	1.20	1.18	1.15	1.11
300	2.65	2.54	2.44	2.35	2.28	2.21	2.15	2.10	2.05	2.01	1.97	1.94	1.91	1.88	1.85	1.83	1.80	1.76	1.72	1.66
400	3.53	3.38	3.25	3.14	3.04	2.95	2.87	2.80	2.74	2.68	2.63	2.58	2.54	2.50	2.47	2.43	2.40	2.35	2.29	2.21
500	4.41	4.22	4.06	3.92	3.80	3.69	3.59	3.50	3.42	3.35	3.28	3.23	3.17	3.12	3.08	3.04	3.00	2.94	2.86	2.76
600	5.29	5.07	4.87	4.70	4.55	4.42	4.30	4.20	4.10	4.02	3.94	3.87	3.81	3.75	3.70	3.65	3.60	3.52	3.43	3.31
700	6.17	5.91	5.69	5.49	5.31	5.16	5.02	4.90	4.79	4.69	4.60	4.52	4.44	4.37	4.31	4.25	4.20	4.11	4.00	3.86
800	7.05	6.76	6.50	6.27	6.07	5.89	5.74	5.60	5.47	5.36	5.25	5.16	5.07	5.00	4.93	4.86	4.80	4.70	4.57	4.41
900	7.94	7.60	7.31	7.05	6.83	6.63	6.45	6.29	6.15	6.02	5.91	5.80	5.71	5.62	5.54	5.47	5.40	5.28	5.14	4.96
1000	8.82	8.44	8.12	7.84	7.59	7.37	7.17	6.99	6.84	6.69	6.56	6.45	6.34	6.24	6.16	6.08	6.00	5.87	5.71	5.51

EXHIBIT 21-3 AMORTIZATION SCHEDULE

287

EQUAL MONTHLY PAYMENTS NECESSARY TO AMORTIZE A LOAN

6¼%

TERM AMOUNT	1 YEARS	1½ YEARS	2 YEARS	2½ YEARS	3 YEARS	3½ YEARS	4 YEARS	4½ YEARS	5 YEARS	5½ YEARS	6 YEARS	6½ YEARS	7 YEARS	7½ YEARS	8 YEARS	9 YEARS	10 YEARS	11 YEARS	12 YEARS	13 YEARS
$100	8.62	5.84	4.45	3.61	3.06	2.66	2.36	2.13	1.95	1.80	1.67	1.57	1.48	1.40	1.33	1.22	1.13	1.05	.99	.94
200	17.24	11.67	8.89	7.22	6.11	5.32	4.72	4.26	3.89	3.59	3.34	3.13	2.95	2.79	2.66	2.43	2.25	2.10	1.98	1.88
300	25.86	17.51	13.34	10.83	9.17	7.98	7.08	6.39	5.84	5.39	5.01	4.70	4.42	4.19	3.98	3.64	3.37	3.15	2.97	2.82
400	34.48	23.34	17.78	14.44	12.22	10.63	9.44	8.52	7.78	7.18	6.68	6.26	5.90	5.58	5.31	4.86	4.50	4.20	3.96	3.76
500	43.10	29.18	22.22	18.05	15.27	13.29	11.80	10.65	9.73	8.98	8.35	7.82	7.37	6.98	6.64	6.07	5.62	5.25	4.95	4.69
600	51.71	35.01	26.67	21.66	18.33	15.95	14.16	12.78	11.67	10.77	10.02	9.39	8.84	8.37	7.96	7.28	6.74	6.30	5.94	5.63
700	60.33	40.85	31.11	25.27	21.38	18.60	16.52	14.91	13.62	12.57	11.69	10.95	10.32	9.77	9.29	8.50	7.86	7.35	6.93	6.57
800	68.95	46.68	35.55	28.88	24.43	21.26	18.88	17.04	15.56	14.36	13.36	12.51	11.79	11.16	10.62	9.71	8.99	8.40	7.92	7.51
900	77.57	52.52	40.00	32.49	27.49	23.92	21.24	19.17	17.51	16.15	15.03	14.08	13.26	12.56	11.94	10.92	10.11	9.45	8.90	8.45
1000	86.19	58.35	44.44	36.10	30.54	26.58	23.60	21.30	19.45	17.95	16.70	15.64	14.73	13.95	13.27	12.13	11.23	10.50	9.89	9.38

6¼%

TERM AMOUNT	14 YEARS	15 YEARS	16 YEARS	17 YEARS	18 YEARS	19 YEARS	20 YEARS	21 YEARS	22 YEARS	23 YEARS	24 YEARS	25 YEARS	26 YEARS	27 YEARS	28 YEARS	29 YEARS	30 YEARS	32 YEARS	35 YEARS	40 YEARS
$100	.90	.86	.83	.80	.78	.76	.74	.72	.70	.69	.68	.66	.65	.64	.64	.63	.62	.61	.59	.57
200	1.79	1.72	1.66	1.60	1.55	1.51	1.47	1.43	1.40	1.37	1.35	1.32	1.30	1.28	1.27	1.25	1.24	1.21	1.18	1.14
300	2.69	2.58	2.48	2.40	2.32	2.26	2.20	2.15	2.10	2.06	2.02	1.98	1.95	1.92	1.90	1.87	1.85	1.81	1.77	1.71
400	3.58	3.43	3.31	3.19	3.09	3.01	2.93	2.86	2.80	2.74	2.69	2.64	2.60	2.56	2.53	2.50	2.47	2.42	2.35	2.28
500	4.48	4.29	4.13	3.99	3.87	3.76	3.66	3.57	3.49	3.42	3.36	3.30	3.25	3.20	3.16	3.12	3.08	3.02	2.94	2.84
600	5.37	5.15	4.96	4.79	4.64	4.51	4.39	4.29	4.19	4.11	4.03	3.96	3.90	3.84	3.79	3.74	3.70	3.62	3.53	3.41
700	6.27	6.01	5.78	5.58	5.41	5.26	5.12	5.00	4.89	4.79	4.70	4.62	4.55	4.48	4.42	4.37	4.32	4.22	4.11	3.98
800	7.16	6.86	6.61	6.38	6.18	6.01	5.85	5.71	5.59	5.48	5.37	5.28	5.20	5.12	5.05	4.99	4.93	4.83	4.70	4.55
900	8.06	7.72	7.43	7.18	6.96	6.76	6.58	6.43	6.29	6.16	6.05	5.94	5.85	5.76	5.68	5.61	5.55	5.43	5.29	5.11
1000	8.95	8.58	8.26	7.98	7.73	7.51	7.31	7.14	6.98	6.84	6.72	6.60	6.50	6.40	6.31	6.24	6.16	6.03	5.88	5.68

EXHIBIT 21-3 CONT.

288

EQUAL MONTHLY PAYMENTS NECESSARY TO AMORTIZE A LOAN

6½%

TERM AMOUNT	1 YEARS	1½ YEARS	2 YEARS	2½ YEARS	3 YEARS	3½ YEARS	4 YEARS	4½ YEARS	5 YEARS	5½ YEARS	6 YEARS	6½ YEARS	7 YEARS	7½ YEARS	8 YEARS	9 YEARS	10 YEARS	11 YEARS	12 YEARS	13 YEARS
$100	8.63	5.85	4.46	3.63	3.07	2.67	2.38	2.15	1.96	1.81	1.69	1.58	1.49	1.41	1.34	1.23	1.14	1.07	1.01	.96
200	17.26	11.70	8.91	7.25	6.13	5.34	4.75	4.29	3.92	3.62	3.37	3.16	2.97	2.82	2.68	2.46	2.28	2.13	2.01	1.91
300	25.89	17.54	13.37	10.87	9.20	8.01	7.12	6.43	5.87	5.42	5.05	4.73	4.46	4.23	4.02	3.68	3.41	3.19	3.01	2.86
400	34.52	23.39	17.82	14.49	12.26	10.68	9.49	8.57	7.83	7.23	6.73	6.31	5.94	5.63	5.36	4.91	4.55	4.25	4.01	3.81
500	43.15	29.23	22.28	18.11	15.33	13.35	11.86	10.71	9.79	9.04	8.41	7.88	7.43	7.04	6.70	6.13	5.68	5.32	5.01	4.76
600	51.78	35.08	26.73	21.73	18.39	16.02	14.23	12.85	11.74	10.84	10.09	9.46	8.91	8.45	8.04	7.36	6.82	6.38	6.02	5.71
700	60.41	40.93	31.19	25.35	21.46	18.68	16.61	14.99	13.70	12.65	11.77	11.03	10.40	9.85	9.38	8.58	7.95	7.44	7.02	6.66
800	69.04	46.77	35.64	28.97	24.52	21.35	18.98	17.13	15.66	14.45	13.45	12.61	11.88	11.26	10.71	9.81	9.09	8.50	8.02	7.61
900	77.67	52.62	40.10	32.59	27.59	24.02	21.35	19.27	17.61	16.26	15.13	14.18	13.37	12.67	12.05	11.03	10.22	9.57	9.02	8.57
1000	86.30	58.46	44.55	36.21	30.65	26.69	23.72	21.41	19.57	18.07	16.81	15.76	14.85	14.07	13.39	12.26	11.36	10.63	10.02	9.52

6½%

TERM AMOUNT	14 YEARS	15 YEARS	16 YEARS	17 YEARS	18 YEARS	19 YEARS	20 YEARS	21 YEARS	22 YEARS	23 YEARS	24 YEARS	25 YEARS	26 YEARS	27 YEARS	28 YEARS	29 YEARS	30 YEARS	32 YEARS	35 YEARS	40 YEARS
$100	.91	.88	.84	.82	.79	.77	.75	.73	.72	.70	.69	.68	.67	.66	.65	.64	.64	.62	.61	.59
200	1.82	1.75	1.68	1.63	1.58	1.53	1.50	1.46	1.43	1.40	1.38	1.36	1.33	1.32	1.30	1.28	1.27	1.24	1.21	1.18
300	2.73	2.62	2.52	2.44	2.36	2.30	2.24	2.19	2.14	2.10	2.06	2.03	2.00	1.97	1.95	1.92	1.90	1.86	1.82	1.76
400	3.64	3.49	3.36	3.25	3.15	3.06	2.99	2.92	2.86	2.80	2.75	2.71	2.66	2.63	2.59	2.56	2.53	2.48	2.42	2.35
500	4.55	4.36	4.20	4.06	3.94	3.83	3.73	3.65	3.57	3.50	3.44	3.38	3.33	3.28	3.24	3.20	3.17	3.10	3.03	2.93
600	5.45	5.23	5.04	4.87	4.72	4.59	4.48	4.38	4.28	4.20	4.12	4.06	3.99	3.94	3.89	3.84	3.80	3.72	3.63	3.52
700	6.36	6.10	5.88	5.68	5.51	5.36	5.22	5.10	5.00	4.90	4.81	4.73	4.66	4.59	4.53	4.48	4.43	4.34	4.23	4.10
800	7.27	6.97	6.72	6.49	6.30	6.12	5.97	5.83	5.71	5.60	5.50	5.41	5.32	5.25	5.18	5.12	5.06	4.96	4.84	4.69
900	8.18	7.84	7.56	7.31	7.08	6.89	6.72	6.56	6.42	6.30	6.18	6.08	5.99	5.90	5.83	5.76	5.69	5.58	5.44	5.27
1000	9.09	8.72	8.40	8.12	7.87	7.65	7.46	7.29	7.13	7.00	6.87	6.76	6.65	6.56	6.48	6.40	6.33	6.20	6.05	5.86

EXHIBIT 21-3 CONT.

289

EQUAL MONTHLY PAYMENTS NECESSARY TO AMORTIZE A LOAN

6¾%

TERM AMOUNT	1 YEARS	1½ YEARS	2 YEARS	2½ YEARS	3 YEARS	3½ YEARS	4 YEARS	4½ YEARS	5 YEARS	5½ YEARS	6 YEARS	6½ YEARS	7 YEARS	7½ YEARS	8 YEARS	9 YEARS	10 YEARS	11 YEARS	12 YEARS	13 YEARS
$100	8.65	5.86	4.47	3.64	3.08	2.68	2.39	2.16	1.97	1.82	1.70	1.59	1.50	1.42	1.36	1.24	1.15	1.08	1.02	.97
200	17.29	11.72	8.94	7.27	6.16	5.36	4.77	4.31	3.94	3.64	3.39	3.18	3.00	2.84	2.71	2.48	2.30	2.16	2.04	1.93
300	25.93	17.58	13.40	10.90	9.23	8.04	7.15	6.46	5.91	5.46	5.08	4.77	4.50	4.26	4.06	3.72	3.45	3.23	3.05	2.90
400	34.57	23.43	17.87	14.53	12.31	10.72	9.54	8.61	7.88	7.28	6.78	6.35	5.99	5.68	5.41	4.96	4.60	4.31	4.07	3.86
500	43.21	29.29	22.33	18.16	15.39	13.40	11.92	10.77	9.85	9.09	8.47	7.94	7.49	7.10	6.76	6.20	5.75	5.38	5.08	4.83
600	51.85	35.15	26.80	21.80	18.46	16.08	14.30	12.92	11.82	10.91	10.16	9.53	8.99	8.52	8.11	7.43	6.89	6.46	6.10	5.79
700	60.49	41.01	31.27	25.43	21.54	18.76	16.69	15.07	13.78	12.73	11.86	11.12	10.48	9.94	9.46	8.67	8.04	7.53	7.11	6.76
800	69.13	46.86	35.73	29.06	24.62	21.44	19.07	17.22	15.75	14.55	13.55	12.70	11.98	11.36	10.81	9.91	9.19	8.61	8.13	7.72
900	77.78	52.72	40.20	32.69	27.69	24.12	21.45	19.38	17.72	16.37	15.24	14.29	13.48	12.78	12.16	11.15	10.34	9.68	9.14	8.69
1000	86.42	58.58	44.66	36.32	30.77	26.80	23.84	21.53	19.69	18.18	16.93	15.88	14.98	14.20	13.51	12.39	11.49	10.76	10.16	9.65

6¾%

TERM AMOUNT	14 YEARS	15 YEARS	16 YEARS	17 YEARS	18 YEARS	19 YEARS	20 YEARS	21 YEARS	22 YEARS	23 YEARS	24 YEARS	25 YEARS	26 YEARS	27 YEARS	28 YEARS	29 YEARS	30 YEARS	32 YEARS	35 YEARS	40 YEARS
$100	.93	.89	.86	.83	.81	.78	.77	.75	.73	.72	.71	.70	.69	.68	.67	.66	.65	.64	.63	.61
200	1.85	1.77	1.71	1.66	1.61	1.56	1.53	1.49	1.46	1.43	1.41	1.39	1.37	1.35	1.33	1.32	1.30	1.28	1.25	1.21
300	2.77	2.66	2.56	2.48	2.41	2.34	2.29	2.24	2.19	2.15	2.11	2.08	2.05	2.02	1.99	1.97	1.95	1.91	1.87	1.82
400	3.69	3.54	3.42	3.31	3.21	3.12	3.05	2.98	2.92	2.86	2.81	2.77	2.73	2.69	2.66	2.63	2.60	2.55	2.49	2.42
500	4.61	4.43	4.27	4.13	4.01	3.90	3.81	3.72	3.65	3.58	3.52	3.46	3.41	3.36	3.32	3.28	3.25	3.19	3.11	3.02
600	5.54	5.31	5.12	4.96	4.81	4.68	4.57	4.47	4.37	4.29	4.22	4.15	4.09	4.03	3.98	3.94	3.90	3.82	3.73	3.63
700	6.46	6.20	5.98	5.78	5.61	5.46	5.33	5.21	5.10	5.01	4.92	4.84	4.77	4.71	4.65	4.59	4.55	4.46	4.35	4.23
800	7.38	7.08	6.83	6.61	6.41	6.24	6.09	5.95	5.83	5.72	5.62	5.53	5.45	5.38	5.31	5.25	5.19	5.10	4.98	4.83
900	8.30	7.97	7.68	7.43	7.21	7.02	6.85	6.70	6.56	6.43	6.32	6.22	6.13	6.05	5.97	5.91	5.84	5.73	5.60	5.44
1000	9.22	8.85	8.54	8.26	8.01	7.80	7.61	7.44	7.29	7.15	7.03	6.91	6.81	6.72	6.64	6.56	6.49	6.37	6.22	6.04

EXHIBIT 21-3 CONT.

EQUAL MONTHLY PAYMENTS NECESSARY TO AMORTIZE A LOAN

7%

TERM AMOUNT	1 YEARS	1½ YEARS	2 YEARS	2½ YEARS	3 YEARS	3½ YEARS	4 YEARS	4½ YEARS	5 YEARS	5½ YEARS	6 YEARS	6½ YEARS	7 YEARS	7½ YEARS	8 YEARS	9 YEARS	10 YEARS	11 YEARS	12 YEARS	13 YEARS
$100	8.66	5.87	4.48	3.65	3.09	2.70	2.40	2.17	1.99	1.83	1.71	1.60	1.51	1.44	1.37	1.26	1.17	1.09	1.03	.98
200	17.31	11.74	8.96	7.29	6.18	5.39	4.79	4.33	3.97	3.66	3.41	3.20	3.02	2.87	2.73	2.51	2.33	2.18	2.06	1.96
300	25.96	17.61	13.44	10.93	9.27	8.08	7.19	6.50	5.95	5.49	5.12	4.80	4.53	4.30	4.10	3.76	3.49	3.27	3.09	2.94
400	34.62	23.48	17.91	14.58	12.36	10.77	9.58	8.66	7.93	7.32	6.82	6.40	6.04	5.73	5.46	5.01	4.65	4.36	4.12	3.92
500	43.27	29.35	22.39	18.22	15.44	13.46	11.98	10.83	9.91	9.15	8.53	8.00	7.55	7.16	6.83	6.26	5.81	5.45	5.15	4.90
600	51.92	35.22	26.87	21.86	18.53	16.15	14.37	12.99	11.89	10.98	10.23	9.60	9.06	8.59	8.19	7.51	6.97	6.54	6.18	5.87
700	60.57	41.08	31.35	25.51	21.62	18.84	16.77	15.15	13.87	12.81	11.94	11.20	10.57	10.02	9.55	8.76	8.13	7.62	7.20	6.85
800	69.23	46.95	35.82	29.15	24.71	21.54	19.16	17.32	15.85	14.64	13.64	12.80	12.08	11.46	10.91	10.01	9.29	8.71	8.23	7.83
900	77.88	52.82	40.30	32.79	27.79	24.23	21.56	19.48	17.83	16.47	15.35	14.40	13.59	12.89	12.28	11.26	10.45	9.80	9.26	8.81
1000	86.53	58.69	44.78	36.44	30.88	26.92	23.95	21.65	19.81	18.30	17.05	16.00	15.10	14.32	13.64	12.51	11.62	10.89	10.29	9.79

7%

TERM AMOUNT	14 YEARS	15 YEARS	16 YEARS	17 YEARS	18 YEARS	19 YEARS	20 YEARS	21 YEARS	22 YEARS	23 YEARS	24 YEARS	25 YEARS	26 YEARS	27 YEARS	28 YEARS	29 YEARS	30 YEARS	32 YEARS	35 YEARS	40 YEARS
$100	.94	.90	.87	.84	.82	.80	.78	.76	.75	.73	.72	.71	.70	.69	.68	.68	.67	.66	.64	.63
200	1.88	1.80	1.74	1.68	1.64	1.59	1.56	1.52	1.49	1.46	1.44	1.42	1.40	1.38	1.36	1.35	1.34	1.31	1.28	1.25
300	2.81	2.70	2.61	2.52	2.45	2.39	2.33	2.28	2.24	2.19	2.16	2.13	2.10	2.07	2.04	2.02	2.00	1.97	1.92	1.87
400	3.75	3.60	3.47	3.36	3.27	3.16	3.11	3.04	2.98	2.92	2.88	2.83	2.79	2.76	2.72	2.69	2.67	2.62	2.56	2.49
500	4.68	4.50	4.34	4.20	4.08	3.98	3.88	3.80	3.72	3.65	3.59	3.54	3.49	3.44	3.40	3.37	3.33	3.27	3.20	3.11
600	5.62	5.40	5.21	5.04	4.90	4.77	4.66	4.56	4.47	4.38	4.31	4.25	4.19	4.13	4.08	4.04	4.00	3.93	3.84	3.73
700	6.55	6.30	6.08	5.88	5.71	5.56	5.43	5.31	5.21	5.11	5.03	4.95	4.88	4.82	4.76	4.71	4.66	4.58	4.48	4.36
800	7.49	7.20	6.94	6.72	6.53	6.36	6.21	6.07	5.95	5.84	5.75	5.66	5.58	5.51	5.44	5.38	5.33	5.23	5.12	4.98
900	8.42	8.09	7.81	7.56	7.34	7.15	6.98	6.83	6.70	6.57	6.46	6.37	6.28	6.20	6.12	6.05	5.99	5.89	5.75	5.60
1000	9.36	8.99	8.63	8.40	8.16	7.95	7.76	7.59	7.44	7.30	7.18	7.07	6.97	6.88	6.80	6.73	6.66	6.54	6.39	6.22

EXHIBIT 21-3 CONT.

EQUAL MONTHLY PAYMENTS NECESSARY TO AMORTIZE A LOAN

7¼%

TERM AMOUNT	1 YEARS	1½ YEARS	2 YEARS	2½ YEARS	3 YEARS	3½ YEARS	4 YEARS	4½ YEARS	5 YEARS	5½ YEARS	6 YEARS	6½ YEARS	7 YEARS	7½ YEARS	8 YEARS	9 YEARS	10 YEARS	11 YEARS	12 YEARS	13 YEARS
$100	8.67	5.88	4.49	3.66	3.10	2.71	2.41	2.18	2.00	1.85	1.72	1.62	1.53	1.45	1.38	1.27	1.18	1.11	1.05	1.00
200	17.33	11.76	8.98	7.31	6.20	5.41	4.82	4.36	3.99	3.69	3.44	3.23	3.05	2.89	2.76	2.53	2.35	2.21	2.09	1.99
300	26.00	17.64	13.47	10.97	9.30	8.11	7.22	6.53	5.98	5.53	5.16	4.84	4.57	4.34	4.13	3.79	3.53	3.31	3.13	2.98
400	34.66	23.52	17.96	14.62	12.40	10.82	9.63	8.71	7.97	7.37	6.87	6.45	6.09	5.78	5.51	5.06	4.70	4.41	4.17	3.97
500	43.33	29.40	22.45	18.28	15.50	13.52	12.04	10.88	9.96	9.21	8.59	8.06	7.61	7.22	6.88	6.32	5.88	5.51	5.21	4.96
600	51.99	35.28	26.94	21.93	18.60	16.22	14.44	13.06	11.96	11.06	10.31	9.67	9.13	8.67	8.26	7.58	7.05	6.61	6.26	5.96
700	60.65	41.16	31.43	25.59	21.70	18.93	16.85	15.24	13.95	12.90	12.02	11.29	10.66	10.11	9.64	8.85	8.22	7.72	7.30	6.95
800	69.32	47.04	35.91	29.24	24.80	21.63	19.25	17.41	15.94	14.74	13.74	12.90	12.18	11.55	11.01	10.11	9.40	8.82	8.34	7.94
900	77.98	52.92	40.40	32.90	27.90	24.33	21.66	19.59	17.93	16.58	15.46	14.51	13.70	13.00	12.39	11.37	10.57	9.92	9.38	8.93
1000	86.65	58.80	44.89	36.55	31.00	27.03	24.07	21.76	19.92	18.42	17.17	16.12	15.22	14.44	13.76	12.64	11.75	11.02	10.42	9.92

7¼%

TERM AMOUNT	14 YEARS	15 YEARS	16 YEARS	17 YEARS	18 YEARS	19 YEARS	20 YEARS	21 YEARS	22 YEARS	23 YEARS	24 YEARS	25 YEARS	26 YEARS	27 YEARS	28 YEARS	29 YEARS	30 YEARS	32 YEARS	35 YEARS	40 YEARS
$100	.95	.92	.89	.86	.84	.81	.80	.78	.76	.75	.74	.73	.72	.71	.70	.69	.69	.68	.66	.64
200	1.90	1.83	1.77	1.71	1.67	1.62	1.59	1.55	1.52	1.50	1.47	1.45	1.43	1.41	1.40	1.38	1.37	1.35	1.32	1.28
300	2.85	2.74	2.65	2.57	2.50	2.43	2.38	2.33	2.28	2.24	2.21	2.17	2.14	2.12	2.09	2.07	2.05	2.02	1.97	1.92
400	3.80	3.66	3.53	3.42	3.33	3.24	3.17	3.10	3.04	2.99	2.94	2.90	2.86	2.82	2.79	2.76	2.73	2.69	2.63	2.56
500	4.75	4.57	4.41	4.28	4.16	4.05	3.96	3.85	3.80	3.73	3.67	3.62	3.57	3.53	3.49	3.45	3.42	3.36	3.29	3.20
600	5.70	5.48	5.29	5.13	4.99	4.86	4.75	4.65	4.56	4.48	4.41	4.34	4.28	4.23	4.18	4.14	4.10	4.03	3.94	3.84
700	6.65	6.40	6.18	5.98	5.82	5.67	5.54	5.42	5.32	5.22	5.14	5.06	5.00	4.93	4.88	4.83	4.78	4.70	4.60	4.48
800	7.60	7.31	7.06	6.84	6.65	6.48	6.33	6.19	6.08	5.97	5.87	5.79	5.71	5.64	5.57	5.52	5.46	5.37	5.26	5.12
900	8.55	8.22	7.94	7.69	7.48	7.29	7.12	6.97	6.84	6.72	6.61	6.51	6.42	6.34	6.27	6.20	6.14	6.04	5.91	5.76
1000	9.50	9.13	8.82	8.55	8.31	8.10	7.91	7.74	7.59	7.46	7.34	7.23	7.14	7.05	6.97	6.89	6.83	6.71	6.57	6.40

EXHIBIT 21-3 CONT.

EQUAL MONTHLY PAYMENTS NECESSARY TO AMORTIZE A LOAN

7½%

TERM AMOUNT	1 YEARS	1½ YEARS	2 YEARS	2½ YEARS	3 YEARS	3½ YEARS	4 YEARS	4½ YEARS	5 YEARS	5½ YEARS	6 YEARS	6½ YEARS	7 YEARS	7½ YEARS	8 YEARS	9 YEARS	10 YEARS	11 YEARS	12 YEARS	13 YEARS
$100	8.68	5.90	4.50	3.67	3.12	2.72	2.42	2.19	2.01	1.86	1.73	1.63	1.54	1.46	1.39	1.28	1.19	1.12	1.06	1.01
200	17.36	11.79	9.00	7.34	6.23	5.43	4.84	4.38	4.01	3.71	3.46	3.25	3.07	2.92	2.78	2.56	2.38	2.23	2.12	2.02
300	26.03	17.68	13.50	11.00	9.34	8.15	7.26	6.57	6.02	5.57	5.19	4.88	4.61	4.37	4.17	3.83	3.57	3.35	3.17	3.02
400	34.71	23.57	18.00	14.67	12.45	10.86	9.68	8.76	8.02	7.42	6.92	6.50	6.14	5.83	5.56	5.11	4.75	4.46	4.23	4.03
500	43.38	29.46	22.50	18.33	15.56	13.58	12.09	10.94	10.02	9.27	8.65	8.12	7.67	7.29	6.95	6.39	5.94	5.58	5.28	5.03
600	52.06	35.35	27.00	22.00	18.67	16.29	14.51	13.13	12.03	11.13	10.38	9.75	9.21	8.74	8.34	7.66	7.13	6.69	6.34	6.04
700	60.74	41.24	31.50	25.67	21.78	19.01	16.93	15.32	14.03	12.98	12.11	11.37	10.74	10.20	9.72	8.94	8.31	7.81	7.39	7.04
800	69.41	47.13	36.00	29.33	24.89	21.72	19.35	17.51	16.04	14.83	13.84	13.00	12.28	11.65	11.11	10.21	9.50	8.92	8.45	8.05
900	78.09	53.03	40.50	33.00	28.00	24.44	21.77	19.69	18.04	16.69	15.57	14.62	13.81	13.11	12.50	11.49	10.69	10.04	9.50	9.05
1000	86.76	58.92	45.00	36.66	31.11	27.15	24.18	21.88	20.04	18.54	17.30	16.24	15.34	14.57	13.89	12.77	11.88	11.15	10.56	10.06

7½%

TERM AMOUNT	14 YEARS	15 YEARS	16 YEARS	17 YEARS	18 YEARS	19 YEARS	20 YEARS	21 YEARS	22 YEARS	23 YEARS	24 YEARS	25 YEARS	26 YEARS	27 YEARS	28 YEARS	29 YEARS	30 YEARS	32 YEARS	35 YEARS	40 YEARS
$100	.97	.93	.90	.87	.85	.83	.81	.79	.78	.77	.75	.74	.73	.73	.72	.71	.70	.69	.68	.66
200	1.93	1.86	1.80	1.74	1.69	1.65	1.62	1.58	1.55	1.53	1.50	1.48	1.46	1.45	1.43	1.42	1.40	1.38	1.35	1.32
300	2.89	2.79	2.69	2.61	2.54	2.48	2.42	2.37	2.33	2.29	2.25	2.22	2.19	2.17	2.14	2.12	2.10	2.07	2.03	1.98
400	3.86	3.71	3.59	3.48	3.38	3.30	3.23	3.16	3.10	3.05	3.00	2.96	2.92	2.89	2.86	2.83	2.80	2.76	2.70	2.64
500	4.82	4.64	4.48	4.35	4.23	4.13	4.03	3.95	3.88	3.81	3.75	3.70	3.65	3.61	3.57	3.53	3.50	3.44	3.38	3.30
600	5.78	5.57	5.38	5.22	5.07	4.95	4.84	4.74	4.65	4.57	4.50	4.44	4.38	4.33	4.28	4.24	4.20	4.13	4.05	3.95
700	6.75	6.49	6.28	6.09	5.92	5.77	5.64	5.53	5.43	5.33	5.25	5.18	5.11	5.05	5.00	4.95	4.90	4.82	4.72	4.61
800	7.71	7.42	7.17	6.95	6.76	6.60	6.45	6.32	6.20	6.10	6.00	5.92	5.84	5.77	5.71	5.65	5.60	5.51	5.40	5.27
900	8.67	8.35	8.07	7.82	7.61	7.42	7.26	7.11	6.98	6.86	6.75	6.66	6.57	6.49	6.42	6.36	6.30	6.20	6.07	5.93
1000	9.64	9.28	8.96	8.69	8.45	8.25	8.06	7.90	7.75	7.62	7.50	7.39	7.30	7.21	7.13	7.06	7.00	6.88	6.75	6.59

EXHIBIT 21-3 CONT.

293

EQUAL MONTHLY PAYMENTS NECESSARY TO AMORTIZE A LOAN

8%   **8%**

TERM AMOUNT	1 YEARS	1½ YEARS	2 YEARS	2½ YEARS	3 YEARS	3½ YEARS	4 YEARS	4½ YEARS	5 YEARS	5½ YEARS	6 YEARS	6½ YEARS	7 YEARS	7½ YEARS	8 YEARS	9 YEARS	10 YEARS	11 YEARS	12 YEARS	13 YEARS
$100	8.70	5.92	4.53	3.69	3.14	2.74	2.45	2.22	2.03	1.88	1.76	1.65	1.56	1.49	1.42	1.31	1.22	1.15	1.09	1.04
200	17.40	11.83	9.05	7.38	6.27	5.48	4.89	4.43	4.06	3.76	3.51	3.30	3.12	2.97	2.83	2.61	2.43	2.29	2.17	2.07
300	26.10	17.75	13.57	11.07	9.41	8.22	7.33	6.64	6.09	5.64	5.26	4.95	4.68	4.45	4.25	3.91	3.64	3.43	3.25	3.10
400	34.80	23.66	18.10	14.76	12.54	10.96	9.77	8.85	8.12	7.52	7.02	6.60	6.24	5.93	5.66	5.21	4.86	4.57	4.33	4.14
500	43.50	29.58	22.62	18.45	15.67	13.69	12.21	11.06	10.14	9.39	8.77	8.25	7.80	7.41	7.07	6.51	6.07	5.71	5.42	5.17
600	52.20	35.49	27.14	22.14	18.81	16.43	14.65	13.27	12.17	11.27	10.52	9.89	9.36	8.89	8.49	7.82	7.28	6.85	6.50	6.20
700	60.90	41.40	31.66	25.83	21.94	19.17	17.09	15.48	14.20	13.15	12.28	11.54	10.92	10.37	9.90	9.12	8.50	8.00	7.58	7.24
800	69.60	47.32	36.19	29.52	25.07	21.91	19.54	17.69	16.23	15.03	14.03	13.19	12.47	11.85	11.31	10.42	9.71	9.14	8.66	8.27
900	78.29	53.23	40.71	33.20	28.21	24.64	21.98	19.91	18.25	16.91	15.78	14.84	14.03	13.34	12.73	11.72	10.92	10.28	9.75	9.30
1000	86.99	59.15	45.23	36.89	31.34	27.38	24.42	22.12	20.28	18.78	17.54	16.49	15.59	14.82	14.14	13.02	12.14	11.42	10.83	10.34

8%   **8%**

TERM AMOUNT	14 YEARS	15 YEARS	16 YEARS	17 YEARS	18 YEARS	19 YEARS	20 YEARS	21 YEARS	22 YEARS	23 YEARS	24 YEARS	25 YEARS	26 YEARS	27 YEARS	28 YEARS	29 YEARS	30 YEARS	32 YEARS	35 YEARS	40 YEARS
$100	1.00	.96	.93	.90	.88	.86	.84	.83	.81	.80	.79	.78	.77	.76	.75	.74	.74	.73	.72	.70
200	1.99	1.92	1.85	1.80	1.75	1.71	1.68	1.65	1.62	1.59	1.57	1.55	1.53	1.51	1.50	1.48	1.47	1.45	1.43	1.40
300	2.98	2.87	2.78	2.70	2.63	2.57	2.51	2.47	2.42	2.39	2.35	2.32	2.29	2.27	2.25	2.22	2.21	2.17	2.14	2.09
400	3.97	3.83	3.70	3.60	3.50	3.42	3.35	3.29	3.23	3.18	3.13	3.09	3.06	3.02	2.99	2.96	2.94	2.90	2.85	2.79
500	4.96	4.78	4.63	4.50	4.38	4.28	4.19	4.11	4.04	3.97	3.92	3.86	3.82	3.78	3.74	3.70	3.67	3.62	3.56	3.48
600	5.95	5.74	5.55	5.39	5.25	5.13	5.02	4.93	4.84	4.77	4.70	4.64	4.58	4.53	4.49	4.44	4.41	4.34	4.27	4.18
700	6.94	6.69	6.48	6.29	6.13	5.99	5.86	5.75	5.65	5.56	5.48	5.41	5.34	5.28	5.23	5.18	5.14	5.07	4.98	4.87
800	7.94	7.65	7.40	7.19	7.00	6.84	6.70	6.57	6.45	6.35	6.26	6.18	6.11	6.04	5.98	5.92	5.88	5.79	5.69	5.57
900	8.93	8.61	8.33	8.09	7.88	7.70	7.53	7.39	7.26	7.15	7.04	6.95	6.87	6.79	6.73	6.66	6.61	6.51	6.40	6.26
1000	9.92	9.56	9.25	8.99	8.75	8.55	8.37	8.21	8.07	7.94	7.83	7.72	7.63	7.55	7.47	7.40	7.34	7.24	7.11	6.96

EXHIBIT 21-3 CONT.

294

EQUAL MONTHLY PAYMENTS NECESSARY TO AMORTIZE A LOAN

8½%

TERM AMOUNT	1 YEARS	1½ YEARS	2 YEARS	2½ YEARS	3 YEARS	3½ YEARS	4 YEARS	4½ YEARS	5 YEARS	5½ YEARS	6 YEARS	6½ YEARS	7 YEARS	7½ YEARS	8 YEARS	9 YEARS	10 YEARS	11 YEARS	12 YEARS	13 YEARS
$100	8.73	5.94	4.55	3.72	3.16	2.77	2.47	2.24	2.06	1.91	1.78	1.68	1.59	1.51	1.44	1.33	1.24	1.17	1.12	1.07
200	17.45	11.88	9.10	7.43	6.32	5.53	4.93	4.48	4.11	3.81	3.56	3.35	3.17	3.02	2.88	2.66	2.48	2.34	2.23	2.13
300	26.17	17.82	13.64	11.14	9.48	8.29	7.40	6.71	6.16	5.71	5.34	5.02	4.76	4.52	4.32	3.99	3.72	3.51	3.34	3.19
400	34.89	23.75	18.19	14.85	12.63	11.05	9.86	8.95	8.21	7.61	7.12	6.70	6.34	6.03	5.76	5.32	4.96	4.68	4.45	4.25
500	43.61	29.69	22.73	18.56	15.79	13.81	12.33	11.18	10.26	9.52	8.89	8.37	7.92	7.54	7.20	6.64	6.20	5.85	5.56	5.31
600	52.34	35.63	27.28	22.28	18.95	16.57	14.79	13.42	12.31	11.42	10.67	10.04	9.51	9.04	8.64	7.97	7.44	7.02	6.67	6.37
700	61.06	41.56	31.82	25.99	22.10	19.33	17.26	15.65	14.37	13.32	12.45	11.72	11.09	10.55	10.08	9.30	8.68	8.19	7.78	7.43
800	69.78	47.50	36.37	29.70	25.26	22.09	19.72	17.89	16.42	15.22	14.23	13.39	12.67	12.06	11.52	10.63	9.92	9.35	8.89	8.49
900	78.50	53.44	40.92	33.41	28.42	24.85	22.19	20.12	18.47	17.12	16.01	15.06	14.26	13.56	12.96	11.96	11.16	10.52	10.00	9.56
1000	87.22	59.37	45.46	37.12	31.57	27.62	24.65	22.36	20.52	19.03	17.78	16.74	15.84	15.07	14.40	13.28	12.40	11.69	11.11	10.62

8½%

TERM AMOUNT	14 YEARS	15 YEARS	16 YEARS	17 YEARS	18 YEARS	19 YEARS	20 YEARS	21 YEARS	22 YEARS	23 YEARS	24 YEARS	25 YEARS	26 YEARS	27 YEARS	28 YEARS	29 YEARS	30 YEARS	32 YEARS	35 YEARS	40 YEARS
$100	1.02	.99	.96	.93	.91	.89	.87	.86	.84	.83	.82	.81	.80	.79	.79	.78	.77	.76	.75	.74
200	2.04	1.97	1.91	1.86	1.82	1.78	1.74	1.71	1.68	1.66	1.64	1.62	1.60	1.58	1.57	1.55	1.54	1.52	1.50	1.47
300	3.06	2.96	2.87	2.79	2.72	2.66	2.61	2.56	2.52	2.48	2.45	2.42	2.39	2.37	2.35	2.33	2.31	2.28	2.25	2.20
400	4.08	3.94	3.82	3.72	3.63	3.55	3.48	3.41	3.36	3.31	3.27	3.23	3.19	3.16	3.13	3.10	3.08	3.04	2.99	2.94
500	5.10	4.93	4.78	4.65	4.53	4.43	4.34	4.27	4.20	4.14	4.08	4.03	3.99	3.95	3.91	3.88	3.85	3.80	3.74	3.67
600	6.12	5.91	5.73	5.57	5.44	5.32	5.21	5.12	5.04	4.96	4.90	4.84	4.78	4.74	4.69	4.65	4.62	4.56	4.49	4.40
700	7.14	6.90	6.69	6.50	6.34	6.20	6.08	5.97	5.87	5.79	5.71	5.64	5.58	5.52	5.47	5.43	5.39	5.32	5.23	5.14
800	8.16	7.88	7.64	7.43	7.25	7.09	6.95	6.82	6.71	6.61	6.53	6.45	6.38	6.31	6.25	6.20	6.16	6.08	5.98	5.87
900	9.18	8.87	8.60	8.36	8.15	7.97	7.82	7.68	7.55	7.44	7.34	7.25	7.17	7.10	7.04	6.98	6.93	6.83	6.73	6.60
1000	10.20	9.85	9.55	9.29	9.06	8.86	8.68	8.53	8.39	8.27	8.16	8.06	7.97	7.89	7.82	7.75	7.69	7.59	7.47	7.34

EXHIBIT 21-3 CONT.

EQUAL MONTHLY PAYMENTS NECESSARY TO AMORTIZE A LOAN

9%

TERM AMOUNT	1 YEARS	1½ YEARS	2 YEARS	2½ YEARS	3 YEARS	3½ YEARS	4 YEARS	4½ YEARS	5 YEARS	5½ YEARS	6 YEARS	6½ YEARS	7 YEARS	7½ YEARS	8 YEARS	9 YEARS	10 YEARS	11 YEARS	12 YEARS	13 YEARS
$100	8.75	5.96	4.57	3.74	3.18	2.79	2.49	2.26	2.08	1.93	1.81	1.70	1.61	1.54	1.47	1.36	1.27	1.20	1.14	1.09
200	17.50	11.92	9.14	7.47	6.36	5.57	4.98	4.52	4.16	3.86	3.61	3.40	3.22	3.07	2.94	2.71	2.54	2.40	2.28	2.18
300	26.24	17.88	13.71	11.21	9.54	8.36	7.47	6.78	6.23	5.78	5.41	5.10	4.83	4.60	4.40	4.07	3.81	3.59	3.42	3.27
400	34.99	23.84	18.88	14.94	12.72	11.14	9.96	9.04	8.31	7.71	7.22	6.80	6.44	6.13	5.87	5.42	5.07	4.79	4.56	4.36
500	43.73	29.80	22.85	18.68	15.90	13.93	12.45	11.30	10.38	9.64	9.02	8.50	8.05	7.66	7.33	6.78	6.34	5.99	5.70	5.45
600	52.48	35.76	27.42	22.41	19.08	16.71	14.94	13.56	12.46	11.56	10.82	10.19	9.66	9.20	8.80	8.13	7.61	7.18	6.83	6.54
700	61.22	41.72	31.90	26.15	22.26	19.50	17.42	15.82	14.54	13.49	12.62	11.89	11.27	10.73	10.26	9.49	8.87	8.38	7.97	7.63
800	69.97	47.68	36.55	29.88	25.44	22.28	19.91	18.08	16.61	15.42	14.43	13.59	12.88	12.26	11.73	10.84	10.14	9.57	9.11	8.72
900	78.71	53.64	41.12	33.62	28.62	25.07	22.40	20.34	18.69	17.34	16.23	15.29	14.49	13.79	13.19	12.19	11.41	10.77	10.25	9.81
1000	87.46	59.60	45.69	37.35	31.80	27.85	24.89	22.59	20.76	19.27	18.03	16.99	16.09	15.32	14.66	13.55	12.67	11.97	11.39	10.90

9%

TERM AMOUNT	14 YEARS	15 YEARS	16 YEARS	17 YEARS	18 YEARS	19 YEARS	20 YEARS	21 YEARS	22 YEARS	23 YEARS	24 YEARS	25 YEARS	26 YEARS	27 YEARS	28 YEARS	29 YEARS	30 YEARS	32 YEARS	35 YEARS	40 YEARS
$100	1.05	1.02	.99	.96	.94	.92	.90	.89	.88	.86	.85	.84	.84	.83	.82	.82	.81	.80	.79	.78
200	2.10	2.03	1.97	1.92	1.88	1.84	1.80	1.77	1.75	1.72	1.70	1.68	1.67	1.65	1.64	1.63	1.61	1.60	1.57	1.55
300	3.15	3.05	2.96	2.88	2.81	2.76	2.70	2.66	2.62	2.58	2.55	2.52	2.50	2.47	2.45	2.44	2.42	2.39	2.36	2.32
400	4.20	4.06	3.94	3.84	3.75	3.67	3.60	3.54	3.49	3.44	3.40	3.36	3.33	3.30	3.27	3.25	3.22	3.19	3.14	3.09
500	5.25	5.08	4.93	4.80	4.69	4.59	4.50	4.43	4.36	4.30	4.25	4.20	4.16	4.12	4.09	4.06	4.03	3.98	3.92	3.86
600	6.30	6.09	5.91	5.76	5.62	5.51	5.40	5.31	5.23	5.16	5.10	5.04	4.99	4.94	4.90	4.87	4.83	4.78	4.71	4.63
700	7.35	7.10	6.90	6.72	6.56	6.42	6.30	6.20	6.10	6.02	5.95	5.88	5.82	5.77	5.72	5.68	5.64	5.57	5.49	5.40
800	8.40	8.12	7.88	7.68	7.50	7.34	7.20	7.08	6.97	6.88	6.79	6.72	6.65	6.59	6.54	6.49	6.44	6.37	6.28	6.18
900	9.45	9.13	8.87	8.63	8.43	8.26	8.10	7.97	7.85	7.74	7.64	7.56	7.48	7.41	7.35	7.30	7.25	7.16	7.06	6.95
1000	10.49	10.15	9.85	9.59	9.37	9.17	9.00	8.85	8.72	8.60	8.49	8.40	8.31	8.24	8.17	8.11	8.05	7.96	7.84	7.72

EXHIBIT 21-3 CONT.

296

EQUAL MONTHLY PAYMENTS NECESSARY TO AMORTIZE A LOAN

9½%

9½%

TERM AMOUNT	1 YEARS	1½ YEARS	2 YEARS	2½ YEARS	3 YEARS	3½ YEARS	4 YEARS	4½ YEARS	5 YEARS	5½ YEARS	6 YEARS	6½ YEARS	7 YEARS	7½ YEARS	8 YEARS	9 YEARS	10 YEARS	11 YEARS	12 YEARS	13 YEARS
$100	8.77	5.99	4.60	3.76	3.21	2.81	2.52	2.29	2.11	1.96	1.83	1.73	1.64	1.56	1.50	1.39	1.30	1.23	1.17	1.12
200	17.54	11.97	9.19	7.52	6.41	5.62	5.03	4.57	4.21	3.91	3.66	3.45	3.27	3.12	2.99	2.77	2.59	2.45	2.34	2.24
300	26.31	17.95	13.78	11.28	9.61	8.43	7.54	6.85	6.31	5.86	5.49	5.17	4.91	4.68	4.48	4.15	3.89	3.68	3.50	3.36
400	35.08	23.94	18.37	15.04	12.82	11.24	10.05	9.14	8.41	7.81	7.31	6.90	6.54	6.24	5.97	5.53	5.18	4.90	4.67	4.48
500	43.85	29.92	22.96	18.79	16.02	14.05	12.57	11.42	10.51	9.76	9.14	8.62	8.18	7.79	7.46	6.91	6.47	6.12	5.84	5.60
600	52.62	35.90	27.55	22.55	19.22	16.85	15.08	13.70	12.61	11.71	10.97	10.34	9.81	9.35	8.95	8.29	7.77	7.35	7.00	6.72
700	61.38	41.88	32.15	26.31	22.43	19.66	17.59	15.99	14.71	13.66	12.80	12.07	11.45	10.91	10.44	9.67	9.06	8.57	8.17	7.84
800	70.15	47.87	36.74	30.07	25.63	22.47	20.10	18.27	16.81	15.61	14.62	13.79	13.08	12.47	11.93	11.05	10.36	9.80	9.34	8.95
900	78.92	53.85	41.33	33.83	28.81	25.28	22.62	20.55	18.91	17.57	16.45	15.51	14.71	14.02	13.42	12.43	11.65	11.02	10.50	10.07
1000	87.69	59.83	45.92	37.58	32.04	28.09	25.13	22.84	21.01	19.52	18.28	17.24	16.35	15.58	14.92	13.81	12.94	12.24	11.67	11.19

TERM AMOUNT	14 YEARS	15 YEARS	16 YEARS	17 YEARS	18 YEARS	19 YEARS	20 YEARS	21 YEARS	22 YEARS	23 YEARS	24 YEARS	25 YEARS	26 YEARS	27 YEARS	28 YEARS	29 YEARS	30 YEARS	32 YEARS	35 YEARS	40 YEARS
$100	1.08	1.05	1.02	.99	.97	.95	.94	.92	.91	.90	.89	.88	.87	.86	.86	.85	.85	.84	.83	.82
200	2.16	2.09	2.03	1.98	1.94	1.90	1.87	1.84	1.81	1.79	1.77	1.75	1.74	1.72	1.71	1.70	1.69	1.67	1.65	1.63
300	3.24	3.14	3.05	2.97	2.91	2.85	2.80	2.76	2.72	2.68	2.65	2.63	2.60	2.58	2.56	2.54	2.53	2.50	2.47	2.44
400	4.32	4.18	4.06	3.96	3.88	3.80	3.73	3.67	3.62	3.58	3.54	3.50	3.47	3.44	3.41	3.39	3.37	3.33	3.29	3.25
500	5.40	5.23	5.08	4.95	4.84	4.75	4.67	4.59	4.53	4.47	4.42	4.37	4.33	4.30	4.26	4.24	4.21	4.16	4.11	4.06
600	6.48	6.27	6.09	5.94	5.81	5.70	5.60	5.51	5.43	5.36	5.30	5.25	5.20	5.16	5.12	5.08	5.05	5.00	4.93	4.87
700	7.55	7.31	7.11	6.93	6.78	6.65	6.53	6.43	6.34	6.26	6.18	6.12	6.06	6.01	5.97	5.93	5.89	5.83	5.76	5.68
800	8.63	8.36	8.12	7.92	7.75	7.60	7.46	7.34	7.24	7.15	7.07	6.99	6.93	6.87	6.82	6.77	6.73	6.66	6.58	6.49
900	9.71	9.40	9.14	8.91	8.72	8.54	8.39	8.26	8.15	8.04	7.95	7.87	7.80	7.73	7.67	7.62	7.57	7.49	7.40	7.30
1000	10.79	10.45	10.15	9.90	9.68	9.49	9.33	9.18	9.05	8.93	8.83	8.74	8.66	8.59	8.52	8.47	8.41	8.32	8.22	8.11

EXHIBIT 21-3 CONT.

EQUAL MONTHLY PAYMENTS NECESSARY TO AMORTIZE A LOAN

10%

TERM AMOUNT	1 YEARS	1½ YEARS	2 YEARS	2½ YEARS	3 YEARS	3½ YEARS	4 YEARS	4½ YEARS	5 YEARS	5½ YEARS	6 YEARS	6½ YEARS	7 YEARS	7½ YEARS	8 YEARS	9 YEARS	10 YEARS	11 YEARS	12 YEARS	13 YEARS
$100	8.80	6.01	4.62	3.79	3.23	2.84	2.54	2.31	2.13	1.98	1.86	1.75	1.67	1.59	1.52	1.41	1.33	1.26	1.20	1.15
200	17.59	12.02	9.23	7.57	6.46	5.67	5.08	4.62	4.25	3.96	3.71	3.50	3.33	3.17	3.04	2.82	2.65	2.51	2.40	2.30
300	26.38	18.02	13.85	11.35	9.69	8.50	7.61	6.93	6.38	5.93	5.56	5.25	4.99	4.76	4.56	4.23	3.97	3.76	3.59	3.45
400	35.17	24.03	18.46	15.13	12.91	11.33	10.15	9.23	8.50	7.91	7.42	7.00	6.65	6.34	6.07	5.64	5.29	5.01	4.79	4.60
500	43.96	30.03	23.08	18.91	16.14	14.16	12.69	11.54	10.63	9.88	9.27	8.75	8.31	7.92	7.59	7.04	6.61	6.26	5.98	5.74
600	52.75	36.04	27.69	22.69	19.37	17.00	15.22	13.85	12.75	11.86	11.12	10.50	9.97	9.51	9.11	8.45	7.93	7.52	7.18	6.89
700	61.55	42.04	32.31	26.47	22.59	19.83	17.76	16.16	14.88	13.84	12.97	12.25	11.63	11.09	10.63	9.86	9.26	8.77	8.37	8.04
800	70.34	48.05	36.92	30.25	25.82	22.66	20.30	18.46	17.00	15.81	14.83	13.99	13.29	12.68	12.14	11.27	10.58	10.02	9.57	9.19
900	79.13	54.06	41.54	34.04	29.05	25.49	22.83	20.77	19.13	17.79	16.68	15.74	14.95	14.26	13.66	12.68	11.90	11.27	10.76	10.34
1000	87.92	60.06	46.15	37.82	32.27	28.32	25.37	23.08	21.25	19.76	18.53	17.49	16.61	15.84	15.18	14.08	13.22	12.52	11.96	11.48

10%

TERM AMOUNT	14 YEARS	15 YEARS	16 YEARS	17 YEARS	18 YEARS	19 YEARS	20 YEARS	21 YEARS	22 YEARS	23 YEARS	24 YEARS	25 YEARS	26 YEARS	27 YEARS	28 YEARS	29 YEARS	30 YEARS	32 YEARS	35 YEARS	40 YEARS
$100	1.11	1.08	1.05	1.03	1.00	.99	.97	.96	.94	.93	.92	.91	.91	.90	.89	.89	.88	.87	.86	.85
200	2.22	2.15	2.10	2.05	2.00	1.97	1.94	1.91	1.88	1.86	1.84	1.82	1.81	1.79	1.78	1.77	1.76	1.74	1.72	1.70
300	3.33	3.23	3.14	3.07	3.00	2.95	2.90	2.86	2.82	2.79	2.76	2.73	2.71	2.69	2.67	2.65	2.64	2.61	2.58	2.55
400	4.44	4.30	4.19	4.09	4.00	3.93	3.87	3.81	3.76	3.71	3.67	3.64	3.61	3.58	3.56	3.53	3.52	3.48	3.44	3.40
500	5.55	5.38	5.23	5.11	5.00	4.91	4.83	4.76	4.70	4.64	4.59	4.55	4.51	4.48	4.44	4.42	4.39	4.35	4.30	4.25
600	6.65	6.45	6.28	6.13	6.00	5.89	5.80	5.71	5.63	5.57	5.51	5.46	5.41	5.37	5.33	5.30	5.27	5.22	5.16	5.10
700	7.76	7.53	7.33	7.15	7.00	6.87	6.76	6.66	6.57	6.50	6.43	6.37	6.31	6.26	6.22	6.18	6.15	6.09	6.02	5.95
800	8.87	8.60	8.37	8.17	8.00	7.86	7.73	7.61	7.51	7.42	7.34	7.27	7.21	7.16	7.11	7.06	7.03	6.96	6.88	6.80
900	9.98	9.68	9.42	9.20	9.00	8.84	8.69	8.56	8.45	8.35	8.26	8.18	8.11	8.05	8.00	7.95	7.90	7.83	7.74	7.65
1000	11.09	10.75	10.46	10.22	10.00	9.82	9.66	9.51	9.39	9.28	9.18	9.09	9.01	8.95	8.88	8.83	8.78	8.70	8.60	8.50

EXHIBIT 21-3 CONT.

PERCENTAGE OF PRINCIPAL UNPAID AT END OF 5-10-15 YEARS BY INTEREST RATE

5 YEARS

LOAN TERM	6%	6½%	6.9%	7%	7.2%	7½%	7⅝%	8%	9%	10%
10 Years	57	58	59	59	59	59	59	60	61	62
15 Years	76	77	77	77	78	78	78	79	80	81
20 Years	85	86	86	86	86	87	87	88	89	90
25 Years	90	91	91	91	91	92	92	92	93	94
30 Years	93	94	94	94	94	95	95	95	96	97

10 YEARS

LOAN TERM	6%	6½%	6.9%	7%	7.2%	7½%	7⅝%	8%	9%	10%
15 Years	44	44	45	45	46	46	46	47	49	50
20 Years	64	66	66	67	67	68	68	69	71	73
25 Years	76	77	78	79	79	80	80	81	83	84
30 Years	84	85	86	86	86	87	87	88	89	91

15 YEARS

LOAN TERM	6%	6½%	6.9%	7%	7.2%	7½%	7⅝%	8%	9%	10%
20 Years	37	38	39	39	39	40	40	41	43	45
25 Years	58	59	60	61	61	62	62	64	66	69
30 Years	71	72	74	74	75	75	76	77	79	81

EXHIBIT 21-4 REMAINING LOAN BALANCE

299

Table of Income Conversions

Per Hour	Per Week	Per Month	Per Year
1.65	66.00	286.00	3,432.00
1.70	68.00	294.67	3,536.00
1.75	70.00	303.33	3,640.00
1.80	72.00	312.00	3,744.00
1.85	74.00	320.67	3,848.00
1.90	76.00	329.33	3,952.00
1.95	78.00	338.00	4,056.00
2.00	80.00	346.67	4,160.00
2.05	82.00	355.33	4,264.00
2.10	84.00	364.00	4,368.00
2.15	86.00	372.67	4,472.00
2.20	88.00	381.33	4,576.00
2.25	90.00	390.00	4,680.00
2.30	92.00	398.67	4,784.00
2.35	94.00	407.33	4,888.00
2.40	96.00	416.00	4,992.00
2.45	98.00	424.67	5,096.00
2.50	100.00	433.33	5,200.00
2.55	102.00	442.00	5,304.00
2.60	104.00	450.67	5,408.00
2.65	106.00	459.33	5,512.00
2.70	108.00	468.00	5,616.00
2.75	110.00	476.67	5,720.00
2.80	112.00	485.33	5,824.00
2.85	114.00	494.00	5,928.00
2.90	116.00	502.67	6,032.00
2.95	118.00	511.33	6,136.00
3.00	120.00	520.00	6,240.00
3.05	122.00	528.67	6,344.00
3.10	124.00	537.33	6,448.00
3.15	126.00	546.00	6,552.00
3.20	128.00	554.67	6,656.00
3.25	130.00	563.33	6,760.00
3.30	132.00	572.00	6,864.00
3.35	134.00	580.67	6,968.00
3.40	136.00	589.33	7,072.00
3.45	138.00	598.00	7,176.00
3.50	140.00	606.67	7,280.00
3.55	142.00	615.33	7,384.00
3.60	144.00	624.00	7,488.00
3.65	146.00	632.67	7,592.00
3.70	148.00	641.33	7,696.00
3.75	150.00	650.00	7,800.00
3.80	152.00	658.67	7,904.00
3.85	154.00	667.33	8,008.00
3.90	156.00	676.00	8,112.00
3.95	158.00	684.67	8,216.00
4.00	160.00	693.33	8,320.00
4.05	162.00	702.00	8,424.00
4.10	164.00	710.67	8,528.00
4.15	166.00	719.33	8,632.00
4.20	168.00	728.00	8,736.00
4.25	170.00	736.67	8,840.00
4.30	172.00	745.33	8,944.00
4.35	174.00	754.00	9,048.00
4.40	176.00	762.67	9,152.00
4.45	178.00	771.33	9,256.00
4.50	180.00	780.00	9,360.00
4.55	182.00	788.67	9,464.00
4.60	184.00	797.33	9,568.00
4.65	186.00	806.00	9,672.00
4.70	188.00	814.67	9,776.00
4.75	190.00	823.33	9,880.00
4.80	192.00	832.00	9,984.00
4.85	194.00	840.67	10,088.00
4.90	196.00	849.33	10,192.00
4.95	198.00	858.00	10,296.00
5.00	200.00	866.66	10,400.00
5.05	202.00	875.27	10,504.00
5.10	204.00	884.00	10,608.00
5.20	208.00	901.34	10,816.00
5.30	212.00	918.67	11,024.00
5.40	216.00	936.00	11,232.00
5.50	220.00	953.34	11,440.00
5.60	224.00	970.67	11,648.00
5.70	228.00	988.00	11,856.00
5.80	232.00	1005.34	12,064.00
5.90	236.00	1022.67	12,272.00
6.00	240.00	1040.00	12,480.00
6.10	244.00	1057.33	12,688.00
6.20	248.00	1074.67	12,896.00
6.30	252.00	1092.00	13,104.00
6.40	256.00	1109.33	13,312.00
6.50	260.00	1126.67	13,520.00
6.60	264.00	1144.00	13,728.00
6.70	268.00	1161.33	13,936.00
6.80	272.00	1178.67	14,144.00
6.90	276.00	1196.00	14,352.00
7.00	280.00	1213.33	14,560.00
7.10	284.00	1230.67	14,763.00
7.20	288.00	1248.00	14,976.00
7.30	292.00	1265.33	15,184.00
7.40	296.00	1282.67	15,392.00
7.50	300.00	1300.00	15,600.00

EXHIBIT 21-5 INCOME CONVERSIONS

Income to Monthly Payment Ratios

Monthly Payment Including Taxes, Ins.	Income Required At:			Monthly Payment Including Taxes, Ins.	Income Required At:		
	4 to 1	4½ to 1	5 to 1		4 to 1	4½ to 1	5 to 1
90	360.00	405.00	450.00	170	680.00	765.00	850.00
91	364.00	410.00	455.00	175	700.00	788.00	875.00
92	368.00	414.00	460.00	180	720.00	810.00	900.00
93	372.00	419.00	465.00	185	740.00	833.00	925.00
94	376.00	423.00	470.00	190	760.00	855.00	950.00
95	380.00	428.00	475.00	200	800.00	900.00	1000.00
96	384.00	432.00	480.00	205	820.00	923.00	1025.00
97	388.00	436.00	485.00	210	840.00	945.00	1050.00
98	392.00	441.00	490.00	215	860.00	968.00	1075.00
99	396.00	445.00	495.00	220	880.00	990.00	1100.00
100	400.00	450.00	500.00	225	900.00	1013.00	1125.00
101	404.00	454.00	505.00	230	920.00	1035.00	1150.00
102	408.00	459.00	510.00	235	940.00	1058.00	1175.00
103	412.00	463.00	515.00	240	960.00	1080.00	1200.00
104	416.00	468.00	520.00	245	980.00	1103.00	1225.00
105	420.00	472.00	525.00	250	1000.00	1125.00	1250.00
106	424.00	477.00	530.00	255	1020.00	1148.00	1275.00
107	428.00	481.00	535.00	260	1040.00	1170.00	1300.00
108	432.00	486.00	540.00	265	1060.00	1193.00	1325.00
109	436.00	490.00	545.00	270	1080.00	1215.00	1350.00
110	440.00	495.00	550.00	275	1100.00	1238.00	1375.00
115	460.00	518.00	575.00	280	1120.00	1260.00	1400.00
120	480.00	540.00	600.00	285	1140.00	1283.00	1425.00
125	500.00	563.00	625.00	290	1160.00	1305.00	1450.00
130	520.00	585.00	650.00	295	1180.00	1328.00	1475.00
135	540.00	608.00	675.00	300	1200.00	1350.00	1500.00
140	560.00	630.00	700.00	310	1240.00	1395.00	1550.00
145	580.00	653.00	725.00	320	1280.00	1440.00	1600.00
150	600.00	675.00	750.00	330	1320.00	1485.00	1650.00
155	620.00	698.00	775.00	340	1360.00	1530.00	1700.00
160	640.00	720.00	800.00	350	1400.00	1575.00	1750.00
165	660.00	743.00	825.00				

EXHIBIT 21-6 RATIO OF INCOME TO MONTHLY PAYMENTS

301

MONTHLY TAX AND INSURANCE PRO-RATER

Principal Amount of Tax or Fire Insurance	1/12th of Principal	1/36th of Principal	Principal Amount of Tax or Fire Insurance	1/12th of Principal	1/36th of Principal
$70	$5.83	$1.94	$440	$36.67	$12.22
75	6.25	2.08	445	37.08	12.36
80	6.67	2.22	450	37.50	12.50
85	7.08	2.36	455	37.92	12.63
90	7.50	2.50	460	38.33	12.77
95	7.92	2.64	465	38.75	12.91
100	8.33	2.78	470	39.17	13.05
105	8.75	2.92	475	39.58	13.19
110	9.17	3.06	480	40.00	13.33
115	9.58	3.20	485	40.42	13.47
120	10.00	3.33	490	40.83	13.61
125	10.42	3.47	495	41.25	13.75
130	10.83	3.61	500	41.67	13.88
135	11.25	3.75	505	42.08	14.02
140	11.67	3.89	510	42.50	14.16
145	12.08	4.03	515	42.93	14.30
150	12.50	4.17	520	43.33	14.44
155	12.92	4.31	525	43.75	14.58
160	13.33	4.44	530	44.17	14.72
165	13.75	4.58	535	44.58	14.86
170	14.17	4.72	540	45.00	15.00
175	14.58	4.86	545	45.42	15.13
180	15.00	5.00	550	45.83	15.27
185	15.42	5.14	555	46.25	15.41
190	15.83	5.28	560	46.67	15.55
195	16.25	5.42	565	47.08	15.69
200	16.67	5.56	570	47.50	15.83
205	17.08	5.69	575	47.92	15.97
210	17.50	5.83	580	48.33	16.11
215	17.92	5.97	585	48.75	16.25
220	18.33	6.11	590	49.17	16.38
225	18.75	6.25	595	49.58	16.52
230	19.17	6.39	600	50.00	16.66
235	19.58	6.53	605	50.42	16.80
240	20.00	6.67	610	50.83	16.94
245	20.42	6.81	615	51.25	17.08
250	20.83	6.94	620	51.67	17.22
255	21.25	7.08	625	52.08	17.36
260	21.67	7.22	630	52.50	17.50
265	22.08	7.36	635	52.92	17.63
270	22.50	7.50	640	53.33	17.77
275	22.92	7.64	645	53.75	17.91
280	23.33	7.78	650	54.17	18.05
285	23.75	7.92	655	54.58	18.19
290	24.17	8.06	660	55.00	18.33
295	24.58	8.19	665	55.42	18.48
300	25.00	8.33	670	55.83	18.61
305	25.42	8.47	675	56.25	18.75
310	25.83	8.61	680	56.67	18.88
315	26.25	8.75	685	57.08	19.02
320	26.67	8.89	690	57.50	19.16
325	27.08	9.03	695	57.92	19.30
330	27.50	9.17	700	58.33	19.44
335	27.92	9.31	705	58.75	19.58
340	28.33	9.44	710	59.17	19.72
345	28.75	9.58	715	59.58	19.86
350	29.17	9.72	720	60.00	20.00
355	29.58	9.86	725	60.42	20.13
360	30.00	10.00	730	60.83	20.27
365	30.42	10.14	735	61.25	20.41
370	30.83	10.28	740	61.67	20.55
375	31.25	10.42	745	62.08	20.69
380	31.67	10.56	750	62.50	20.83
385	32.08	10.69	755	62.92	20.97
390	32.50	10.83	760	63.33	21.11
395	32.92	10.97	765	63.75	21.25
400	33.33	11.11	770	64.17	21.38
405	33.75	11.25	775	64.58	21.52
410	34.17	11.38	780	65.00	21.66
415	34.58	11.52	785	65.42	21.80
420	35.00	11.66	790	65.83	21.94
425	35.42	11.80	795	66.25	22.08
430	35.83	11.94	800	66.67	22.22
435	36.25	12.08			

EXHIBIT 21-7 PRORATIONS

Glossary

The format and definitions of words and phrases found in this glossary were extracted from the California Department of Real Estate Reference Book, 1971 Edition. In some instances, revisions may have been made to the above state publication.

DEFINITIONS OF REAL ESTATE WORDS AND PHRASES

A. L. T. A. Title Policy: A type of title insurance policy issued by title insurance companies which expands the risks normally insured against under the standard type policy to include unrecorded mechanic's liens; unrecorded physical easements; facts a physical survey would show; water and mineral rights; and rights of parties in possession, such as tenants and buyers under unrecorded instruments.

Abatement of Nuisance: Extinction or termination of a nuisance.

Abstract of Judgment: A condensation of the essential provisions of a court judgment.

Abstract of Title: A summary or digest of the conveyances, transfers, and any other facts relied on as evidence of title, together with any other elements of record which may impair the title.

Acceleration Clause: Clause in trust deed or mortgage giving lender right to call all sums owing him to be immediately due and payable upon the happening of a certain event.

Acceptance: When the seller or agent's principal agrees to the terms of the agreement of sale and approves the negotiation on the part of the agent and acknowledges receipt of the deposit in subscribing to the agreement of sale, that act is termed an acceptance.

Access Right: The right of an owner to have ingress and egress to and from his property.

Accretion: An addition to land from natural causes as, for example, from gradual action of the ocean or river waters.

Accrued Depreciation: The difference between the cost of replacement new as of the date of the appraisal and the present appraised value.

Acknowledgment: A formal declaration before a duly authorized officer by a person who has executed an instrument that such execution is his act and deed.

Acoustical tile: Blocks of fiber, mineral or metal, with small holes or rough-textured surface to absorb sound, used as covering for interior walls and ceilings.

Acquisition: The act or process by which a person procures property.

Acre: A measure of land equaling 160 square rods, or 4,840 square yards, or 43,560 square feet, or a tract about 208.71 feet square.

Administrator: A person appointed by the probate court to administer the estate of a person deceased.

Ad Valorem: According to valuation.

Adverse Possession: The open and notorious possession and occupancy under an evident claim or right, in denial or opposition to the title of another claimant.

Affidavit: A statement or declaration reduced to writing sworn to or affirmed before some officer who has authority to administer an oath or affirmation.

Affirm: To confirm, to aver, to ratify, to verify.

Agency: The relationship between principal and agent which arises out of a contract, either expressed or implied, written or oral, wherein the agent is employed by the principal to do certain acts dealing with a third party.

Agent: One who represents another from whom he has derived authority.

Agreement of Sale: A written agreement or contract between seller and purchaser in which they reach a meeting of minds on the terms and conditions of the sale.

Alienation: The transferring of property to another; the transfer of property and possession of lands, or other things, from one person to another.

Alluvion: (Alluvium) Soil deposited by accretion. Increase of earth on a shore or bank of a river.

Amenities: Satisfaction of enjoyable living to be derived from a home; conditions of agreeable living or a beneficial influence arising from the location or improvements.

Amortization: The liquidation of a financial obligation on an installment basis; also, recovery, over a period, of cost or value.

Appraisal: An estimate and opinion of value; a conclusion resulting from the analysis of facts.

Appraiser: One qualified by education, training and experience who is hired to estimate the value of real and personal property based on experience, judgment, facts, and use of formal appraisal processes.

Appurtenance: Something annexed to another thing which may be transferred incident to it. That which belongs to another thing, as a barn, dwelling, garage, or orchard is incident to the land to which it is attached.

Assessed Valuation: A valuation placed upon property by a public officer or board, as a basis for taxation.

Assessed Value: Value placed on property as a basis for taxation.

Assessment: The valuation of property for the purpose of levying a tax or the amount of the tax levied.

Assessor: The official who has the responsibility of determining assessed values.

Assignment: A transfer or making over to another of the whole of any property, real or personal, in possession or in action, or of any estate or right therein.

Assignor: One who assigns or transfers property.

Assigns; Assignees: Those to whom property shall have been transferred.

Assumption Agreement: An undertaking or adoption of a debt or obligation primarily resting upon another person.

Assumption of Mortgage: The taking of title to property by a grantee, wherein he assumes liability for payment of an existing note secured by a mortgage or deed of trust against the property; becoming a co-guarantor for the payment of a mortgage or deed of trust note.

Attachment: Seizure of property by court order, usually done to have it available in event a judgment is obtained in a pending suit.

Attest: To affirm to be true or genuine; an official act establishing authenticity.

Attorney in Fact: One who is authorized to perform certain acts for another under a power of attorney; power of attorney may be limited to a specific act or acts, or be general.

Avulsion: The sudden tearing away or removal of land by action of water flowing over or through it.

Backfill: The replacement of excavated earth into a hole or against a structure.

Balloon Payment: Where the final installment payment on a note is greater than the preceding installment payments and it pays the note in full, such final installment is termed a balloon payment.

Baseboard: A board placed against the wall around a room next to the floor.

Base and Meridian: Imaginary lines used by surveyors to find and describe the location of private or public lands.

Base Molding: Molding used at top of baseboard.

Base Shoe: Molding used at junction of baseboard and floor. Commonly called a carpet strip.

Batten: Narrow strips of wood or metal used to cover joints, interiorly or exteriorly; also used for decorative effect.

Beam: A structural member transversely supporting a load.

Bearing Wall or Partition: A wall or partition supporting any vertical load in addition to its own weight.

Bench Marks: A location indicated on a durable marker by surveyors.

Beneficiary: (1) One entitled to the benefit of a trust; (2) One who receives profit from an estate, the title of which is vested in a trustee; (3) The lender on the security of a note and deed of trust.

Bequeath: To give or hand down by will; to leave by will.

Bequest: That which is given by the terms of a will.

Betterment: An improvement upon property which increases the property value and is considered as a capital asset as distinguished from repairs or replacements where the original character or cost is unchanged.

Bill of Sale: A written instrument given to pass title of personal property from vendor to the vendee.

Blacktop: Asphalt paving used in streets and driveways.

Blanket Mortgage: A single mortgage which covers more than one piece of real estate.

Blighted Area: A declining area in which real property values are seriously affected by destructive economic forces, such as encroaching inharmonious property usages, infiltration of lower social and economic classes of inhabitants, and/or rapidly depreciating buildings.

Board foot: A unit of measurement of lumber; one foot wide, one foot long, one inch thick; 144 cubic inches.

Bona Fide: In good faith, without fraud.

Bracing: Framing lumber nailed at an angle in order to provide rigidity.

Breach: The breaking of a law, or failure of duty, either by omission or commission.

Breezeway: A covered porch or passage, open on two sides, connecting house and garage or two parts of the house.

Bridging: Small wood or metal pieces used to brace floor joists.

B.T.U.: British thermal unit. The quantity of heat required to raise the temperature of one pound of water one degree Fahrenheit.

Building Line: A line set by law a certain distance from a street line in front of which an owner cannot build on his lot. (A setback line.)

Building Paper: A heavy waterproofed paper used as sheathing in wall or roof construction as a protection against air passage and moisture.

Built-in: Cabinets or similar features built as part of the house.

Bundle of Rights: Beneficial interests or rights.

Capital Assets: Assets of a permanent nature used in the production of an income, such as: land, buildings, machinery, and equipment, etc. Under income tax law, it is usually distinguishable from "inventory" which comprises assets held for sale to customers in ordinary course of the taxpayers' trade or business.

Capitalization: In appraising, determining value of property by considering net income and percentage of reasonable return on the investment.

Capitalization Rate: The rate of interest which is considered a reasonable return on the investment, and used in the process of determining value based upon net income.

Casement Window: Frames of wood or metal, which swing outward.

Caveat Emptor: Let the buyer beware. The buyer must examine the goods or property and buy at his own risk.

Chain of Title: A history of conveyances and encumbrances affecting the title from the time the original patent was granted, or as far back as records are available.

Chattel Mortgage: A personal property mortgage. (See definition of *Security Agreement* and *Security Interest*.)

Chattel Real: An estate related to real estate, such as a lease on real property.

Chattels: Goods or every species of property movable or immovable which are not real property.

Circuit Breaker: An electrical device which automatically interrupts an electric circuit when an overload occurs; may be used instead of a fuse to protect each circuit and can be reset.

Clapboard: Boards usually thicker at one edge used for siding.

Cloud on the Title: Any conditions revealed by a title search which affect the title to property; usually relatively unimportant items but which cannot be removed without a quitclaim deed or court action.

Collar Beam: A beam that connects the pairs of opposite roof rafters above the attic floor.

Collateral: This is the property subject to the security interest. (See definition of *Security Interest.*)

Collateral Security: A separate obligation attached to contract to guarantee its performance; the transfer of property or of other contracts, or valuables, to insure the performance of a principal agreement.

Collusion: An agreement between two or more persons to defraud another of his rights by the forms of law, or to obtain an object forbidden by law.

Color of Title: That which appears to be good title but which is not title in fact.

Combed Plywood: A grooved building material used primarily for interior finish.

Commercial Acre: A term applied to the remainder of an acre of newly subdivided land after the area devoted to streets, sidewalks and curbs, etc., has been deducted from the acre.

Commercial Paper: Bills of exchange used in commercial trade.

Commission: An agent's compensation for performing the duties of his agency; in real estate practice, a percentage of the selling price of property, percentage of rentals, etc.

Commitment: A pledge or a promise or firm agreement.

Common Law: The body of law that grew from customs and practices developed and used in England "since the memory of man runneth not to the contrary."

Community Property: Property accumulated through joint efforts of husband and wife living together.

Compaction: Whenever extra soil is added to a lot to fill in low places or to raise the level of the lot, the added soil is often too loose and soft to sustain the weight of buildings. Therefore, it is necessary to compact the added soil so that it will carry the weight of buildings without the danger of their tilting, settling or cracking.

Competent: Legally qualified.

Compound Interest: Interest paid on original principal and also on the accrued and unpaid interest which has accumulated.

Condemnation: The act of taking private property for public use by a political subdivision; declaration that a structure is unfit for use.

Conditional Commitment: A commitment of a definite loan amount

307

for some future unknown purchaser of satisfactory credit standing.

Conditional Sale Contract: A contract for the sale of property stating that delivery is to be made to the buyer, title to remain vested in the seller until the conditions of the contract have been fulfilled. (See definition of *Security Interest.*)

Condominium: A system of individual fee ownership of units in a multi-family structure, combined with joint ownership of common areas of the structure and the land. (Sometimes referred to as a vertical subdivision.)

Conduit: Usually a metal pipe in which electrical wiring is installed.

Confession of Judgment: An entry of judgment upon the debtor's voluntary admission or confession.

Confirmation of Sale: A court approval of the sale of property by an executor, administrator, guardian or conservator.

Consideration: Anything of value given to induce entering into a contract; it may be money, personal services, or even love and affection.

Constructive Notice: Notice given by the public records.

Contract: An agreement, either written or oral, to do or not to do certain things.

Consumer Goods: These are goods used or bought for use primarily for personal, family or household purposes.

Conversion: Change from one character or use to another.

Conveyance: The transfer of the title of land from one to another. It denotes an instrument which carries from one person to another an interest in land.

Corporation: A group or body of persons established and treated by law as an individual or unit with rights and liabilities or both, distinct and apart from those of the persons composing it.

A corporation is a creature of law having certain powers and duties of a natural person. Being created by law it may continue for any length of time the law prescribes.

Counterflashing: Flashing used on chimneys at roofline to cover shingle flashing and to prevent moisture entry.

Covenant: Agreements written into deeds and other instruments promising performance or nonperformance of certain acts or stipulating certain uses or nonuses of the property.

C.P.M.: Certified Property Manager; a member of the Institute of Real Property Management of the National Association of Real Estate Boards.

Crawl Hole: Exterior or interior opening permitting access underneath building, as required by building codes.

C.R.E.A.: California Real Estate Association.

Curtail Schedule: A listing of the amounts by which the principal sum of an obligation is to be reduced by partial payments and of the dates when each payment will become payable.

Curtesy: The right which a husband has in a wife's estate at her death.

Damages: The indemnity recoverable by a person who has sustained an injury, either in his person, property, or relative rights, through the act or default of another.

Debtor: This is the party who "owns" the property which is subject to the Security Interest. Previously he was known as the *mortgagor* or the *pledgor*, etc.

Deciduous Trees: Lose their leaves in the autumn and winter.

Deck: Usually an open porch on the roof of a ground or lower floor, porch or wing.

Dedication: An appropriation of land by its owner for some public use accepted for such use by authorized public officials on behalf of the public.

Deed: Written instrument which, when properly executed and delivered, conveys title.

Default: Failure to fulfill a duty or promise or to discharge an obligation; omission or failure to perform any act.

Defeasance Clause: The clause in a mortgage that gives the mortgagor the right to redeem his property upon the payment of his obligations to the mortgagee.

Deferred Maintenance: Existing but unfulfilled requirements for repairs and rehabilitation.

Deficiency Judgment: A judgment given when the security pledge for a loan does not satisfy the debt upon its default.

Depreciation: Loss of value in real property brought about by age, physical deterioration or functional or economic obsolescence. Broadly, a loss in value from any cause.

Desist and Refrain Order: The Real Estate Commissioner is empowered by law to issue an order directing a person to desist and refrain from committing an act in violation of the real estate law.

Deterioration: Impairment of condition. One of the causes of depreciation and reflecting the loss in value brought about by wear and tear, disintegration, use in service, and the action of the elements.

Devisee: One who receives a bequest made by will.

Devisor: One who bequeaths by will.

Directional Growth: The location or direction toward which the residential sections of a city are destined or determined to grow.

Documentary Transfer Tax: A state enabling act allowing a county to adopt a documentary transfer tax to apply on all transfer of real property located in the county. Notice of payment is entered on face of the deed or on a separate paper filed with the deed. The tax applies when the consideration (exclusive of the value of any lien or encumbrance attaching to property at time of sale and not removed or replaced upon consummation of the sale) exceeds $100. Tax is computed at the rate of 55 cents for each $500 of consideration or fraction thereof.

Donee: A person to whom a gift is made.

Donor: A person who makes a gift.

Dower: The right which a wife has in her husband's estate at his death.

Duress: Unlawful constraint exercised upon a person whereby he is forced to do some act against his will.

Easement: Created by grant or agreement for a specific purpose, an easement is the right, privilege or interest which one party has in the land of another. (Example: right of way.)

Eaves: The lower part of a roof projecting over the wall.

Economic Life: The period over which a property will yield a return on the investment, over and above the economic or ground rent due to land.

Eminent Domain: The right of the government to acquire property for necessary public or quasi-public use by condemnation; the owner must be fairly compensated.

Encroachment: Trespass; the building of a structure or construction of any improvements, partly or wholly on the property of another.

Encumbrance: Anything which affects or limits the fee simple title to property, such as mortgages, easements or restrictions of any kind. Liens are special encumbrances which make the property security for the payment of a debt or obligation, such as mortgages and taxes.

Equity: The interest or value which an owner has in real estate over and above the liens against it; branch of remedial justice by and through which relief is afforded to suitors in courts of equity.

Equity of Redemption: The right to redeem property during the foreclosure period, such as a mortgagor's right to redeem within a year after foreclosure sale.

Erosion: The wearing away of land by the action of water, wind or glacial ice.

Escalator Clause: A clause in a contract providing for the upward or downward adjustment of certain items to cover specified contingencies.

Escheat: The reverting of property to the State when heirs capable of inheriting are lacking.

Escrow: The deposit of instruments and funds with instructions to a third neutral party to carry out the provisions of an agreement or contract; when everything is deposited to enable carrying out the instructions, it is called a complete or perfect escrow.

Estate: As applied to the real estate practice, the term signifies the quantity of interest, share, right, equity, of which riches or fortune may consist, in real property. The degree, quantity, nature, and extent of interest which a person has in real property.

Estate for Life: A freehold estate, not of inheritance, but which is held by the tenant for his own life or the life or lives of one or more other persons, or for an indefinite period which may endure for the life or lives of persons in being and beyond the period of life.

Estate for Years: An interest in lands by virtue of a contract for the possession of them for a definite and limited period of time. A lease may be said to be an estate for years.

Estate of Inheritance: An estate which may descend to heirs. All freehold estates are estates of inheritance, except estates for life.

Estate of Will: The occupation of lands and tenements by a tenant for an indefinite period, terminable by one or both parties.

Estoppel: A doctrine which bars one from asserting rights which are inconsistent with a previous position or representation.

Ethics: That branch of moral science, idealism, justness, and fairness, which treats of the duties which a member of a profession or craft owes to the public, to his clients or patron, and to his professional brethren or members.

Exclusive Agency Listing: A written instrument giving one agent the right to sell property for a specified time but reserving the right of the owner to sell the property himself without the payment of a commission.

Exclusive Right to Sell Listing: A written agreement between owner and agent giving agent the right to collect a commission if the property is sold by anyone during the term of his agreement.

Execute: To complete, to make, to perform, to do, to follow out; to execute a deed, to make a deed, including especially signing, sealing, and delivery; to execute a contract is to perform the contract, to follow out to the end, to complete.

Executor: A person named in a will to carry out its provisions as to the disposition of the estate of a person deceased.

Expansible House: Home designed for further expansion and additions in the future.

Expansion Joint: A bituminous fiber strip used to separate units of concrete to prevent cracking due to expansion as a result of temperature changes.

Facade: Front of a building.

Fee: An estate of inheritance in real property.

Fee Simple: In modern estates, the terms "Fee" and "Fee Simple" are substantially synonymous. The term "Fee" is of Old English derivation.

"Fee Simple Absolute" is an estate in real property, by which the owner has the greatest power over the title which it is possible to have, being an absolute estate. In modern use, it expressly establishes the title of real property in the owner, without limitation or end. He may dispose of it by sale, or trade or will, as he chooses.

Fiduciary: A person in a position of trust and confidence, as between principal and broker; broker as fiduciary owes certain loyalty which cannot be breached under rules of agency.

Financing Statement: This is the instrument which is filed in order to give public notice of the security interest and thereby protect the interest of the secured parties in the collateral. See definitions of *Security Interest and Secured Party.*

Finish Floor: Finish floor strips are applied over wood joists, deadening felt and diagonal subflooring before finish floor is installed; finish floor is the final covering on the floor: wood, linoleum, cork, tile or carpet.

Fire Stop: A solid, tight closure of a concealed space, placed to prevent the spread of fire and smoke through such a space.

Fixtures: Appurtenances attached to the land or improvements, which usually cannot be removed without agreement as they become real property; examples: plumbing fixtures, store fixtures built into the property, etc.

Flashing: Sheet metal or other material used to protect a building from seepage of water.

Footing: The base or bottom of a foundation wall, pier, or column.

Foreclosure: Procedure whereby property pledged as security for a debt is sold to pay the debt in event of default in payments or terms.

311

Forfeiture: Loss of money or anything of value, due to failure to perform.

Foundation: The supporting portion of a structure below the first floor construction, or below grade, including the footings.

Fraud: The intentional and successful employment of any cunning, deception, collusion, or artifice, used to circumvent, cheat or deceive another person, whereby that person acts upon it to the loss of his property and to his legal injury.

Front Foot: Property measurement for sale or valuation purposes; the property measures by the front foot on its street line—each front foot extending the depth of the lot.

Frostline: The depth of frost penetration in the soil. Varies in different parts of the country. Footings should be placed below this depth to prevent movement.

Furring: Strips of wood or metal applied to a wall or other surface to even it, to form an air space, or to give the wall an appearance of greater thickness.

Gable Roof: A pitched roof with sloping sides.

Gambrel Roof: A curb roof, having a steep lower slope with a flatter upper slope above.

Gift Deed: A deed for which the consideration is love and affection and where there is no material consideration.

Girder: A large beam used to support beams, joists and partitions.

Grade: Ground level at the foundation.

Graduated Lease: Lease which provides for a varying rental rate, often based upon future determination; sometimes rent is based upon result of periodical appraisals; used largely in long-term leases.

Grant: A technical term made use of in deeds of conveyance of lands to import a transfer.

Grantee: The purchaser; a person to whom a grant is made.

Grantor: Seller of property; one who signs a deed.

Grid: A chart used in rating the borrower risk, property, and the neighborhood.

Gross Income: Total income from property before any expenses are deducted.

Ground Lease: An agreement for the use of the land only, sometimes secured by improvements placed on the land by the user.

Ground Rent: Earnings of improved property credited to earnings of the ground itself after allowance is made for earnings of improvements; often termed *economic rent.*

Header: A beam placed perpendicular to joists and to which joists are nailed in framing for chimney, stairway, or other opening.

Highest and Best Use: An appraisal phrase meaning that use which at the time of an appraisal is most likely to produce the greatest net return to the land and/or buildings over a given period of time; that use which will produce the greatest amount of amenities or profit. This is the starting point for appraisal.

Hip Roof: A pitched roof with sloping sides and ends.

Holder in Due Course: One who has taken a note, check or bill of exchange in due course:

(1) Before it was overdue;

(2) In good faith and for value;

(3) Without knowledge that it has been previously dishonored and without notice of any defect at the time it was negotiated to him.

Homestead: A home upon which the owner or owners have recorded a Declaration of Homestead, as provided by California Statutes; protects home against judgments up to specified amounts.

Hundred Percent Location: A city retail business location which is considered the best available for attracting business.

Hypothecate: To give a thing as security without the necessity of giving up possession of it.

Incompetent: One who is mentally incompetent, incapable; any person who, though not insane, is, by reason of old age, disease, weakness of mind, or any other cause, unable, unassisted, to properly manage and take care of himself or his property and by reason thereof would be likely to be deceived or imposed upon by artful or designing persons.

Increment: An increase. Most frequently used to refer to the increase of value of land that accompanies population growth and increasing wealth in the community. The term unearned increment is used in this connection since values are supposed to have increased without effort on the part of the owner.

Indirect Lighting: The light is reflected from the ceiling or other object external to the fixture.

Indorsement: The act of signing one's name on the back of a check or a note, with or without further qualification.

Injunction: A writ or order issued under the seal of a court to restrain one or more parties to a suit or proceeding from doing an act which is deemed to be inequitable or unjust in regard to the rights of some other party or parties in the suit or proceeding.

Installment Note: A note which provides that payments of a certain sum or amount be paid on the dates specified in the instrument.

Instrument: A written legal document; created to effect the rights of the parties.

Interest Rate: The percentage of a sum of money charged for its use.

Intestate: A person who dies having made no will, or one which is defective in form, in which case his estate descends to his heirs at law or next of kin.

Involuntary Lien: A lien imposed against property without consent of an owner; example: taxes, special assessments, federal income tax liens, etc.

Irrevocable: Incapable of being recalled or revoked; unchangeable.

Irrigation Districts: Quasi-political districts created under special laws to provide for water services to property owners in the district; an operation governed to a great extent by law.

Jalousie: A slatted blind or shutter, like a venetian blind but used on the exterior to protect against rain as well as to control sunlight.

Jamb: The side post or lining of a doorway, window or other opening.

Joint: The space between the adjacent surfaces of two components joined and held together by nails, glue, cement, mortar, etc.

Joint Note: A note signed by two or more persons who have equal liability for payment.

Joint Tenancy: Joint ownership by two or more persons with right of survivorship; all joint tenants own equal interest and have equal rights in the property.

Joist: One of a series of parallel beams to which the boards of a floor and ceiling laths are nailed, and supported in turn by larger beams, girders, or bearing walls.

Judgment: The final determination of a court of competent jurisdiction of a matter presented to it; money judgments provide for the payment of claims presented to the court, or are awarded as damages, etc.

Jurisdiction: The authority by which judicial officers take cognizance of and decide causes; the power to hear and determine a cause; the right and power which a judicial officer has to enter upon the inquiry.

Laches: Delay or negligence in asserting one's legal rights.

Land Contract: A contract ordinarily used in connection with the sale of property in cases where the seller does not wish to convey title until all or a certain part of the purchase price is paid by the buyer; often used when property is sold on small down payment.

Lateral Support: the support which the soil of an adjoining owner gives to his neighbors' land.

Lath: A building material of wood, metal, gypsum, or insulating board fastened to the frame of a building to act as a plaster base.

Lease: A contract between owner and tenant, setting forth conditions upon which tenant may occupy and use the property, and the term of the occupancy.

Legal Description: A description recognized by law; a description by which property can be definitely located by reference to government surveys or approved recorded maps.

Lessee: One who contracts to rent property under a lease contract.

Lessor: An owner who enters into a lease with a tenant.

Lien: A form of encumbrance which usually makes property security for the payment of a debt or discharge of an obligation. Example: judgments, taxes, mortgages, deeds of trust, etc.

Limited Partnership: A partnership composed of some partners whose contribution and liability are limited.

Lintel: A horizontal board that supports the load over an opening such as a door or window.

Lis Pendens: Suit pending, usually recorded so as to give constructive notice of pending litigation.

Listing: An employment contract between principal and agent authorizing the agent to perform services for the principal involving the latter's property; listing contracts are entered into for the purpose of securing persons to buy, lease or rent property. Employment of an agent by a prospective purchaser or lessee to locate property for purchase or lease may be considered a listing.

Louver: An opening with a series of horizontal slats set at an angle to permit ventilation without admitting rain, sunlight, or vision.

M.A.I.: Designates a person who is a member of the American Institute of Appraisers of the National Association of Real Estate Boards.

Margin of Security: The difference between the amount of the mortgage loan(s) and the appraised value of the property.

Marginal Land: Land which barely pays the cost of working or using.

Market Price: The price paid regardless of pressures, motives or intelligence.

Market Value: (1) The price at which a willing seller would sell and a willing buyer would buy, neither being under abnormal pressure; (2) As defined by the courts, is the highest price estimated in terms of money which a property will bring if exposed for sale in the open market allowing a reasonable time to find a purchaser with knowledge of property's use and capabilities for use.

Marketable Title: Merchantable title; title free and clear of objectionable liens or encumbrances.

Material Fact: A fact is material if it is one which the agent should realize would be likely to affect the judgment of the principal in giving his consent to the agent to enter into the particular transaction on the specified terms.

Meridians: Imaginary north-south lines which intersect base lines to form a starting point for the measurement of land.

Metes and Bounds: A term used in describing the boundary lines of land, setting forth all the boundary lines together with their terminal points and angles.

Minor: All persons under 21 years of age, except that any person lawfully married who is 18 or over is deemed an adult person for the purpose of entering into any engagement or transaction respecting property.

Molding: Usually patterned strips used to provide ornamental variation of outline or contour, such as cornices, bases, window and door jambs.

Monument: A fixed object and point established by surveyors to establish land locations.

Moratorium: The temporary suspension, usually by statute, of the enforcement of liability for debt.

Mortgage: An instrument recognized by law by which property is hypothecated to secure the payment of a debt or obligation; procedure for foreclosure in event of default is established by statute.

Mortgage Contracts with Warrants: Warrants make the mortgage more attractive to the lender by providing both the greater security that goes with a mortgage, and the opportunity of a greater return through the right to buy either stock in the borrower's company or a portion of the income property itself.

Mortgage Guaranty Insurance: Insurance against financial loss available to mortgage lenders from Mortgage Guaranty Insurance Corporation, a private company organized in 1956.

Mortgagee: One to whom a mortgagor gives a mortgage to secure a loan or performance of an obligation, a lender. (See definition of *Secured Party.*)

Mortgagor: One who gives a mortgage on his property to secure a loan or assure performance of an obligation; a borrower. (See definition of *debtor.*)

315

Multiple Listing: A listing, usually an exclusive right to sell, taken by a member of an organization composed of real estate brokers, with the provisions that all members will have the opportunity to find an interested client; a co-operative listing.

Mutual Water Company: A water company organized by or for water users in a given district with the object of securing an ample water supply at a reasonable rate; stock is issued to users.

NAREB: National Association of Real Estate Boards.

Negotiable: Capable of being negotiated; assignable or transferable in the ordinary course of business.

Net Listing: A listing which provides that the agent may retain as compensation for his services all sums received over and above a net price to the owner.

Note: A signed written instrument acknowledging a debt and promising payment.

Notice of Nonresponsibility: A notice provided by law designed to relieve a property owner from responsibility for the cost of work done on the property or materials furnished therefor; notice must be verified, recorded and posted.

Notice to Quit: A notice to a tenant to vacate rented property.

Obsolescence: Loss in value due to reduced desirability and usefulness of a structure because its design and construction become obsolete; loss because of becoming old-fashioned and not in keeping with modern needs, with consequent loss of income.

Offset Statement: Statement by owner of property or owner of lien against property, setting forth the present status of liens against said property.

Open-end Mortgage: A mortgage containing a clause which permits the mortgagor to borrow additional money after the loan has been reduced, without rewriting the mortgage.

Open Listing: An authorization given by a property owner to a real estate agent wherein said agent is given the nonexclusive right to secure a purchaser; open listings may be given to any number of agents without liability to compensate any except the one who first secures a buyer ready, willing and able to meet the terms of the listing, or secures the acceptance by the seller of a satisfactory offer.

Option: A right given for a consideration to purchase or lease a property upon specified terms within a specified time.

Oral Contract: A verbal agreement; one which is not reduced to writing.

Orientation: Placing a house on its lot with regard to its exposure to the rays of the sun, prevailing winds, privacy from the street and protection from outside noises.

Overhang: The part of the roof extending beyond the walls, to shade buildings and cover walks.

Over Improvement: An improvement which is not the highest and best use for the site on which it is placed by reason of excess size or cost.

Par Value: Market value, nominal value.

Partition Action: Court proceedings by which co-owners seek to sever their joint ownership.

Partnership: A decision of the California Supreme Court has defined a partnership in the following terms: "A partnership as between partners themselves may be defined to be a contract of two or more persons to unite their property, labor or skill, or some of them, in prosecution of some joint or lawful business, and to share the profits in certain proportions."

Parquet Floor: Hardwood flooring laid in squares or patterns.

Participation: In addition to base interest on mortgage loans on income properties, a small percentage of gross income is required, sometimes predicated on certain conditions being fulfilled, such as minimum occupancy or a percentage of net income after expenses, debt service and taxes.

Party Wall: A wall erected on the line between two adjoining properties, which are under different ownership, for the use of both properties.

Patent: Conveyance of title to government land.

Penny: The term, as applied to nails, serves as a measure of nail length and is abbreviated by the letter "d".

Percentage Lease: Lease on property, the rental for which is determined by amount of business done by the lessee; usually a percentage of gross receipts from the business with provision for a minimum rental.

Perimeter Heating: Baseboard heating, or any system in which the heat registers are located along the outside walls of a room, especially under the windows.

Personal Property: Any property which is not real property.

Pier: A column of masonry, usually rectangular in horizontal cross section, used to support other structural members.

Pitch: The incline or rise of a roof.

Plate: A horizontal board placed on a wall or supported on posts or studs to carry the trusses of a roof or rafters directly; a shoe, or base member as of a partition or other frame; a small flat board placed on or in a wall to support girders, rafters, etc.

Pledge: The depositing of personal property by a debtor with a creditor as security for a debt or engagement.

Pledgee: One who is given a pledge or a security. (See definition of *Secured Party.*)

Pledgor: One who offers a pledge or gives security. (See definition of *debtor.*)

Plottage Increment: The appreciation in unit value created by joining smaller ownerships into one large single ownership.

Plywood: Laminated wood made up in panels; several thicknesses of wood glued together with grain at different angles for strength.

Police Power: The right of the State to enact laws and enforce them for the order, safety, health, morals and general welfare of the public.

Power of Attorney: An instrument authorizing a person to act as the agent of the person granting it, and a general power authorizing the

317

agent to act generally in behalf of the principal. A special power limits the agent to a particular or specific act as: a landowner may grant an agent special power of attorney to convey a single and specific parcel of property. Under the provisions of a general power of attorney, the agent having the power may convey any or all property of the principal granting the general power of attorney.

Prefabricated house: A house manufactured and sometimes partly assembled, before delivery to building site.

Prepayment Penalty: Penalty for the payment of a mortgage or trust deed note before it actually becomes due.

Prescription: The securing of title to property by adverse possession; by occupying it for the period determined by law barring action for recovery.

Presumption: A rule of law that courts and judges shall draw a particular inference from a particular fact, or from particular evidence, unless and until the truth of such inference is disproved.

Prima Facie: Presumptive on its face.

Principal: The employer of an agent.

Privity: Mutual relationship to the same rights of property, contractual relationship.

Procuring Cause: That cause originating from series of events that, without break in continuity, results in the prime object of an agent's employment producing a final buyer.

Proration of Taxes: To divide or prorate the taxes equally or proportionately to time of use.

Purchase and Installment Saleback: Involves purchase of the property upon completion of construction and immediate saleback on a long-term installment contract.

Purchase of Land, Leaseback and Leasehold Mortgages: An arrangement whereby land is purchased by the lender and leased back to the developer with a mortgage negotiated on the resulting leasehold of the income property constructed. The lender receives an annual ground rent, plus a percentage of income from the property.

Purchase and Leaseback: Involves the purchase of property subject to an existing mortgage and immediate leaseback.

Purchase Money Mortgage or Trust Deed: A trust deed or mortgage given as part or all of the purchase consideration for property.

Quantity Survey: A highly technical process in arriving at cost estimate of new construction, and sometimes referred to in the building trade as the *price take-off* method. It involves a detailed estimate of the quantities of raw material (lumber, plaster, brick, cement, etc.) used, as well as the current price of the material and installation costs. These factors are all added together to arrive at the cost of a structure. It is usually used by contractors and experienced estimators.

Quarter round: A molding that presents a profile of a quarter circle.

Quiet Enjoyment: Right of an owner to the use of property without interference of possession.

Quiet Title: A court action brought to establish title; to remove a cloud on the title.

318

Quitclaim Deed: A deed to relinquish any interest in property which the grantor may have.

Radiant Heating: A method of heating, usually consisting of coils or pipes placed in the floor, wall, or ceiling.

Rafter: One of a series of boards of a roof designed to support roof loads. The rafters of a flat roof are sometimes called *roof joists.*

Range: A strip of land six miles wide determined by a government survey, running in a north-south direction.

Ratification: The adoption or approval of an act performed on behalf of a person without previous authorization.

Real Estate Board: An organization whose members consist primarily of real estate brokers and salesmen.

Real Estate Trust: A special arrangement under Federal and State law whereby investors may pool funds for investments in real estate and mortgages and yet escape corporation taxes.

Realtor: A real estate broker holding active membership in a real estate board affiliated with the National Association of Real Estate Boards.

Recapture: The rate of interest necessary to provide for the return of an investment. Not to be confused with interest rate, which is a rate of interest on an investment.

Reconveyance: The transfer of the title of land from one person to the immediate preceding owner. This particular instrument or transfer is commonly used in California when the performance or debt is satisfied under the terms of a deed of trust, when the trustee conveys the title he has held on condition back to the owner.

Redemption: Buying back one's property after a judicial sale.

Reformation: An action to correct a mistake in a deed or other document.

Release Clause: This is a stipulation that upon the payment of a specific sum of money to the holder of a trust deed or mortgage, the lien of the instrument as to a specific described lot or area shall be removed from the blanket lien on the whole area involved.

Remainder: An estate which vests after the termination of the prior estate, such as a life estate.

Rescission of Contract: The abrogation or annulling of contract; the revocation or repealing of contract by mutual consent by parties to the contract, or for cause by either party to the contract.

Reservation: A right retained by a grantor in conveying property.

Restriction: The term as used relating to real property means the owner of real property is restricted or prohibited from doing certain things relating to the property, or using the property for certain purposes. For instance, the requirement in a deed that a lot may be used for the construction of not more than a one-party dwelling, costing not less than ten thousand dollars ($10,000), is termed to be a restriction; also a legislative ordinance affecting all properties in a given area, requiring that improvements on property shall not be constructed any closer than 25 feet of the street curb, is a restriction by operation of law.

319

Reversion: The right to future possession or enjoyment by the person, or his heirs, creating the preceding estate.

Reversionary Interest: The interest which a person has in lands or other property, upon the termination of the preceding estate.

Ridge: The horizontal line at the junction of the top edges of two sloping roof surfaces. The rafters at both slopes are nailed at the ridge.

Ridge Board: The board placed on edge at the ridge of the roof to support the upper ends of the rafters; also called roof tree, ridge piece, ridge plate or ridgepole.

Right of Survivorship: Right to acquire the interest of a deceased joint owner; distinguishing feature of a joint tenancy.

Right of Way: A privilege operating as an easement upon land, whereby the owner does by grant, or by agreement, give to another the right to pass over his land, to construct a roadway, or use as a roadway, a specific part of his land, or the right to construct through and over his land, telephone, telegraph, or electric power lines, or the right to place underground water mains, gas mains, or sewer mains.

Riparian Rights: The right of a landowner to water on, under, or adjacent to his land.

Riser: The upright board at the back of each step of a stairway. In heating, a riser is a duct slanted upward to carry hot air from the furnace to the room above.

Roman Brick: Thin brick of slimmer proportions than standard building brick.

Sales Contract: A contract by which buyer and seller agree to terms of a sale.

Sale-leaseback: A situation where the owner of a piece of property wishes to sell the property and retain occupancy by leasing it from the buyer.

Sandwich Lease: A leasehold interest which lies between the primary lease and the operating lease.

Sash: Wood or metal frames containing one or more window panes.

Satisfaction: Discharge of mortgage or trust deed lien from the records upon payment of the evidenced debt.

Scribing: Fitting woodwork to an irregular surface.

Seal: An impression made to attest the execution of an instrument.

Secondary Financing: A loan secured by a second mortgage or trust deed on real property.

Secured Party: This is the party having the security interest. Thus the *mortgagee,* the *conditional seller,* the *pledgee,* etc., are all now referred to as the secured party.

Security Agreement: An agreement between the secured party and the debtor which creates the security interest.

Security Interest: A term designating the interest of the creditor in the property of the debtor in all types of credit transactions. It thus replaces such terms as the following: *chattel mortgage; pledge; trust receipt; chattel trust; equipment trust; conditional sale; inventory lien;* etc.

Section: Section of land is established by government survey and contains 640 acres.

Separate Property: Property owned by a husband or wife which is not community property; property acquired by either spouse prior to marriage or by gift or devise after marriage.

Septic Tank: An underground tank in which sewage from the house is reduced to liquid by bacterial action and drained off.

Set-back Ordinance: An ordinance prohibiting the erection of a building or structure between the curb and the set-back line.

Severalty Ownership: Owned by one person only. Sole ownership.

Shake: A hand-split shingle, usually edge grained.

Sheathing: Structural covering usually boards, plywood, or wallboards, placed over exterior studding or rafters of a house.

Sheriff's Deed: Deed given by court order in connection with sale of property to satisfy a judgment.

Sill: The lowest part of the frame of a house, resting on the foundation and supporting the uprights of the frame. The board or metal forming the lower side of an opening, as a door sill, window sill, etc.

Sinking Fund: Fund set aside from the income from property which, with accrued interest, will eventually pay for replacement of the improvements.

Soil Pipe: Pipe carrying waste out from the house to the main sewer line.

Sole or *Sole plate:* A member, usually a 2 by 4, on which wall and partition studs rest.

Span: The distance between structural supports such as walls, columns, piers, beams, girders, and trusses.

Special Assessment: Legal charge against real estate by a public authority to pay cost of public improvements such as: street lights, sidewalks, street improvements, etc.

Specific Performance: An action to compel performance of an agreement, e.g., sale of land.

S.R.A.: Designates a person who is a member of the Society of Real Estate Appraisers.

Statute of Frauds: State law which provides that certain contracts must be in writing in order to be enforceable at law. Examples: real property lease for more than one year; agent's authorization to sell real estate.

Straight Line Depreciation: Definite sum set aside annually from income to pay cost of replacing improvements, without reference to interest it earns.

String, Stringer: A timber or other support for cross members. In stairs, the support on which the stair treads rest.

Studs or *Studding:* Vertical supporting timbers in the walls and partitions.

Subject to Mortgage: When a grantee takes a title to real property subject to mortgage, he is not responsible to the holder of the promissory note for the payment of any portion of the amount due. The most that he can lose in the event of a foreclosure is his equity in the property. See also "assumption of mortgage" in this section. In neither case is the original maker of the note released from his responsibility.

Sublease: A lease given by a lessee.

Subordinate: To make subject to, or junior to.

Subordination Clause: Clause in a junior or a second lien permitting retention of priority for prior liens. A subordination clause may also be used in a first deed of trust permitting it to be subordinated to subsequent liens as, for example, the liens of construction loans.

Subpoena: A process to cause a witness to appear and give testimony.

Subrogation: The substitution of another person in place of the creditor, to whose rights he succeeds in relation to the debt. The doctrine is used very often where one person agrees to stand surety for the performance of a contract by another person.

Surety: One who guarantees the performance of another : Guarantor.

Survey: The process by which a parcel of land is measured and its area is ascertained.

Tax Sale: Sale of property after a period of nonpayment of taxes.

Tenancy in Common: Ownership by two or more persons who hold undivided interest, without right of survivorship; interests need not be equal.

Tentative Map: The Subdivision Map Act requires subdividers to submit initially a tentative map of their tract to the local planning commission for study. The approval or disapproval of the planning commission is noted on the map. Thereafter a final map of the tract embodying any changes requested by the planning commission is required to be filed with the planning commission.

Tenure in Land: The mode or manner by which an estate in lands is held.

Termites: Ant-like insects which feed on wood.

Termite Shield: A shield, usually of noncorrodible metal, placed on top of the foundation wall or around pipes to prevent passage of termites.

Testator: One who leaves a will in force at his death.

Threshold: A strip of wood or metal beveled on each edge and used above the finished floor under outside doors.

Time Is the Essence: One of the essential requirements to forming of a binding contract; contemplates a punctual performance.

Title: Evidence that owner of land is in lawful possession thereof, an instrument evidencing such ownership.

Title Insurance: Insurance written by a title company to protect property owner against loss if title is imperfect.

Topography: Nature of the surface of land; topography may be level, rolling, mountainous.

Torrens Title: System of title records provided by state law (no longer used in California).

Tort: A wrongful act; wrong, injury; violation of a legal right.

Township: A territorial subdivision six miles long, six miles wide and containing 36 sections, each one mile square.

Trade Fixtures: Articles of personal property annexed to real property, but which are necessary to the carrying on of a trade and are removable by the owner.

Trade-in: An increasingly popular method of guaranteeing an owner a minimum amount of cash on sale of his present property to permit him to purchase another. If the property is not sold within a specified time at the listed price, the broker agrees to arrange financing to purchase the property at an agreed upon discount.

Treads: Horizontal boards of a stairway.

Trim: The finish materials in a building, such as moldings, applied around openings (window trim, door trim) or at the floor and ceiling (baseboard, cornice, picture molding).

Trust Deed: Deed given by borrower to trustee to be held pending fulfillment of an obligation, which is ordinarily repayment of a loan to a beneficiary.

Trustee: One who holds property in trust for another to secure the performance of an obligation.

Trustor: One who deeds his property to a trustee to be held as security until he has performed his obligation to a lender under terms of a deed of trust.

Undue Influence: Taking any fraudulent or unfair advantage of another's weakness of mind, or distress or necessity.

Unearned Increment: An increase in value of real estate due to no effort on the part of the owner; often due to increase in population.

Uniform Commercial Code: Effective January 1, 1965. Establishes a unified and comprehensive scheme for regulation of security transactions in personal property, superseding the existing statutes on chattel mortgages, conditional sales, trust receipts, assignment of accounts receivable and others in this field.

Unit-in-place Method: The cost of erecting a building by estimating the cost of each component part, i.e. foundations, floors, walls, windows, ceilings, roofs, etc. (including labor and overhead).

Urban Property: City property; closely settled property.

Usury: On a loan, claiming a rate of interest greater than that permitted by law.

Valid: Having force, or binding force; legally sufficient and authorized by law.

Valley: The internal angle formed by the junction of two sloping sides of a roof.

Valuation: Estimated worth or price. Estimation. The act of valuing by appraisal.

Vendee: A purchaser; buyer.

Vendor: A seller; one who disposes of a thing in consideration of money.

Veneer: Thin sheets of wood.

Vent: A pipe installed to provide a flow of air to or from a drainage system or to provide a circulation of air within such system to protect trap seals from siphonage and back pressure.

Verification: Sworn statement before a duly qualified officer to correctness of contents of an instrument.

Vested: Bestowed upon someone; secured by someone, such as title to property.

Void: To have no force or effect; that which is unenforceable.

Voidable: That which is capable of being adjudged void, but is not void unless action is taken to make it so.

Voluntary Lien: Any lien placed on property with consent of, or as a result of, the voluntary act of the owner.

Wainscoting: Wood lining of an interior wall; lower section of a wall when finished differently from the upper part.

Waive: To relinquish, or abandon; to forego a right to enforce or require anything.

Warranty Deed: A deed used to convey real property which contains warranties of title and quiet possession, and the grantor thus agrees to defend the premises against the lawful claims of third persons. It is commonly used in other states but not in California where the grant deed has supplanted it. The modern practice of securing title insurance policies has reduced the importance of express and implied warranty in deeds.

Waste: The destruction, or material alteration of, or injury to premises by a tenant for life or years.

Water Table: Distance from surface of ground to a depth at which natural groundwater is found.

Wrap Around Mortgage: Involves the borrower entering into a second mortgage. This arrangement represents the means by which he can add to his development without refinancing the first mortgage at substantially higher current rates.

Zone: The area set off by the proper authorities for specific use; subject to certain restrictions or restraints.

Zoning: Act of city or county authorities specifying type of use to which property may be put in specific areas.

Index

325

C